SOBRIETY AND BEYOND

by
Father John Doe
(Father Ralph Pfau)

I asked for bread; God gave a stone instead.
And ACCEPTING, I pillowed there my weary head;
Then angels made a ladder of my dreams,
Which upward to celestial mountains led.
And when I woke beneath the morning's beams,
Around my resting place fresh manna lay;
And, praising God, I went upon my way—
For I was fed—and I
Was HAPPY
IN SOBRIETY AND BEYOND!

• • •

Hazelden
Center City, MN 55012-0176

1-800-328-9000
1-612-257-1331 (FAX)
http://www.hazelden.org

First published 1955 by SMT Guild, Inc.,
Indianapolis. First published by Hazelden 1998

FOREWORD

No matter how degraded an alcoholic may be; no matter how confused his or her thinking might be; no matter how burdened may his soul or body be; somewhere deep within his heart and soul there is that deathless urge found in all such people to reach out beyond the sordidness, the deceit, the folly, the ignorance, the immorality, the sham, the materialism, and the hypocrisy of this world to grasp that elusive something which spells kinship with the lovely, and the beautiful and the divine in life. His perfectionist nature—so sensitive and so attuned to the eternal cravings—has always and anon reached for the pinnacle in every endeavor. Nothing in life was ever less than perfection, albeit ever blocked by some strange unseen force. In his work, his play, his love—he ever strove with might and main for the best. But, again, in his search—so endless; so heart-rending—time and time again he ended in defeat—which wrenched from the depth of his agonized soul the cry:

> *"How can my dream break through the darkness,*
> *When always this 'thing,' this vile 'thing'*
> *Hangs as a satanic chalice above the threshold of night, . . .*
> *So that none may pass?"*

And like the "Hound of Heaven,"

> *"He fled Him down the nights,*
> *And down the days—*
> *Down the labyrinthine ways of his own mind*
> *He sped . . ."*

UNTIL one day—along that frenzied raceway which is the life of the alcoholic there appeared a stairway—with Twelve Steps

—leading not only to sobriety, but beyond sobriety to happiness, and peace of mind and contentment.

This stairway called Alcoholics Anonymous, a hundred and fifty thousand men and women have climbed today—to SOBRIETY AND BEYOND. The following pages are a compilation of the writings of one such alcoholic originally published as The Golden Books, and are now offered in one volume basically unchanged so that, God willing, many, many others, both alcoholics and non-alcoholics, may profit from these simple, unpedantic, straightforward outpourings of the alcoholic soul—so that you, dear readers, may also find and maintain that peace beyond sobriety.

—Another John Doe

ALCOHOLISM

Alcoholism is fast becoming the most discussed problem of the day. Seldom a week passes without some national publication publishing an article dealing with the situation. More and more frequently, public speakers, particularly in the educational and moral fields, are contributing their thinking toward a possible solution of the problem; and we do not believe any sane person will deny the appalling fact that alcoholism itself is increasing by leaps and bounds, and is fast invading the area of the late teens and the early twenties. As recently as six years ago, one seldom met anyone in Alcoholics Anonymous under the age of forty; today, it is very common to find as members of these groups, individuals—both men and women—in their late teens and early twenties. The writer has met, here and there, a member as young as seventeen years of age already acutely alcoholic. We also know that alcoholism, today, is rated fourth as a national public health menace. Each year fifteen thousand men and women die as a result of alcoholism. Last year it cost industry in the United States $1,255,300,000.

Still, the present methods of dealing with the problem (with the possible exception of the almost miraculous work of Alcoholics Anonymous), are in many cases expensive, sometimes barbaric; almost always punitive; and they seldom rehabilitate nor do they prevent; and perhaps, what is worse, is the persistent attitudes of many of our outstanding public speakers, educators and writers, who still dogmatically condemn the labelling of alcoholism as a sickness, and make light of the work of such organizations as the Yale School for Alcoholic Studies, Alcoholics Anonymous, etc.

At this juncture, before attempting to answer such criticisms, we had better first clarify our own terms, lest we, too, become confused in our discussion of this problem. So, first of all, let us define what is meant by "Alcoholism," and whom do we classify as an "alcoholic."

We have all heard down through the years many wrong definitions of an alcoholic. Let us analyze some of the more common: "An alcoholic is an individual who drinks alone." Undoubtedly, in the past, many a father or mother has given such advice to their sons, "Son, never drink alone, and you will not become an alcoholic." Also, many well meaning doctors, psychiatrists, and clergymen have given the same advice. However, the fact is that there are thousands of alcoholics who never drink alone. As soon as they start drinking they want people; they are gregarious; they get "telephonitis." Their primary desire is NOT to be alone. Yet, these people are very acutely alcoholic.

Others have advised the potential alcoholic that "an alcoholic is the individual who drinks in the morning." And then very dogmatically taught their charges, "If you don't drink in the morning, you are not an alcoholic." In reality, the writer has met alcoholics who had never taken a drink in the morning. He remembers one particular person in Alcoholics Anonymous who had had that advice given to him in his youth, so in order not to become an alcoholic, he fought off daily, the shakes and the jitters, and the nervousness, and what-have-you, for years, with Bromo Seltzer, the barbitals, aspirin, etc., until *NOON*—then, he could drink to his heart's content, and not become (so he thought), and alcoholic! He has now been a member of A.A. for seven years!

Then, there was the common error of advice, "always stay with two or three drinks, and you will not become an alcoholic." What such well meaning guardians of the morals seemed not to know at all was, that an alcoholic IN SPITE OF ALL THINGS HE MAY DO TO AVOID IT, cannot stay with two or three drinks—or for that matter fifty drinks—and stop. Furthermore, there are certain types of alcoholics who become "drunk" on as little as a very few drinks, nor do they ever increase their intake, but still continue to become drunk.

Then we have the classical advice used down through the years by parents, doctors, clergymen, and all well meaning persons, "stick with beer—the light stuff—and you'll never become an alcoholic." It is the rare alcoholic who somewhere along the course of his drinking days has not encountered such advice.

Many actually attempted to drink nothing but beer, and still they became alcoholics. As a matter of fact, there are a few alcoholics here and there who have never drunk strong liquor. And we all know that the "wino" is very common among the alcoholic ranks.

Other well meaning persons have advised, "never drink every day and you will not become an alcoholic." The so called "periodic" alcoholic demonstrates the fallacy of such advice. They are individuals who may go for weeks, months, even years, and never touch nor desire a drop of alcohol. Then such a one goes off on a "binge" or two, three or four weeks, or months before sobering up.

We feel that when we analyze the true causes of alcoholism the reader will readily see that the above definitions and advice have nothing to do with true alcoholism, and will realize that it doesn't make any difference how, when, where, or why the individual drinks. *WHAT HAPPENS TO THE PERSONALITY WHEN THE ALCOHOLIC DRINKS DETERMINES THE CONDITION OF ALCOHOLISM.* And along this line of thought we find that the most commonly accepted definition of an alcoholic is: *ONE WHO HAVING TAKEN ONE DRINK CANNOT GUARANTEE HIS BEHAVIOR,* or medically speaking, *AN ALLERGY OF THE BODY COUPLED WITH AN OBSESSION OF THE MIND.* Therefore, an alcoholic is an individual who having begun to drink cannot tell when he is going to stop. In his personality is a definite allergy so that when alcohol enters into his system, then and there begins the complete obsession or compulsion of the mind leading to excessive consumption.

All alcoholics are excessive drinkers; but not all excessive drinkers are alcoholics. The Yale School of Alcoholism tells us (1950) that in the United States there are five million[1] individuals who drink to excess. In other words, there are five million people who regularly get drunk. But of that five million, only about nine hundred thousand[1] may be classified as alcoholics, and as sick people. And we maintain that willful ex-

---

[1] **The writer feels that both of these figures are too low.**

cessive drinking is still sinful; but we also maintain that alcoholism, in which the excessive drinking is symptomatic of an underlying personality disorder, is a sickness, a highly complex one, and often a fatal one.

Now what are the principal objections to the approach to the problem of alcoholism as a sickness?

First, to quote one writer. "This teaching would excuse the drinker who foresees that this excessive drinking might lead to alcoholism and to disasters that may happen in it."

But it would no more excuse such an individual than would the teaching that diabetes, or syphilis, or neurosis, or heart disease, is a sickness. Certainly in many cases of such illness, the patient was willfully responsible for bringing on his condition, but here and now no one would dare deny that he or she is a very sick individual. And to those objectors who maintain that alcoholism was brought on through sinful actions of excessive drinking (as undoubtedly is true in many cases) we answer that so also were other illnesses. Syphilis, for example is brought about practically always through sinful actions. Yet here and now, no one will dare deny that syphilis is a very definite and dangerous sickness. Let us not confuse causes with present circumstances.

Another objection: Many writers decry the use of the dictum, "Once an alcoholic, always an alcoholic." To quote, "One implication of this teaching is that an alcoholic is not morally responsible who has been dry, say five or more years, and then becomes intoxicated or drunk." Rather the contrary! Such conviction—once an alcoholic, always an alcoholic—is the only thing that will bring about the realization that therefore, he is responsible always and at all times to avoid even the first drink. The saying "once an alcoholic, always an alcoholic" simply means that once a person has crossed that invisible line into the realms of chronic alcoholism, he never again can take one drink and guarantee his behavior. For until the day he dies he will remain an alcoholic, having an allergy of such a nature that even though he be dry ten, twenty, thirty, yes even forty years, one drink will set off the compulsion of mind and excess.

An interesting example of the above factor occurred in the writer's experience several years ago. A certain individual had not taken a drink for forty-one years. During this time he had been absolutely dry. However, for some reason or excuse, he took a drink. Within one week he was in the psychopathic ward of the city hospital with delirium tremens. ONCE AN ALCOHOLIC—ALWAYS AN ALCOHOLIC.

What is needed today more than anything else in all approaches to the problem is CLARIFICATION AND UNDERSTANDING, INSTEAD OF THE HURLING OF DOGMATIC "TIS'S" AND "TAINT'S" without even a semi-understanding of the realities of the problem.

Now let us try to find, in as far as we can, the actual cause of the condition of alcoholism. And in doing so, let us keep in mind that the excessive drinking itself is not the sickness, but only the symptom of the underlying disease—a condition similar to the innumerable irritations that are external signs of internal infections in various sicknesses.

Much has been learned in the past decade concerning the cause of alcoholism. And in our analysis of the condition, we find that there are many contributory causes which are not in reality causes, but merely circumstances, aggravating the underlying causes. Their name is legion. To name but a few: environment, nervousness, pain, illness, home and marital conditions, etc. Actually, these are not causes but merely occasions. For example one hears the remark, "Well, I don't blame so and so for getting drunk. If I had a wife like he has to live with, I would get drunk too." What such a person does not realize is that so-and-so's wife is not the cause of his drinking (although many times she may be an aggravating factor), and that if she were removed as a circumstance in his life (IF HE IS AN ALCOHOLIC), he would continue to get drunk. The same analysis may be applied to any other circumstance, such as job, boss, finance, etc., which we so often wrongly blame as the cause of the alcoholic's drinking.

The primary cause of alcoholism is not positively known in the present knowledge of the problem. Nor do we believe that the cause in most instances is singular, but usually a combination of causes. However, we are of the opinion that to date the best defined cause for alcoholism is the one given by Dr. Edward Strecker, Psyc.D., head psychiatrist of Pennsylvania University. He defines the cause of alcoholism as " 'Momism' mixed with alcohol." By this is meant that the average alcoholic is the individual who was pampered or neglected in childhood, usually on the part of the mother. In the first instance—in the case of the over-pampered child—the individual grows to adult life and tends to retreat from life. Although this tendency is present in most human beings to a certain extent, it is emphatically obvious in the alcoholic personality, and because of this childhood emotional damage, which now may not even be in the consciousness, will cause *abnormal* insecurity and fear. If such is mixed with a regular intake of alcohol, the fear element is released and dominates the personality. Likewise, in the case of the neglected child, fear is instilled from childhood, and through regular alcoholic intake, is accentuated beyond control. Thus, we find that the basic ingredient in every alcoholic personality is an ABNORMAL FEAR element that lies behind and motivates most of the abnormal and inhuman behavior of the alcoholic which is so trying to, and misunderstood by, those nearest and dearest to him.

This abnormal condition of fear is responsible for the four basic traits found in every alcoholic: sensitivity, childishness, egocentricity, and grandiosity. These are usually operative in the area of the subconscious. They are manifested in the consciousness by *irritability, defiance, pouting, bragadoccio, quarreling, loneliness, depression, elation, reticence, aggressiveness, stubbornness, determination, dishonesty, nervousness, restlessness, frustration, and selfishness.*

All these "quirks" of the alcoholic personality stem from the basic abnormal fear motive. It is the reason that an alcoholic must be approached, not with the idea of correcting the above "faults," but *WITH THE HOPE OF INSTILLING FAITH AND CONFIDENCE TO OFFSET THE BASIC ELEMENT OF FEAR.* It is also the reason that criticizing, condemning, making fun of, or frightening the alcoholic only accentuates his alcoholism because it only deepens his fear and insecurity. A normal person who pouts does so because he has been hurt; on the other hand, when the alcoholic apparently pouts he often times does so because he has been frightened. It is true that his fears are very abnormal, but it is also true that they are present, and we must face facts and not indulge in wishful thinking. *PRACTICALLY EVERY ALCOHOLIC WHO HAS ACHIEVED SOBRIETY, HAS ACHIEVED IT, AND MAINTAINS IT, BECAUSE SOMEONE, SOMEWHERE, REBUILT HIS HUMAN CONFIDENCE, AND THUS LED HIM AGAIN TO A CONFIDENCE AND FAITH IN THE DIVINE, WHICH ULTIMATELY IS THE ONLY REAL SECURITY.*

We find that there are in general three basic types of alcoholics:

1. *THE NEUROTIC.* (Some were neurotic before they began to drink; others became neurotic through excessive drinking.) These alcoholics have a definite neurosis as a part of their alcoholic condition. Which came first is irrelevant. They comprise 80 per cent of all alcoholics.
2. *THE SIMPLE ADDICT.* These individuals apparently have no neurosis but still are unable to control their drinking, no matter how much they try. They comprise 15 per cent of all alcoholics.
3. *THE PSYCHOPATH.* Such have a mental disease along with their alcoholism. These comprise 5 per cent of all alcoholics.

The next question that logically presents itself is the responsiblity of the alcoholic. Is the alcoholic, on the average, responsible for his excessive drinking?

It is impossible to answer this question with a dogmatic statement. A thorough analysis must of necessity be left to essays of broader scope than our present one. Suffice it for the present to give Father Ford's conclusion to this excellent analysis of moral responsibility in alcoholism.[1] "The average alcoholic is

[1] Cf. DEPTH PSYCHOLOGY AND COMPULSION—ALCOHOLISM AND MORAL RESPONSIBILITY, 1951, by John C. Ford, S.J., Weston College Press, Weston, Mass.

sick in body, mind, and soul and usually cannot stop drinking without help. HIS RESPONSIBILITY IS GENERALLY DIMINISHED TO A CONSIDERABLE EXTENT, BUT EACH ALCOHOLIC, EACH DRINKING EPISODE, AND EVEN EACH ACT OF DRINKING MUST BE JUDGED SEPARATELY."

One of the most damaging attitudes that has become a definite obstacle to the solution of the problem of alcoholism is the refusal on the part of the average individual to admit the existence of the problem. Ostrich-like they bury their heads in the sand with false shame, and whether personally, or in the family, or in business, or in any other organization, they bow their heads, close their eyes, and meekly sputter, "We ain't got no problem."

For some strange reason most people would rather be called anything under the sun than an alcoholic, wherefore it is only by an understanding of what alcoholism really is, will such ever be brought to admit the problem. It must be brought out into the open, and all available therapies used to treat the situation. Thanks be to God, in the past decade, many organizations and individuals have contributed much to the knowledge and mode of solving the problem of alcoholism.

In past years there have been primarily three agencies treating the problem: the doctors, the psychiatrists, and the clergy. However, in spite of the many sincere endeavors on the part of these good men, their success, they will tell you, has been practically nil.

The doctors in the past have always approached alcoholism as a physical condition. And there are some, even today, who hope that eventually a pill, or an injection, or a hormone will be discovered to cure alcoholism. We think not. Their success has been about 2.1 per cent.

The average psychiatrist in the past has treated alcoholism as a purely mental disease. About 3 per cent of their alcoholic patients remain sober.

The clergy, the priests, have in most instances in the past approached the alcoholic with a moral solution, and have deemed alcoholism as a purely moral condition. Although we shall never know the many instances of cure through the Grace of God in the confessional, most priests will tell you that their success with a true alcoholic has been most discouraging.

Why all this failure? Why this lack of success? Why, with the best that professional men could give, have so few alcoholics achieved and maintained sobriety down through the years? To answer this question let us analyze their approach. What did the average doctor tell the alcoholic who came to him for help and advice? "If you don't stop drinking you will die." That is precisely what the alcoholic has been afraid of! So he left the doctor's office with more fear and with a confused idea that maybe a little drink might make dying a little less hard. So he reached for another fifth.

What did the psychiatrist tell the alcoholic? "If you don't stop drinking, you will go insane." Many times the alcoholic has feared just that! Perhaps he has had a stop or two at the asylum! And to make insanity more bearable, he too, in his confusion of fear and frantically attempting security, reaches for another fifth.

IN ALL THESE CASES THE CONDITION THAT WAS CAUSING THE EXCESSIVE DRINKING WAS ONLY ACCENTUATED, AND THE CONDITION BECAME WORSE. THE ALCOHOLIC BECAME MORE FEARFUL THAN EVER. HE DRANK THE MORE.

And then along came Alcoholics Anonymous, a group of individuals who have had the amazing percentage of success of 50 per cent from initial contact; another 25 per cent after difficulties; the other 25 per cent they rate still as unsolved problem drinkers. Today (1955) they number 150,000 members.

Why the success of Alcoholics Anonymous? We feel that there are five principal reasons for their phenomenal success:

1. Their threefold approach to the problem as a physical, mental, and spiritual sickness, wherein they maintain that unless there be adjustment of personality on all three levels, there will not be permanent sobriety.

2. The reviving of the alcoholic's confidence, chiefly by being approached by another alcoholic. Members of A.A. maintain that the ability to establish this 'contact of confidence' is a gift of the Almighty to all recovered alcoholics. It is here that FEAR IS REPLACED.
3. There deep conviction that 'ONCE AN ALCOHOLIC, ALWAYS AN ALCOHOLIC'; that in the present knowledge of the problem, alcoholism may be ARREST-ED, but cannot be CURED.
4. Their aim at placing ultimate security and sobriety upon the only true source of security—Almighty God.
5. The application of the time-valued 'group therapy,' especially since many 'eccentricities' may remain for a long time after initial sobriety, and such are hardly ever understood by non-alcoholics.

The core of their program consists of Twelve Steps, simple and solid; its meat is the practicing of their conviction that 'only an alcoholic can FULLY understand another alcoholic.' It is all something like the story of the little boy at the puppy sale who hesitatingly edged up to the seller and said, 'Please, mister, I'd like to buy a puppy. How much do they cost?"

"They're ten dollars."

The child's face fell. "I only got $1.63. I heard you had one with a bad leg. How much is he?"

"But that one will never walk perfectly. You wouldn't want him."

Hiking up his pant-leg, the little boy showed a brace, "I don't walk so good either, mister, and I reckon that's just the puppy I want. He'll need some understanding for a long time, till he gets used to it. I did."

Today a hundred and fifty thousand men and women are sober because someone understood their problem—and now are enjoying

SOBRIETY AND BEYOND

BEYOND SOBRIETY

"Sought through prayer and meditation . . ."

BEYOND sobriety lies serenity, and beneath all true serenity lies a deep spiritual life through which must run "the golden thread which binds the hearts of men about the feet of God": PRAYER AND MEDITATION.

In order to have a clear mind in considering the subject of prayer and meditation, a true concept of the nature of spirituality is paramount. Many have much difficulty with the so-called 'spiritual side' of the program, because they have a distorted idea of what is meant by the term 'spiritual.' To many, such a term conjures up in their minds innumerable prayers, a long face, isolation, *in*human qualities of human association, a retreating gait, somber groanings, and what-have-you. Nothing could be farther from the truth, for a truly spiritual man is a saint, and a saint is very human—but one who has built his life and his actions on *God's* will and not his own. Spiritual men and women are happy—they have no conflicts—for their will is trained to be always subject to the will of God. As St. Theresa put it with two pertinent remarks: "A saint sad is a sad saint" and "Lord, deliver me from sour-faced saints." Spiritual men and women are normal, whereas the grotesque figure conjured above is very abnormal. They keep such people locked up. A spiritual person is one who does *what* he has to do, *when* he has to do it, in the *best* way he can do it and who gets the guidance, the strength, and the success from God through humble prayer and meditation. They realize that whether they pray or eat or work or play or sleep, they do it all for the honor and glory of God and thus they praise God in doing His Will.

Some obtain their wrong idea of spirituality and sanctity from the pictures and statues of the saints. In order to denote sanctity, they are usually depicted in a 'saintly' pose *but* we should not conclude from this fact that their whole life was consumed in such pose. Do we think for a moment that St. Joseph went around day after day with a lily in one hand and the Christ Child in the other! ? Or that St. Aloysius spent all of his days on some side altar dressed in cassock and surplice and his hands clasped in prayer! ? The lily in St. Joseph's hand simply denotes his perpetual chastity; the Christ Child in his arm denotes his role as protector of God's Son. St. Joseph was a carpenter and as such had to work every day to support Mary and Jesus. He had to put up with all the inconveniences of life the same as you and I. He laughed, and wept, and ate, and slept, and talked with friends, and suffered and died—even as you and I. But he did all of these things as *God* willed them—and *that* made him a saint.

With this idea of spirituality and sanctity in mind, we can easily understand that even the oft-used term 'spiritual angle' or 'spiritual side' is a misnomer. As one outstanding member once remarked, "spiritual SIDE? The *whole* program is spiritual." And those who decry it, or who so naïvely remark that they can accept *all* of the program but the 'spiritual side' are woefully ignorant of the meaning of spirituality. Their statement is a contradiction in terms. As a member once remarked to the writer after a long attempt to discredit the 'spiritual side,' "There is no doubt but that my seven years of sobriety is a *miracle*." You figure out that one.

Have you ever analyzed the twelve steps and eliminated those steps that are spiritual? It is very interesting—let's try it—

1. *WE ADMITTED WE WERE POWERLESS OVER ALCOHOL THAT OUR LIVES HAD BECOME UNMANAGEABLE.*

There's nothing spiritual about this admission. Any drunk can truthfully make it. So we will keep this one—we admit we are in a 'mess.'

2. *CAME TO BELIEVE THAT A POWER GREATER THAN OURSELVES COULD RESTORE US TO SANITY.*

Came to belief in God—in spiritual things. If we do not accept the 'spiritual side' of the program then we must eliminate this step. . . .

3. *MADE A DECISION TO TURN OUR WILL AND OUR LIVES OVER TO THE CARE OF GOD . . .*

Here we make a decision to lead a *spiritual* life, a life surrendered to the Will of God . . . so we must eliminate this step too. . . .

4. *MADE A SEARCHING AND FEARLESS MORAL INVENTORY OF OURSELVES . . .*

"A *moral* inventory" — morality postulates a law — the *moral* law. Without God and His Commandments we could not have a moral law. We take this inventory in order that we might adjust ourselves to this moral law—which again is to live a spiritual life. So step four is out. . . .

5. *ADMITTED TO GOD . . .*

There's God again, so that's out. . . .

6. *WERE ENTIRELY READY TO HAVE GOD . . .*

God . . . that's out. . . .

7. *HUMBLY ASKED HIM . . .*

We can't do it if there is no *spiritual* side . . . we can't use this step, it's spiritual. . . .

8. *MADE A LIST OF ALL THE PERSONS WE HAD HARMED AND WERE WILLING TO MAKE AMENDS . . .*

Justice and rights . . . again postulating the law of God . . . but there's no 'spiritual side' . . . no submission to God's Will and Law . . . no restitution . . . no taking of the eighth step. . . .

9. *MADE DIRECT AMENDS TO SUCH PEOPLE . . .*

A corollary of step eight . . . emanating from obligations of justice . . . so we can't use this one. . . .

10. *CONTINUED TO TAKE PERSONAL INVENTORY . . . WHEN WRONG . . .*

But only a truly spiritual man need pay attention to right and wrong . . . to morality . . . to God's Law . . . so we discard this step also, it's spiritual. . . .

11. *SOUGHT THROUGH PRAYER AND MEDITATION TO IMPROVE OUR CONSCIOUS CONTACT WITH GOD...*

This step is loaded with the very essence of spirituality... we could never include it....

12. *HAVING HAD A SPIRITUAL EXPERIENCE...*

Spiritual! There could never be a twelfth step if we deny there is a spiritual side....

Now what have we left of the program having thrown out all the steps that are spiritual?

WE ADMITTED THAT WE WERE POWERLESS OVER ALCOHOL THAT OUR LIVES HAD BECOME UNMANAGEABLE!... What a mess! Open the barred gates, Richard!

Therefore, understanding that the leading of a spiritual life is nothing more nor less than the honest effort to live daily in accordance with the known Will of God to the best of our ability, let us proceed to the consideration of the one thing that is the cornerstone of the whole program, the very life fuel of the spiritual life, and the positive unfailing insurance for continued sobriety and happiness. We express this all-important and essential part of the program in the eleventh step: WE SOUGHT THROUGH PRAYER AND MEDITATION TO IMPROVE OUR CONSCIOUS CONTACT WITH GOD AS WE UNDERSTOOD HIM PRAYING ONLY FOR KNOWLEDGE OF HIS WILL FOR US AND THE POWER TO CARRY THAT OUT.

No one will achieve sobriety and happiness and serenity for long unless he or she honestly practices the eleventh step. Thousands of alcoholics have slipped. But experience proves that *every slip* was preceded by a period of neglect of the eleventh step, by a neglect of honest prayer, by a neglect of humbly asking God for the guidance and the strength to remain sober. The writer has made it a point to ask hundreds of men who had slipped whether they had sincerely prayed on the day they began to drink. Only one answered affirmatively, and he qualified his answer with, "I prayed and prayed that *God would not let me get hurt* during this drunk!" This is tantamount to no prayer. We can put it down as an indisputable fact that the one who *humbly* and *sincerely* prays *daily for strength* and *guidance will not slip;* the good Lord will not let him.

On the other hand *all things* are possible to the man who prays. No matter in what condition or how entangled one may be in the problems of life; no matter how long or how much a man has drunk to excess; no matter how low such a person has sunk in the quick-sands of immorality or mental aberrations, *if he prays he will recover!* For alcoholism, unhappiness, wrong-doing, self-pity, resentments, conflicts, and all the host of things that the alcoholic knows so well *cannot* co-exist with prayer. One will be eliminated—either he will stop praying or even the worst of human problems eventually will clear up under the power of God's grace.

There is a story that frequently makes the rounds of the A.A. groups. It is told to exemplify the extreme of self-pity, and goes something like this:

A certain man was feeling so sorry for himself that he was planning suicide. He had decided to jump into the river and end it all. However on his way to the water, while passing through an adjacent meadow he decided that it would not be a bad idea to say a prayer before he consummated his decision. As he knelt down he removed his hat. At that moment a bird was passing above and deposited his 'calling-card' in the center of his bald pate. Looking up the man exclaimed, "See God, that's what I mean! For other people birds *sing!*" There the story ends, but I should like to add a corollary: Did the man say the prayer? If he did, I feel certain he did not jump.

History is full of examples of the power of prayer. Tennyson tells us that "More things are wrought by prayer than this world dreams of." If we only realized it, every happy, normal life is the product of prayer. On the contrary every unhappy, abnormal life is the result of the neglect of prayer.

Striking proof of the power of prayer may be seen in the story of the writing of the Constitution of the United States. The founding fathers had spend weeks in discussion, attempting to draw up the articles to be incorporated into the document. Finally, after much wrangling, Benjamin Franklin arose and addressed the assembled statesmen: "I have lived a long time Sirs, and the longer I live the more convincing proofs I see of this truth: That God governs all the affairs of men. And if a sparrow cannot fall to the ground without His notice, is it possible that an empire can rise without His aid? I believe that without His concurring aid, we shall succeed in this political building no better than the builders of the Tower of Babel. We ourselves shall become a reproach and a by-word through future ages." The next day the assembly was opened with a prayer to God for guidance, and the *same day* the Constitution of the U.S., one of the greatest documents on record, was written!

We know from the Scriptures that as long as Moses knelt with his arms outstretched in prayer, the Israelites were victorious, and that when he ceased to pray they were put to rout. Hundreds of such examples could be given to show the power of prayer in governing the lives of men and nations.

One time a man entered a restaurant to eat. Before partaking of his food he humbly bowed his head in prayer. At the adjoining table were some individuals who decided to make fun of him. "Say, buddy," one of the crowd remarked, "Does everybody where you come from do that before they eat?" "Everybody but the pigs," the man calmly answered, "Pigs don't pray."

In order to even desire to pray we must have *faith* in God—in His existence and in His Omnipotent power. There are some who have trouble here when they come to the program. One person solved his difficulty in this way: "I would rather be wrong on the side of believing in God and finding after death that there is no God, than *not* believing in God here and then finding after death that there is a God." Very logical, very simple.

They tell the story of the atheist who noticed a little girl reading the Bible on the train. He approached her and cynically queried, "Surely you do not believe all that trash you are reading, do you?"

"Certainly I do," the girl guilelessly replied.

"The fable of Adam and Eve?"

"Certainly."

And Cain and Abel?"

"Yes, I do."

"Jonas and the whale?"

"Sure I do."

"Well, how are you going to prove it? I suppose you are going to ask Jonas when you get to heaven?"

"That sounds like a good idea. I think I shall."

"And what are you going to do if Jonas isn't there?"

"Well, then you ask him."

If we *do not* believe in God, little in life makes sense. Life becomes an endless "Why?" with never an answer. For it is only the acceptance of the Divinity, of God—His mercy, His providence, His power, His Wisdom, etc.—that can satisfactorily explain to man's reasoning powers the problems of life. As we read in the A.A. book: "On one proposition the members of A.A. are strikingly agreed. Everyone of them has gained access to, and believes in, a Power greater than themselves... thousands of men and women flatly declare that since they have come to believe in a Power greater than themselves, there has been a revolutionary change in their way of thinking and living... once confused and baffled by the seeming futility of existence, they will show the underlying reasons why they were making such a heavy going of life. Leaving aside the drink question, they will tell you why living was so unsatisfactory... and when thousands of such men and women are able to say that belief in the presence of God is the most important fact of their life, they present a powerful reason why we should have Faith... for deep down in every man, woman and child is the fundamental idea of God. It may be obscured by pomp, calamity, by worship of other things, but in some form or other it is there. For Faith in God and the miracluous manifestations of His Power in human lives are facts as old as man himself...."

Can we doubt it?

Then think of the plight of the atheist at death. One time such a person died and his co-worker, Pat, came to the wake. As he stood beside the bier he began to laugh. One of the bystanders chided him for laughing in the presence of the dead and asked him why he did such a thing. Pat replied: "I can't help it. Only yesterday Mike was telling me that he didn't believe in a life after death, nor in heaven nor hell, nor in God, and when I see him in all those fine clothes in the coffin, I can't help thinking 'the poor fellow, all dressed up and no place to go.'"

In order to pray well our prayers should have certain qualities to make them effective. In the first place they must be SINCERE. We all have had an experience with the "gimme" prayers and prayers backed by a lying promise. "O God, get me out of this mess, and I'll *never* take another drink!" The big liar—he doesn't really want to quit drinking, he simply doesn't want to get hurt.

A very good way to test the sincerity of our prayers is by analyzing the Lord's Prayer which we say at our meetings. In this prayer we pray:

"Our Father who art in heaven,

Hallowed be Thy Name. . . ."

Are we sincere when we say this? Do we really make an effort on our part to avoid profaning God's Name? Or is this prayer merely words to us? Keep your ears open at the meetings and listen, "Two years ago I was on the —— —— drunk in my life!" *Hallowed by Thy Name!*

"*Thy Kingdom Come. . . .*"

This means that we pray that *all* men will come to a knowledge of truth, of God; that *His* providence will prosper; that *His* kingdom will come about both on earth and eternally in heaven. And what do we hear? "That new member there, he's another of those —— Methodists, or Catholics, or Baptists, or Jews!" *Thy* kingdom come! Are we looking for denomination or sincerity?

"*Thy will be done . . .*

On earth as it is in heaven. . . ."

And then we don't acomplish what we set out to do. We don't get the job, or the raise, or the wife nags, or someone crosses us in any one of a thousand ways and we are burned up, resentful, full of self-pity, and if continued, we're drunk. Why, *our* will wasn't done. God's was. If it wasn't God's will it would not have happened, and after all we pray *Thy* will be done, not *my* will be done. Do we *act* as we pray?

Some years ago we attended an anniversary banquet of one of the A.A. groups. After the dinner and talks one of the members sang a song and dedicated it to A.A. The song was "O What a Beautiful Morning, Everything's Going *My* Way." We believe the singer was badly mistaken in his dedication. Certainly his song's theme doesn't fit into A.A. thinking. For, if we would follow through with his thought, many mornings we would moan "O What a Terrible Morning, *Nothing* is Going *My* Way!" That is one of the attitudes that put us in A.A.—extremes of emotion, elation and self-pity. But now we strive to acquire the middle of the road—serenity no matter what comes along—for "Everything's going *His* Way"—and it always will. *"Thy* Will be done!"

"Give us this day our daily bread...."

We pray that God will grant us *sufficient* strength, guidance and blessings to live *today.* Today means twenty-four hours. We don't pray for tomorrow, nor ask the impossible, that God will change the past. We pray only for *today*—and for all that is *necessary* to live this *day, with absolute faith* that God will give us what we need, but not necessarily what we *want.* Yet how many of us worry and stew about what might happen tomorrow, next month, next year?

"Forgive us our trespasses as we forgive
those who trespass against us...."

We have taken an inventory and found quite a mess for which we had been responsible. We found that we were loaded with faults and failings. We asked God to forgive us, "as *we forgive those* who trespass against us." Then someone hurts us, crosses us, contradicts us and we are so loathe to forgive! How often we want to get even! Isn't it a blessed thing that God does not take us at our word? *"As we forgive."*

"Lead us not *into temptation...."*

We are asking that God preserve us from temptation to wrong-doing. It is understood that *we* shall do our part to avoid, as far as we can, the temptation to drink, etc. Do we? Do we avoid taverns, and places where whiskey flows freely, except when *necessity* (not excuses) takes us there? Do we avoid companions who drink to excess? Or rather do we permit a sub-conscious desire to rebuild our "ego" lead us to seek such circumstances? Like the gentleman who remarked, "I go into a tavern every day to drink a 'coke' just to prove to *myself* that I won't take a drink of liquor." He did—drink liquor. Remember Peter's proud boast? "Even though all betray you, *I never will.*" Had he been humble he would have stayed away from the courtyard—the source of temptation. "Lead us not into temptation"—grant us the grace to avoid the occasions of sin, and we will do the foot-work.

"But deliver us from *all* evil."

Not only that which is actually wrong, but *all* evil, all that is not good, all that is not of Thee. Grant us ever to strive to bring our *entire* life in accord with the designs of Thy loving providence and Thy will. Do we guard against small beginning, thoughts, etc., that might grow into a temptation to sin? "Deliver us from *all* evil."

"Amen," which means "so be it"—may our *actions* follow our words. We are told in the A.A. book, "The spiritual life is not a theory, we must *live* it . . .*action* is the magic word."

The second quality our prayer should have is CONFIDENCE. We should pray knowing that God is more anxious to hear our prayers than we are to have them heard. Yet how often we are really surprised when our prayers are answered! They tell the story of the man who had a flat tire and, amid curses and epithets, was having much difficulty removing the tire from the rim. At this point a clergyman came along and suggested that perhaps he would have better luck if he tried prayer instead of cursing. "You're a clergyman," the man replied, "How about you trying it?" Whereupon the reverend gentleman said a prayer, put his hands on the tire, and it fell off. "Well I'll be ——!" cried the clergyman in amazement. The owner of the car smiled wryly to himself.

There should never be any doubt that God wants to and will answer *every* prayer provided we do our part and it be not contrary to His will. And even should our request be contrary to His will, he *will* answer it in another manner. *No prayer ever goes unanswered.* Although Almighty God often refrains for a time in answering our prayers, He does so to make us realize our complete dependence on Him and to teach us patience and constancy.

There was a story on the radio sometime ago which was very dramatically illustrative of the point. It told of a certain individual who became very bitter towards Almighty God because a sudden storm had destroyed the entire yield from his grape arbors. In his resentment he often derided the idea of prayer and the fact of God answering prayers. A short time later his wife suddenly became very ill and was rushed to the hospital. The doctors after examining her informed the husband that there was little hope for her life.

He was permitted to see her for a short time before he left the hospital, and her last words, whispered to him with much effort, were: "Pray for me, Jim."

Pray—pray—pray—the word haunted him, but withal it seemed only to deepen his resentment and bitterness. He went home. As he entered the living room his five-year-old boy ran to him. "Daddy," the lad begged, "Why don't you ask God to bring mommy home?"

"God?" he questioned bitterly. "God's got cotton in His ears!"

"Cotton? What's cotton, daddy?"

"I mean God doesn't hear you. He doesn't answer you."

"He answered my prayers, daddy."

"He answered your prayers? How? You have been asking God for a red scooter for a long time now and haven't got it. If God answered you, what did He say?"

"God said 'No,' daddy!"

There are times, also, when our prayers go unanswered because we do not *do our part.* Instead of not enough confidence, we have 'false confidence' which is nothing more nor less than presumption. They tell the story of the person whose house was burning down. He calmly continued to sit nearby apparently doing nothing. When a passerby asked him why he did not attempt to put out the fire he replied, "I am—I'm praying for rain."

A very good thought to keep in our conscious mind to help us have absolute confidence in God answering our prayers is that primarily God is our *Father,* only secondarily our *Judge.*

The third quality necessary for effective prayer is PERSEVERANCE. It is not sufficient to pray only when danger or temptation is present; to ask once in a while; or to ask for sobriety and then quit praying. We must pray *daily* and *continue* to pray daily. "He who perseveres to the end, he will be saved." Remember the woman in the Gospel story—even apparent direct refusal did not cause her to quit asking. And as a result her prayers were more than answered (Matt. xv; 21-28). Our faith must be such that against all odds we *persevere* in prayer for ultimately our prayer *will* be heard. We must "keep on swimming" like the two little frogs who jumped into the pail of cream. After many futile attempts to get out one gave up and drowned, but the other kept on swimming and finally found that he was sitting on a pail of butter from which he easily jumped to safety.

The fourth quality that our prayers should possess is that they should be DELIBERATE. Remember that prayer is a *two-way* conversation. We not only ask and tell, but we *listen.* Therefore our prayers should not be hurried, and should be free from distractions so that this way be possible. As Christ tells us, "When you pray . . . pray to the Father in secret," i.e., in the *quiet* of our souls devoid of worldly distractions and problems. Thus and thus alone will we be able to hear the Voice of the Divine Master.

There was once a poor boy who had no shoes. Being a very pious lad, he was taunted one day by a passerby, "You say so many prayers, it seems to me that if God heard them He would tell someone to buy you a pair of shoes."

"Please, mister," the boy answered, "I think He does, but they don't listen."

The most important times for prayer are:

1) *In the morning.* It is here that we ask for the strength and the guidance for the day. Many are the ones who fall into sin, because they did not ask God for the strength to avoid wrong; because they did not say their morning prayers; because they *were on their own.* We should keep ever in our conscious minds the *fact*: *No one ever slipped who honestly and sincerely asked God that morning to keep him sober that day.* We do not go to town to shop without money with which to make our purchases. Likewise we *cannot* go through the day sober, and serene, and secure *without* the strength of God which is only given to those who *ask.*

2) *In time of temptation.* When doubtful, agitated, tempted—we should pause and *ask* for the light, the strength, and the guidance. We should always remember that the *Power of God* is at our disposal at *all* times, and in *all* places, and under *all* circumstances for the *asking.* Did you ever try it?

3) *At night.* All of our life we shall remain human and shall be burdened with fallen human nature. From the Scriptures we know that even 'the just man falls seven times a day" and that "if any one says that he is without sin, that man is a liar and the truth is not in him." Therefore *each* evening we should ask forgiveness of the faults of that day. We should renew our resolves. We should make up any wrongs. We should *thank* God for having had sobriety and all the rest of His blessings for another day. The more grateful we are for blessings received, the more blessings will God shower upon us. Even selfish people despise an ingrate.

It is also a very good practice to have a *set* time for our prayers. We are far less apt to forget or omit them if we say them at the same time each day. It is good psychology. It gives us something to hang our will onto. On the other hand a general resolution to 'pray every day' seldom proves effective. It is too indefinite.

Now let us consider the matter of MEDITATION. To most people it seems so difficult, yet in reality it is very simple. It is absolutely necessary for living a good life free from doubts and conflicts. Meditation purifies the mind and motivates the will. It is simply the turning over in our minds of a *truth* (any truth) in order that, becoming a conscious factor in our lives, it will motivate our wills to right action. It is the giving truth a 'good think.' Let us take an example; let's meditate a few moments on *death.*

What is death? Death is the end of life on earth, the end of all that I cherish so much now. Then I shall see no more of this world, shall hear no more the voices of my friends and loved ones, shall no longer breathe nor speak nor move.

Who? I—that big ego that I now pamper so much —*I* am going to die!

When? I don't know—next year? Maybe. Next month? Maybe. Tomorrow? Maybe. *Today?* Could be. The startling fact is that I *may* die at any moment! *I do not know* the day nor the hour, but it could be today!

Where? At home? Away—from friends and loved ones, alone?

By what means? An accident? Disease?

How am I going to die? Sober? Drunk? God forbid, but *many have died drunk!* Shall I die suddenly? Without time to say a prayer? At peace with God or in sin?

Think—think—think—*I* am going to die! I cannot know when or where but *I can know how—if—if*—I live *each* day *prepared to meet my God.*

Now do you think we could very easily go out and take that first drink? Do you think it will be difficult to try to lead a good life today? Will it be so hard to be faithful to prayer today? Not with those thoughts in our mind. We shall probably the more cry out "O God, teach me to pray, so that I may learn to live—and to die." For *as we pray we shall live—and as we live we shall die*—therefore *if we pray well we shall live well*—and *if we live well we shall die well*—and *that is* all that matters.

HUMILITY

"He hath scattered the proud in the conceit of their heart...
He hath exalted the humble"

The entire Twelve Steps of the A.A. Program are based on humility. Without it there can be no actual *taking* of the twelve steps. For without humility the program would be nothing more nor less than a continuation of a life of sham and hypocrisy. Without it prayer would be only an empty collection of words—ineffective and lifeless, whereas "an *humble* and contrite heart God will not despise." Without it there is no alcoholic who can ever hope to achieve permanent sobriety, and happiness and contentment. Many are the souls that are cast aside along life's highway simply because they are too proud to use the means that God has ordained for their rehabilitation and salvation—"He hath scattered the proud in the conceit of their heart."

At the meetings, in private conversation and discussion, wherever A.A.'s are gathered together, humility always comes in for its share of the discussion. It is the most important of the virtues, for without it there can be no true virtue. Yet, at the same time, it is one of the most elusive of all the virtues. When one thinks he is most humble he is usually farthest from possessing any semblance of humility. As one self-deceived writer pharisaically said, "If you haven't read my book on humility, you haven't read anything yet."

The simplest definition of humility is the one given by St. Teresa: "Humility is truth." Therefore its opposite, pride, is nothing but a lie, an inordinate or exaggerated opinion of one's self. That is the precise reason why an alcoholic is usually such a liar, because he is so inordinately proud; that is why the alcoholic has so seldom admitted the truth; and finally that is why the alcoholic has become such a frustrated personality, because he has been working on false premises. Hence the first step becomes the biggest obstacle to the A.A. prospect and yet it is the most important step of the whole program. For without a *full* admission in the first step, the *full* practice of the subsequent steps becomes an impossibility. On the other hand, if one does *fully* admit his real condition in the first step, the other eleven become an absolute necessity. Many of the difficulties with the program stem from the fact that the individual did not or will not honestly and unequivocally admit "that he is powerless over alcohol and that his life has become unmanageable." And this is simply saying that he or she refuses to practice *humility.*

In a way it should not be so hard to admit that one is an alcoholic. If we fully understood the program and the blessings and abilities that come with it. It's something like the story of the bricklayer. One day he and his fellow-worker were discussing the inequalities of life, how some seem to fare so much better than others. "Take for example yourself, Mike," Pat ruefully remarked, "you have a brother that is a Bishop, and here you are a bricklayer." "Yes," Mike replied, "it's a shame, the poor fellow couldn't lay a brick if his life depended on it."

Humility is not a denial of good qualities, for being *truth* it is the admission of *all* qualities both good and bad. We admit our faults and endeavor to remedy them; we admit our abilities, accept them as a gift of God and use them. If one is absolutely truthful in the estimation of himself, that person is humble. He accepts his good qualities, his abilities and his accomplishments as the work of God. Such a person when he comes on the program does not exclaim, "See what I have accomplished," but rather in the words of the great scientist, Samuel B. Morse, marvels at his progress with an exclamation of awe, "What God hath wrought!" His defects he clearly knows and he admits them to God, to himself and to his fellowmen. He looks forward to the elimination of them, not through his own strength or ability, but by the grace and help of a Power greater than himself, a supreme Power whom we call God. Until such an attitude of humble estimation of oneself is achieved, no one will attain contented sobriety on the program, for without humility the program is impossible. One person, after having been apparently on the program for a few weeks, slipped and became very full of self-pity—which is also from pride. He set for his sponsor and crying on his shoulder exclaimed, "And to think I have lost all my pride!" "Swell," his sponsor bluntly remarked, "NOW we can begin."

Humility is the root of all the other virtues and hence the very cornerstone of the program.

It is the root of FAITH. For a firm belief in God demands that we take someone else's word for His attributes. We *must* be open-minded, which is but a synonym for honesty. We must accept things on the word of God; we must be willing to learn more about God; and we must admit that *God alone can restore us to sanity.* Without humility this is impossible.

It is the root of HOPE. The proud man trusts in himself. He has no hope outside of his own puny abilities which in reality are but mere fantasies in his pride-blinded intellect. On the other hand the humble man realizes his helplessness and hopes for all things—for the guidance, for the strength and for the accomplishment—from the goodness of a merciful and omnipotent God.

It is the root of CHARITY. The humble man is good to his fellow man. He is patient, forbearing, tolerant, for he esteems *all* men without exception his brothers under God their common Father. He ever keeps uppermost in his conscious mind, "but for the Grace of God, there go I." And he is ever on the alert to be ready—ready to be a fitting instrument in the hands of God in His Providence of Love.

It is the root of CHASTITY. The humble man realizes the need of Divine Help; he knows his inherent human weakness, and therefore he avoids the occasions of sin.

It is the root of OBEDIENCE. The humble man finds it easy to submit to authority. He knows that he is no longer running the show, that Almighty God has taken over the management of his life. Therefore no matter what circumstances or persons dictate his actions, he gladly accepts all authority as the voice of God—the Divine Will.

And so, with all the virtues, we find that each one is upheld, fortified and practiced only if it rests on true humility.

On the other hand, *pride* is the root of all of our troubles. In some way or other every difficulty or trouble we encounter stems from pride. Frustration of egostistical determinations is basic in every dissension in life—and that is pride. The proud man is truly the *self*-made man—and how he adores his maker! Such a man brooks no interference from God nor man, and that means *trouble*. What kind? Let's analyze a few:

1. *Resentments or self-pity*—The number one twin enemy of all alcoholics. Someone is threatening to or has hurt *me*, and I am either—angry at them, or—sorry for myself. In a way self-pity is but resentment turned around. Resentments usually come first, build up, are completely frustrated and end in self-pity. We have a classic example of this in Judas. Remember the time that Mary Magdalen used the precious spices to anoint Christ? Judas was resentful. "We could sell this and give it to the poor." The liar! He wasn't interested in the poor, he was interested in Judas, in self, in financial gain. *He* was being hurt by this "waste." We know what was the ultimate end of Judas. Restment followed restment, and finally the betrayal and the thirty pieces of silver failed to satisfy his ego—he was completely frustrated—he retreated into a morass of self-pity—and then—suicide. How different the humble man, for example, Peter. St. Peter sinned—seriously. Later he repented—he was sorry. Christ made him the head of His Church. But so was Judas sorry. The difference? Judas was sorry because *he* was hurt; Peter was sorry because he had hurt *Christ*. Judas became a suicide; Peter became a saint. Judas was *proud;* Peter was *humble*. Pride causes resentments; resentments turn into self-pity and suicide, either by the hand or by the bottle. The proud man constantly lives with the slogan, "I want what I want when I want it the way I want it; and if I don't get what I want when I want it the way I want it, then I am angry or I am sorry *for myself . . . Poor me!*"

2. *Criticism*—The plague of every group. It stems from pride. The critical man adopts a slightly different slogan: "I don't like what or the way someone does something and I criticize—*not because it is wrong,* or because it does or will harm

the *common good,* but because it is not what or the way I think it should be, and I criticize to destroy so *I can build me up.*" Wives, families, and superiors could learn much from this. At the bottom of every destructive criticism is pride, vanity and self-conceit. Such people are just like buttons, "always popping off." One time such a person died, and the following remark was overheard at his wake: "Poor Jim, he won't like God!"

3. *Intolerance and bigotry*—Something that keeps many out of A.A. and out of religion. Their pride naïvely suggests: "That's no place for you, it's just a bunch of drunks"; or, "You don't want to go to Church, it's just a bunch of hypocrites." They don't realize, with their pride-distorted minds, that if this were true, they would be perfectly at home!

Pride makes men intolerant of people, whereas humility makes one intolerant only of evil itself. God hates sin, but He loves the sinner. Likewise the tolerant man, not blinded by pride, can see in all men the image of God—whether they are white or black; Catholic, Protestant or Jew; rich or poor; drunk or sober. He knows that A.A. is not for any one class, or race, or creed, for he has finally learned the basic truth of human relationship—the Fatherhood of God and the Brotherhood of man; whereas the proud man is intolerant of other creeds, other races, other classes—not because they are wrong—but *"because they are not like ME."*

4. *Difficulty in submitting to God's Will*—A common difficulty stemming from the refusal to admit that God knows best, that God knows better *than I.* Whereas the humble man in the words of Job is ever willing, "The Lord has given, the Lord has taken away; blessed be the Name of the Lord."

5. *Courting temptation*—A cause of many slips. The proud man puts himself in the way of temptation because he has never *honestly* (humbly) admitted that *he is powerless.* He wants to prove to *himself* that *he* can handle the situation. A temporary member once remarked at one of the meetings, "I go into a tavern every day and drink a 'coke' *to prove to myself that I don't have to take a drink of liquor.*" Yes, he is still drink-

ing—liquor. Another fellow, after one of his frequent slips, moaned, "I can't understand why I slipped; I didn't do anything but *pick up a woman and go to a tavern!*"

6. *Worry and despondency*—Someone has defined worry as "an exaggerated sense of one's own responsibility." That's pride. Such a person forgets or refuses to admit that the outcome of every action of life is *God's responsibility;* we are responsible for only the foot-work. Worry is always the property of the management, and we in A.A. have placed the entire management of our lives in the hands of God. Therefore, the entire results are HIS business not OURS. Of course we must plan, but not the result, only the work.

Despondency or discouragement are very akin to worry. They, too, stem from pride. The proud man easily becomes discouraged. Such a person does not progress as fast as he thinks he should. He thinks *his* efforts should produce results, not realizing that all success is entirely in the hands of God. We need only to make the honest effort. The great danger of despondency is, that being deceived by our pride, we become blind to the truth, and are discouraged at difficulties against which we find no strength *in ourselves;* we fail to see the Omnipotent God whose strength *can never fail.* All that is asked of us is to keep on honestly trying. God knows what a mess we are trying to untangle—but we should always remember the 'when' of the untangling is in the hands of God, not ours.

7. *Boasting*—We read in the A.A. book that we are to tell our story *when it is necessary to help others.* The proud man takes every opportunity to brag of his drinking days, ever trying to top the other fellow's story. Did you ever hear, "Take me for example, *I'm* a real alcoholic—I drank two quarts a day for forty years!"

8. *Lack of contrition*—The proud man blames everyone and everything but himself for his troubles—nervousness, sleeplessness, heredity, environment, family, job, employer, and what have you. He is too proud to admit that for most of his difficulties *he* is to blame; that in most circumstances of life, he

can't change others, but *he* can change. He has an act of contrition of his own making. "Through *your* fault" is his daily slogan. Let's don't forget Judas!

9. *Lack of Serenity*—True peace and serenity are only possible through an humble acceptance of *all* the circumstances of life as the Will of God. The proud man is ever trying to arrange *his* affairs as *he* wants them, and hence is always full of conflicts and discontentments. Let us not forget that discontentment is, in plain English, nothing else but rebellion against the Will of God.

10. *Slips through spiritual pride*—Many a man has come into A.A. and made amazing progress in a very short time. Then, forgetting that all this is a gift of God, he begins to think his progress his own. He becomes like the Pharisees "who trusted in themselves and despised others." Remember the story from scripture? "Two men went up to the temple to pray, the one a Pharisee and the other a Publican. The Pharisee standing prayed thus within himself: "O God, I give Thee thanks that I am not like the rest of men, extortioners, unjust, adulterers, as also is this Publican. I fast twice a week, I pay tithes of all I possess.' But the Publican standing afar off, would not as much as raise his eyes to heaven, but kept striking his breast saying: 'O God, be merciful to me a sinner.' I tell you, this man went back to his home justified rather than the other, for everyone who exalts himself shall be humbled, and he who humbles himself shall be exalted."

Some time ago we had occasion to come face to face with a striking example of spiritual pride. One of the members of a group was condemning certain ones for their failure to do what he thought they ought to do. Then, "Take *me* for example, I go to Communion every morning, I teach my children Catechism—in fact I have arrived at a point where *anything I make up my mind to do I can do it.*" Strewing incense at his own shrine. Stupidly glorifying himself. The sequel? He's still drunk.

The longer we are sober the more it becomes necessary to keep ever in our conscious mind, "I am what I am *by the grace of God.* Isn't it marvelous that God can do so much with such poor material?" Remember vice will always beget vice, but *vain-glory* alone is begotten of virtue.

Examples of difficulties and troubles stemming from pride are endless. On the other hand the rewards of humility are unlimited. We find the perfect *expression* of this in the reply which the Blessed Virgin Mary gave the Angel Gabriel when he told her she was to become the Mother of Christ. It is called the 'Magnificat':

"My soul doth magnify the Lord, And my spirit hath rejoiced in God my Savior, *Because He hath regarded the humility* of His handmaid; For behold from henceforth all generations shall call me blessed...." The greatest honor bestowed on a member of the human race—"The Mother of God"—was given "because He hath regarded the *humility* of His handmaid."

"For *He that is Mighty* hath done great things to me, and holy is His name" ... Not see what *I have done,* but *"What God has wrought."*

"And His mercy is from generation unto generation to them that fear Him."

"He hath showed might in His arm; *He hath scattered the proud in the conceit of their heart"* ... The former A.A.'s who are drinking again have been "scattered in the conceit of their heart."

"He hath put down *the mighty from their seat"* ... the mighty in their own estimation. The "I can do it on my own-ers."

"He hath *exalted the humble"* ... Take a look at the ones who are humbly working the program ... the serenity, the happiness, the success....

"He hath filled *the hungry with good things"* ... Those who *admitted they* were powerless, who were hungry for the help of God....

"And *the rich he hath sent empty away"* ... Did you ever hear them? "I haven't lost my job, I've got money, I've got my family, don't need A.A."

The perfect *example* of humility is Christ. Follow Him through His life, His passion, His death. Heed his word, "Learn of Me, for I am meek and *humble* of heart."

In the A.A. book we read, "As we go through the day, we pause when agitated or doubtful, and ask for the right thought or action. We constantly remind ourselves many times each day "Thy Will be done . . . that we are no longer running the show . . . we are then in much less danger of excitement, fear, anger, worry, self-pity, criticism, or foolish decisions. We become more efficient . . . humbly abandon yourself to God . . . admit your faults to Him and your fellowman . . . it works, it really does."

A retreat master once said:

"The price of real maturity in life is a realization of the mistakes we have made. You young men will be really mature the day you look back on your life and cry out: 'My God, what a mess I've made of things!' That day will be a great day for you, but it will be a day, too, when only a *real deep humility* will enable you, despite the mess of the past, to go forward and do life's work."

"It is easy enough, in the years when life's blood is coursing through our veins to rush on and on from day to day, from week to week, and even from year to year taking each new task in its stride . . . but then sooner or later—unless we fail to learn humility—the day of awakening comes . . . it may come with a blinding flash that seems to tear away the very foundations of life . . . but it must come if we are ever to be mature . . . 'My God, what a mess I've made of things!' As I look back how pitiful is the good done, how sparing my help to others, how innumerable my mistakes, the wrongs, how all-pervading my self-seeking! How seamy the finished product!"

"Is such realization discouraging? Absolutely, unless—unless I fall on my knees and *humbly* admit it all to God, with a heartfelt thanks that He knows and understands and will make allowance, full allowance, for my pitiful human frailty. What else could He—or I—expect? Then from my knees I arise and face the future, trusting far less in myself than ever before, and throwing my full weight on God, *knowing that it will be an easy burden for omnipotence.*"

THE TWELVE STEPS

1. *WE ADMITTED WE WERE POWERLESS OVER ALCOHOL—THAT OUR LIVES HAD BECOME UNMANAGEABLE.*

This is first of all an *admission*—an act of the mind. It is not something calling for strength of *will,* but something that calls for a weakening of a rebellious will—an honest *admission* —a *giving in*—or in plain language a true act of *humility* which is nothing more nor less than absolute honesty. The objective fact that we are powerless perhaps has been there for years, but now we recognize that fact, we *admit it*—we take the first step on the road to honesty and humility which alone can lead to sobriety and happiness.

We admit that we are *powerless.* In the matter of alcohol we have absolutely no control, no will. The statements that are made so often by many well-meaning persons about the alcoholic's will-power being rejuvenated is a lot of nonsense. It is this fallacy that leads many after a period of sobriety to "try it again." Experience proves beyond a doubt that an alcoholic can *never* hope to "rejuvenate" his will-power and again control his drinking—he is *powerless.* He has *no will in the matter of alcohol.*

It was quite interesting to read some time ago about an alcoholic who lived in Dublin, Ireland, in the early part of this century. His name is Matt Talbot.[1] For sixteen years he drank heavily. Finally he came, as we say, to his level. *He made up his mind to do something* about his *drinking* and turned to God for the solution. Through the grace of God he not only remained sober, but for forty years led a very holy and penitential life. Today the cause for his Canonization has been introduced at Rome, and we hope that, in God's Providence, he will be canonized. If and when he is, it will be the first alcoholic that the Catholic Church will have canonized.

---

[1] **Cf. "Matt Talbot and Alcoholics Anonymous"—Published by the Catholic Information Society, N.Y.C.**

It is stated in his biography that he came to realize that in the matter of alcohol *he had no will.* Therefore, as a matter of desperate necessity, he had to turn to Almighty God Who alone could give him permanent sobriety. But all the time he was very conscious of the fact that never again could he ever hope to drink normally. Now this is exactly what we mean when we admit we are *powerless—we have no will in the matter of alcoholic indulgence*—and the strength to remain sober must come from the outside, from Almighty God, a fact we shall consider in the next step.

"Admitted we were powerless *over alcohol.*" That is very plain. Alcohol means *all alcohol*: beer, wine, or what have you. No 'beer experiment' or 'wine experiment'—unless you want to learn the hard way. If you are not fully convinced of this, a little beer will convince you—very dramatically! But we prefer to accept the universal experience which tells us that when we say we are powerless over *alcohol,* we mean *all alcohol*—period.

"That our lives had become unmanageable." We admit that we have drifted away from *normal* living, normal thinking, normal drinking. Anyone who will stop a moment to analyze one of his 'binges' should not have a very difficult time admitting that he has drifted away from normalcy. Certainly normal people don't act the way we invariably did on our binges.

We further admit that we have tried innumerable methods to live, think *and drink* normally—and always failed. We tried medicine, psychiatry, sanataria, etc., and they didn't seem to work. So we have come to a point where we admit that in the managing of our lives we are a complete failure. Again honesty —humility. We *are alcoholic.*

Now at this point come the questions that are much discussed in the meetings: "What is an alcoholic?"; "Am I an alcoholic?"

You have heard some remark that they drank two quarts a day. We never will forget the first meeting that we attended. It so happened that an A.A. from out of town was there and made the very positive statement, "I drank two quarts a day for years!"—it scared the daylights out of us! Now, after a bit of experience in the group, we have a slight suspicion that when one says he drank two quarts a day for years—he is bragging. It certainly is by no means necessary to have drunk so much to be a true alcoholic. It is not even necessary to have drunk daily. Perhaps we needed a drink the next morning, perhaps we did not; perhaps we drank alone, perhaps we didn't; maybe we drank constantly, maybe only periodically. In our opinion, we do not believe any of these factors has any bearing on whether one is an alcoholic or not. For years one person went on the fallacy that when one drank the next morning then and then only was he to be considered an alcoholic. The innumerable days he fought with bromides, aspirin, ASA, barbitals, etc., etc., just to avoid that morning drink! But come noon—he could drink to his heart's content and not be an alcoholic!

What then *is* an alcoholic? We believe the most all-inclusive definition on an alcoholic is: One who having taken *one* drink, cannot absolutely guarantee his behavior; one to whom drinking has become a major problem in his life. It makes little difference how often we drink, how long we drink, or where, when, why or how we drink, *if drinking has become a major problem in our life then we are alcoholic.* And being an alcoholic we know that we cannot take that *first* drink. If we do, the problem of drinking to us will become progressively worse, will bring innumerable other problems in its train, and our lives again will become unmanageable. The end? Insanity or death.

Sincerity and honesty in making this admission in the first step is half the solution. Many slip because somewhere in the back of their minds they retain the false hope that maybe some day, somehow, they again will be able to drink normally. Then that supposed day comes—a drink—and bang, off to the races! One who *fully* takes the first step—once and for all—will *want* and *practice* the other eleven. But one who takes it with some sort of a mental reservation, a mental 'maybe,' will only halfheartedly, if at all, practice the others. To *honestly* and *completely* admit that we are powerless over alcohol—that our lives have become unmanageable is the only door that opens to the Alcoholics Anonymous program.

2. *CAME TO BELIEVE THAT A POWER GREATER THAN OURSELVES COULD RESTORE US TO SANITY.*

"A Power greater than ourselves," i.e., a Power outside and beyond *human* power, the Power which we call *God.* We have tried medicine and many other ways and methods to no avail, so now we are going to try the spiritual. This is not religion. Religion is the *formal* worship of God, and has nothing to do with A.A. nor does A.A. have anything to do with religion. The second step simply means that we came to believe that there is a God, and that God can restore us to normal and happy living. We do not approach this step with an attitude of 'show me,' but with a humble attitude of acceptance, an attitude of faith and humility—with an open mind, willing to learn more about this Power Whom we call God. If a person *won't* admit this, he is rather hopeless and A.A. has little, if anything, to offer. For, the person who refuses to accept the fact that there is anything, or any Power, greater than himself, is rather a hopeless egotist. To his stinted mind, no thing, no person, not even a God can do something more than he in his blinding pride thinks he can do.

However, we do find people who want the A.A. program (and need it!) who *can't* seem to accept the idea of God. There is here a big difference from the one who *won't* accept it. The former is sincere, honest and willing. And in the course of time —in God's own time—such a person will be enabled by the grace of God to see clearly. Experience has borne out this fact time and time again. But the man who *positively refuses to* believe in God hasn't a chance as long as he retains such a negative attitude and bad will. It is clearly stated in the Alcoholics Anonymous book that "No one should have difficulty with the spiritual side of the program. *Willingness, honesty and openmindedness are essentials* of recovery. But they *are indispensable!"*

One man solved his difficulties in this manner: "I've thought a lot about the idea of God, and I found it difficult to believe in God. However, I finally reasoned it out this way—when I die I would rather wake up in the next life finding there is no God, having believed in Him here, than to find there is a God, having *not* believed in Him here." That is very logical.

We find by experience that the firmer and greater our belief in God the greater will be our success in sobriety, the greater our happiness, and the more serene our contentment. The more fully we admit that God, and God alone can restore us to sanity, the more will we seek God as the solution of *all* of our problems and difficulties; and the more willing will we be to make the full decision to turn our life and will over to Him as we do in the third step.

3. *MADE A DECISION TO TURN OUR WILL AN OUR LIVES OVER TO THE CARE OF GOD AS WE UNDERSTOOD HIM.*

This is another decision—a *full* decision with no reservations, no holding back, no "if's," "and's" or "but's." The more complete and unconditional our decision was in step number one, the more readily and fully will we make this decision to turn our lives over to God. It is the mental reservations in the admission that we are powerless over alcohol and that our lives have become unmanageable that often proves a stumbling block in step number three. Many would like to turn *most* of their lives over to the care of God, but certain associations, practices, and relationships—we don't like to let them go. But we should realize, that when we make up our minds to turn our will and our lives over to the care of God, that means without reservation. Therefore all dishonesty, dishonest practices, illicit relationships, and all the many things in our lives *that we know are contrary to the will of God must go.* It is here that we understand fully the meaning of the term "unconditional surrender." And having once and for all fully made this decision of surrender, we will perhaps for the first time in our lives, experience the true meaning of peace and serenity. We will finally begin to live. We shall at last understand what Christ meant when He told us that we must die in order to live—die to all that is of self in order to live to all that is of God—His will, His providence, His Love.

If we are not willing to take this step unconditionally, then as we are advised in the A.A. book, we should pray that God will make us willing—praying both for the will to do and the strength to accomplish. This, for a time, may be necessary for most of us. For, after years away from normal living, from God and His will, it is not going to be so easy to change and we may need to pray daily, even hourly, "God, make we willing to do Thy will."

"As we understood Him." We are above everything else searching for *truth.* Therefore, we don't *make up* a God to fit *us,* but we search for God *according to our honest convictions.* We want a God Who "can restore us to sanity," a "Power greater than ourselves," not a figment of *our* imagination or a product of *our* own will. If we have no clear cut idea of God, we *ask* that *He* give it to us. Isn't it very plain that the making of a God to suit *us* is a contradiction of the admission we made "that *we* were *powerless"?* The safe and sure way is to *humbly* pray, "God, that I may see!"

4. *MADE A SEARCHING AND FEARLESS MORAL INVENTORY OF OURSELVES.*

"Searching and fearless." "To search" means to *carefully* look for. "Fearless" means having no fear of *whatever* we may find. Therefore, when we make a "searching and fearless inventory," we are going to leave *no* nook nor cranny of ourselves, past or present, unturned. We are going to *fearlessly search* for *all* of our defects. We are not going to make a phony list; we have been making such a list for years, and now we are going to replace it with an honest one—item by item. We do not find any successful business man taking an inventory and making wild guesses as to the actual kind and number of his stock in trade. Imagine such a person looking on his shelves and saying, "*About* a dozen of such-and-such," missing half of them. No; he takes his stock item by item. How many of this? Twelve. How many of that? Sixteen—ten good, six soiled. Of course we are going to find a lot of rotten stock, but then what do we expect to find after years of abnormal living and drinking? Some of it is going to be a little putrid and unpleasant, *but it is in the inventory.* That is the basic reason we are taking it—in order to know what has to be eliminated in the next step. They tell of the gentleman who came to his sponsor with twenty-one typewritten pages! He was honest, he knew the real meaning of the terms "searching and fearless"; and he got in return happiness and peace and serenity.

Now we come to the question, "What measuring stick are we to use in taking our inventory?" In other words how are we going to know what is to be eliminated from the stock at hand?

First we have CONSCIENCE. Every human being has been endowed by his Creator with a basic knowledge of good and evil. The alcoholic, who probably has subjected his conscience to a false justification of his antics, should of course precede his inventory with humble prayer for guidance. Again, "O God, that I may see!"

Next we have the TEN COMMANDMENTS of God. They point out definite actions, etc., which are right or wrong. They show us our obligations to God and to our fellowman. They both command and forbid—they are the positive Divine measuring rod.

Then there are the OBLIGATIONS OF OUR STATE OF LIFE—as a married man, a father of a family, a man in business, and all the obligations which we assumed by that particular circumstances in which we live.

We also may have OBLIGATIONS TO OUR CHURCH. In this there are specific obligations as to attendance, church laws, etc., etc.

Again we have the SEVEN FUNDAMENTAL PASSIONS of man: The tendency to pride, envy, greed, lust, gluttony, sloth and anger (which includes that A-1 enemy of all alcoholics—*resentment*). What are we going to do about these? Those who are experienced in such matters tell us that we should 'act contrary.' Therefore, if we tend to be angry and resentful, we should practice the contrary positive act by speaking kindly and doing good to those against whom we are angry or resentful.

This *positive* act will tend to eliminate the negative angry feeling or tendency. If we tend to be gready, we should practice the charity of giving; if we tend to be slothful (which is nothing else but plain laziness) we should endeavor to keep busy; and so on down the list. We do not *worry* about them, nor about getting rid of them, for we shall have them more or less all of our lives. Our job is simply to try *daily* to control them. The ultimate elimination of them is in the hands of God.

The opposite of *love* is HATRED. Hatred for our fellowman comes from a lack of realization that *all* men are children of God our Father. Therefore, if we truly love God and our fellowman, there will be no room for hatred, even for the lowest of His creatures.

"Of ourselves." We in no way permit the faults of others to enter this inventory. We assume full responsibility. It is an inventory of ourselves and *our* faults, not of our wives, nor of our boss, nor of our family, nor of our friends—it is *a searching and fearless moral inventory of ourselves.*

5. *ADMITTED TO GOD, TO OURSELVES, AND TO ANOTHER HUMAN BEING THE EXACT NATURE OF OUR WRONGS.*

First of all this step implies that we have sorrow for what we have done wrong, and that *we* admit that *we* have been responsible for it. This is not self-pity or self-sorrow. It is sorrow that *we* have hurt or offended God and our fellowman, *not that we have been hurt. We* have been loaded with self-pity for years and now, by admitting *our fault* to God, to ourselves and to another human being, we are going to go far in eliminating sorrow for self.

We see the big difference between true sorrow and self-pity in St. Peter and Judas. Judas was sorry, and Peter was sorry, but Judas was sorry because *he had been hurt,* "he repented *himself."* Thus he became full of self-pity, which in turn led to despair and suicide. Peter was sorry because he had denied *Christ.* Peter had contrition, Judas nothing but self-pity.

By no means should we permit ourselves to fumble around in a morass of self-pity, or what is as bad, indulge in self-condemnation. If we do we are liable to start a guilt-complex and our state will be worse than before. We shall be of no use to ourselves nor anybody else.

"We admitted *to ourselves.*" This means that we admitted that *we* are responsible—that all the mess we are in, *we* could have avoided it. For once in our lives we begin to accept responsibility.

"Admitted . . . to *another human being.*" Some might hold back at this, thinking that the admission to God and to themselves is sufficient. But let's remember—we are alcoholics, we want not only sobriety but peace and contentment, and we *need big chunks of humility.* Holding back from this step is nothing more nor less than being too *proud* to let someone else know how loaded we are with faults and failings. It is very indicative that the admission to God and to ourselves was not very honest, and came not from the heart but merely from the lips.

In regard to Catholics they will want to go to confession, but that is not enough, they should have a full discussion of their soul's condition with their confessor, in order that they might receive proper advice and direction in eliminating the *cause* of the wrongs they confess. A non-Catholic may go to anyone he chooses, but all should remember, that if it is to be to a member of the group, it should be with *one who has taken this step,* not with someone who might say, "I never took that step, and look at me, I'm sober." Such a one may be sober *now,* but experience proves that *no one* will achieve contentment and happiness and serenity *unless* they admit their fault to *another human being.* It is the doing of this all-important job that casts out fears, phobias, and dishonesty. And having completed it, we can at last face the world, and anyone in that world, with a clear conscience and a serenity that must be experienced to be understood.

"We admitted . . . the *exact* nature of our wrongs." Again we have honesty. Nothing counts but being honest. No dressing up, no cutting corners, but thoroughly, and honestly and *ex-*

actly admitting the nature of our wrongs. "It works, it really does!"

6. *WERE ENTIRELY READY TO HAVE GOD REMOVE ALL THESE DEFECTS OF CHARACTER.*

We are *ready* and *willing*. We place everything in the hands of God. We are willing to let His Providence work on our character in order to rebuild it. He may use some striking measures, but we are ready. He may put us in circumstances where someone is always aggravating us—that is to teach us *patience*. He may give us association with someone we don't like—that is to teach us *charity* and *tolerance*. He may put us in a position of inferiority—that is to teach us *humility*. He may bring it about that we have to work hard—that is to eliminate *laziness*. He may even give us failure—that is to teach us *courage* and *trust in Him*. All the disappointments, circumstances or whatever He may arrange for us in His Providence, are *all* going to be opportunities to eliminate our defects of character.

The present Archbishop of Indianapolis made a statement shortly after he was appointed to the Archdiocese that fits in exactly with what this step implies. Some of the priests of the Archdiocese called on him to find out what arrangements he wanted to make for his installation as Archbishop. He told them, "You go ahead and make the arrangements, I'll fit in." Now that is what we are saying to Almighty God, "You arrange my life. I have turned it over to Your Providence. *I'll fit in*. Grant me the grace to change the things I can; to accept the things I cannot change; and the wisdom to know the difference." But in *all* things, *Thy will be done!*

7. *HUMBLY ASKED GOD TO REMOVE OUR SHORTCOMINGS.*

Again we have humility. Realizing that the job we are ready to undertake is humanly impossible, we ask Him to do it for us and give us the strength to do the foot-work. We cannot ask Him *once* and then quit—we ask Him *daily*. We cannot ask for the morrow, only for today—twenty-four hours at a time, oftener if necessary. It is normally a slow process, this rejuvenation of our character and personality. But after all, we did not get this way overnight, and we are not going to come into full personality overnight. It is ordinarily a lifetime work. We should always remember that we are working on the most difficult job in life—we are rebuilding, not a house, nor a town, nor a nation, nor a world, but *a man*. That is slow. It is difficult, and we should never be agitated over lack of progress. If we get mad again, if we become resentful, or if all of our faults pop back on occasion, we are not surprised, but we are amazed that we don't do worse. As long as we are honestly doing the foot-work, hand in hand with Almighty God, we know that in His own time, success will be ours—a *gift* from God.

8. *MADE A LIST OF ALL THE PERSONS WE HAD HARMED AND BECAME WILLING TO MAKE AMENDS TO THEM ALL.*

"Made a *list*"—a list of the people *we had harmed*. Why a list? So that seeing these injustices, black on white, they may be the more emphatically impressed on our minds and memories. It is to replace a list that we have carried around in our imaginations for years of the people who, so we thought, were *harming us*. We had resentfully gone along imagining that if we could only change circumstances, we would change; that if people would only change, we would change; that *if we could change others*, we would be all right. As one person remarked, "If you would only make my wife change, I'd be O.K." Nonsense! We can't often change others, but *we* can change—*we* can *"fit in."* And, in making an *honest* list in this step, we are amazed to find that it wasn't others who were harming us, but that *we* had been harming others.

"Made a list of *all* persons we had harmed." Honesty again. We leave out *no one* from this list. Whether friend or foe, whether we like them or not, whether superior or inferior, we make a list of *all* the persons we had harmed. We make no excuses in the odd case where we had also been harmed; we don't say, "Well, maybe I did harm him, but after all look what he did to me"—no "but's," no self-exoneration, no retaliation—*all the* persons *we* had harmed. Difficult? Sure, but only unbending egotism makes it impossible.

"The persons we had *harmed.*" Our injustices will be classified under three heads: *material* wrongs; *moral* wrongs; and *spiritual* wrongs.

Material. The wrongs we have done others in matters of material things: money, damages, injury to persons and property, and any injustice in the material order.

Moral. The injuries we have done to others wherein we have been the direct or indirect cause of his wrongdoings. We have given scandal; led others to wrongdoings by bad example to friends, associates, family, etc.; taught others to do wrong, to drink, steal, etc.; permitted others to drift into evil ways by shirking responsibilities to children, inferiors, etc.

Spiritual. The wrongs we have done by neglect of our obligations to our Church and our God; neglect of prayer and the worship owing to God. Here we find the necessity of penance for *all* our wrongs, over and above the mere restitutions owing in justice and indicated under material and moral wrongs.

"Became willing to make amends to them *all.*" We are willing and *ready.* No hesitancy and still no hurry. We take our time in order to be thorough. We have agreed to *go to any length* to defeat alcohol, therefore we are ready to make amends to them *all*—even our enemies!

9. *MADE DIRECT AMENDS TO SUCH PEOPLE WHEREVER POSSIBLE EXCEPT WHEN TO DO SO WOULD INJURE THEM OR OTHERS.*

"Made *direct* amends." This may seem and actually be difficult, especially to people we don't like, but we have asked for it. We want humility and we know that an alcoholic needs humility more than anything else in the world. This step is a short cut to humility. Ordinarily, if a person has done an injustice, he may make it up without the injured person's knowledge. In such manner he has fulfilled his obligation of *justice,* but he has not practiced *humility.* When we are asked or advised to make amends directly and openly to the ones we have harmed, we are simply being shown the shortest route to the practice of humility. Hence we admit our faults and make restitution *openly* and *directly* to the persons we have harmed. We don't do it in a 'behind the bush' manner—we make *direct* amends.

"Wherever *possible.*" We don't hedge in this matter of making restitution, but in some instances it is either impossible or in the doing of it we would injure *others.* In such cases, under *competent* advice, we turn the matter over to God. This is often the only recourse in matters of scandal where we can only through our prayers and sacrifices humbly petition God to make up to the person we had led to wrongdoing.

Some don't like this idea of leaving it up to God. We wish *we* could make it up. We fail to see the pride that lies hidden in such desire. Or else our weak faith fails to realize that the omnipotent God, on Whom we are relying to restore us to sanity and sobriety, can and will make up all the damage in such cases *if we have the humility to leave it in His hands.* Pride says, "I wish I could make it up"; humility admits, "I can't, God, You do it for me."

So, in circumstances we can't change; in instances where we might do serious harm to others; and in cases where restitution is *impossible,* we place it entirely in the hands of God. But in all of these circumstances, we only do so *on competent advice.* We never trust our own judgment. That is one of the purposes of the discussion of our faults and wrongs with another.

"Injure *them* or *others.*" We take no thought of any possible or even probable injury that might come to *us* in this step. We hesitate *only* when we might injure *others.* It may even be that we might suffer serious inconvenience and have our standing seriously hurt, but "we agreed to go to any length to defeat alcohol." If we haven't, we had better go back to step one and begin over again—*honestly.*

This business of restitution may take a long time. It may ever take years, but it is thoroughness, not haste, that counts. We do not hurry, *nor* do we *needlessly* delay. "Easy does it," but *procrastination* is very destructive of honesty and sincerity.

10. *CONTINUED TO TAKE PERSONAL INVENTORY AND WHEN WE WERE WRONG PROMPTLY ADMITTED IT.*

Here we have a continuation of steps four, eight and nine. When we took our general inventory we had quite a shock. We thought we had a good business, that we were big shots, that *we* didn't have any faults; but when we took stock honestly, we found to our dismay that we weren't much at all and that all the virtues we thought we possessed were falsely labeled. Now we do not intend to have this happen again, so we regularly (daily if possible) take an honest personal inventory. As mentioned previously, in this inventory we don't pay too much attention to *how* we have succeeded, but only to how honestly are we *trying*. The success is up to God, ours is only the foot-work. This conviction will help to avoid indulging in self-pity with some such soliloquy as "I have tried so hard for so long and I still get angry, get hurt, criticize, etc." What do we expect? We should be amazed that we don't do worse. We should always remember that God in judgment is not going to ask how much we have accomplished, but *how honestly and sincerely* did we *try*. And the strongest and the weakest can always sincerely try.

"*Personal* inventory." This is to prevent a relapse into the old fallacy of thinking that others were injuring us. If we strive for a constant and true knowledge of *ourselves,* we won't be so apt to blame others or to judge them. This is a *personal* inventory—*our* faults.

There is one great danger in this regular inventory. When we look for our faults we might concentrate too much on our progress and fall into what we call 'spiritual pride.'[1] For if, through God's grace, we are enabled to eliminate many of our faults, we are liable to take the credit to ourselves, which is pride again and the prelude to a bad collapse. Like the person mentioned in our discussion of humility, we can so easily take the attitude of "See, what *I* have accomplished," instead of the humble admiration of "What *God* has wrought." Many of us have

---

[1] Cf. p. 41.

miraculously eliminated certain faults *by the grace of God.* And by ever being conscious of the fact that *it is God's work,* not ours, we shall avoid the pitfall of spiritual pride. God, in His mercy, often permits many faults to remain—in order to keep us humble.

"When wrong *promptly* admitted it." We don't find excuses or, by pure procrastination, put it off, but we make it up (whatever the wrong may be) *immediately.* Why? Because if we don't, we probably will begin to think the other person was at fault, and resentment will set in, grow and bear fruit—discontent, negative thinking, neglect of prayer and—a little drink might lift our spirits! Remember?

11. *SOUGHT THROUGH PRAYER AND MEDITATION TO IMPROVE OUR CONSCIOUS CONTACT WITH GOD AS WE UNDERSTOOD HIM PRAYING ONLY FOR KNOWLEDGE OF HIS WILL FOR US AND THE POWER TO CARRY THAT OUT.*

We analyzed this step in our discussion of prayer and meditation.[1] However we should bear four thinks always in mind:

1) We must *seek.* We must make an honest effort to learn to pray well and to meditate well—*daily.*

2) We must seek to *improve* our *conscious* contact with God. We cannot stagnate and accept whatever idea of God happens to be ours at the beginning of our sobriety. We must *with an open mind* seek *to improve,* and gradually become more and more *God-conscious.*

3) We must pray for *knowledge of God's will,* not that God will satisfy *our* wills. "Illumine our mind, inflame our heart, strengthen our will!" *"Thy* will be done!"

4) We must *ask* for the *strength* which will constantly remind us that *we are powerless.* And, since we need this Divine assistance daily, we must *daily* ask God for it.

---

[1] Cf. p. 19.

12. *HAVING HAD A SPIRITUAL AWAKENING (EXPERIENCE) AS A RESULT OF THESE STEPS WE TRY TO CARRY THIS MESSAGE TO OTHER ALCOHOLICS AND TO PRACTICE THESE PRINCIPLES IN ALL OUR AFFAIRS.*

"A spiritual *experience of awakening.*" Many are stumped by this. After a period of sobriety, they can't seem to realize that they have had any spiritual experience or awakening. The reason is because many do not understand what the expression signifies. If they would ask themselves: "Who sent someone to explain A.A.? Who enabled me to remain sober for the time I have been dry in spite of frequent craving and temptation? Who enabled me to pray these past weeks or months? Who brought about all of the entire chain of circumstances that brought me to the condition of sobriety I enjoy today? I admitted I was powerless, where did the strength come from?" *God gave it to me.* Each and every circumstance that helped me along the road to sobriety was the *experiencing of spiritual help*—the help of God, a spiritual experience. And, as a result, we have *awakened* to a new sense of values, new attitudes towards life, God and our fellowman—in short we have had a *spiritual awakening.*

Many seem to have great difficulty in achieving this awakening. Those who have such difficulty might well *carefully* retrace the other eleven steps, for in step twelve we have the spiritual awakening *as a result of these steps.* And anyone who does not have this spiritual re-birth and *know* it in all probability has not *honestly* and *thoroughly* taken the first eleven steps, for when they have thus taken them, no one will have to tell them; they *will* have the spiritual awakening and *they will know it.* Each step gives a bit—these are the spiritual experiences. They in turn contribute to the whole which is a spiritual awakening to a new life, the life of grace, or peace, and happiness and serenity. It is not our own work, but *a gift of God,* a reward for our good will and humility. "He hath regarded the humility of his handmaid . . . He hath exalted the humble."

"Try to *carry this message to other alcoholics*"—the so-called 'Twelfth Step Work.' We do it out of a sense of gratitude and of our realization of the need of insurance against a slip. In all of the work of the twelfth step we *give*. We should always remember that the program is essentially a *give* program. We shall receive much, but not unless we give. "Freely have you received, freely give."

Let us consider some of the instances of twelfth step work:

1) We attend meetings *regularly*. This is especially necessary to keep our thinking straight and to insure against a possible let-up on the other steps with the inevitable result, a slip. Many a one has admitted that the first step towards a slip was the missing of the meetings. His insurance lapsed, he got back into his old ways of thinking—and *drinking*. We should never forget that every meeting we attend, *even though* we think *we* do not benefit by the talk, etc., we are *giving* someone a good example and encouragement by our very presence.

2) We make calls on new members *when* we are asked, not only when we *feel* like it. We are practicing charity and unselfishness—vital virtues especially for the alcoholic.

3) We speak at the meetings when asked. It is a part of our contribution. Even though we may not be accomplished public speakers, *everyone* has a message and *our* presentation may have the answer someone has been seeking for a long time.

4) We give financial donations when asked. It is amusing how 'tight' some become on the occasion of a donation being asked. Some who spent hundreds of dollars on liquor, 'squawk' their heads off when asked for fifty cents for the 'kitty.'

5) We own and loan the A.A. book. Many do not have a full knowledge of the program because they have never, or at most only cursorily, read the A.A. book. We should read and re-read it. We certainly do not absorb it in one reading. Some are amazed at certain statements made at meetings, or in conversation, relative to the alcohol problem and its solution which were merely taken,

sometimes 'verbatim,' from the A.A. book. We should *own* the book, *read* the book, and *loan* it to others—it is all part of the twelfth step work.

6) We should encourage those with difficulties and have the patience and charity to listen to their troubles. We should never forget the day when a good listener was a necessity to us when we first came to A.A.

7) We should serve as chairmen and on the various committees when asked to do so. This is also twelfth step work and a wonderful training in both responsibility and unselfishness.

8) We should gladly sponsor new prospects and *conscientiously* accept such responsibility. There has been many a slip because the sponsor was a "one-call-that's-all' A.A. We should realize that the average newcomer needs someone to lean on for awhile—some more, some less—until his thinking clears and he gets both feet on the program. A drowning man needs more than a throw-line to save him. "Freely have you received, freely *give*."

9) Finally we should give of whatever talent we may have been blessed in order that, through us, God may bring others from the darkness of alcoholic fantasy into the light of His grace.

We should do all of these things with a *conscious* idea of sacrifice in order to discipline ourselves away from the habits of selfishness into habits of unselfishness and love. We should, in fine, *work* the program and then we will never need a program for the work at hand.

CHARITY

"... and the greatest of these is CHARITY"

In our past discussions we have considered some of the primary ingredients that go into the twelve steps of the A.A. program. We have first of all seen how in reality the entire program is nothing more nor less than a *spiritual* way of life. The basis of this spiritual life we found to be humility. We also considered the importance of prayer and meditation as a means to obtain the necessary strength and guidance to live the program. Now let us consider another ingredient that is absolutely paramount for the program to run smoothly. This ingredient we call *charity.* Nothing else but true charity will keep out friction and enable an individual or a group of individuals to function smoothly and to live in contentment.

The "how" of charity is strikingly exemplified in the life of St. John. On one occasion when he, with Christ and several of the other Apostles, were visiting a small Samaritan town, the townspeople did not receive them very kindly. To retaliate, St. John urged Christ to "call down upon them the fire of Heaven and destroy them." But towards the end of his life in practically every other paragraph of his writings he urges his disciples to the practice of charity with the words, "Little children, LOVE one another." What a tremendous change had come over one who in deep resentment and hatred had urged injury but now in all things urges LOVE which is but a synonym for charity.

To thoroughly understand how this change can take place in a human being we must first understand the meaning of love. There are many erroneous definitions of love in the modern world. To many people love is synonymous with lust; to others it is merely dependent upon human emotion; and there are some who think that love only aims at possession. All of these conceptions of love seem oblivious of the fact that such "love" is in reality selfishness—the desire to have, to possess, to satisfy SELF. It is true that true love also ultimately seeks possession, but primarily it seeks to give.

Selfishness says, "I want; give ME." True love says, "I want TO GIVE." Hence the quality of our love can always be tested by its willingness to give, to serve, to do FOR the object of our love. If we wish to know whether we really love God we need not bother to consider our emotional reaction to His service; we need only to ask ourselves, "How WILLING are we to SERVE GOD, to GIVE ourselves for Him, to do His will?" Likewise if we wish to know whether we truly love our neighbor we need only to ask, "How WILLING are we to SERVE our neighbor? How WILLING are we to GIVE of our talents, time, etc., for the sake of our neighbor?"—regardless of whether there is human attraction.

Love, although often cloaked in human emotion, is basically a product of the WILL. Therefore the validity of our love either for God or our neighbor is verified by our WILLINGNESS, not by our feelings. We may not be attracted to certain people but this fact in no way prevents us from loving them; from being *willing* to serve them.

All of this leads to the true definition of love which tells us that LOVE IS SACRIFICE. That is the reason that God tells us that He so loved the world as to *give* His only Divine Son for its redemption; That is the reason that Christ tells us that "greater love than this no man has than that he lay down his life for his friend"; and that is the reason that He died for us because His love for man was perfect. Furthermore, the basis of The Fatherhood of God and the brotherhood of man, of which we so often speak, is *love*. That is why difficult things in human relationship become not only easy but desirable to him or her who loves.

One time a very rich man was visiting the leper colony in Louisiana. Seeing the nuns caring for the lepers, binding their wounds and cleansing the filth of their disease—and all of this with a smile—he was so amazed that he told one of the nuns later on that he would not do that for a million dollars. He was stunned when the good nun replied: "Neither would I."

This same factor comes into play in our twelfth-step work when we make a call on a new prospect who is no "tender rose."

We would not do it for a million dollars but we do it because we want to give. We are practicing charity. We are practicing love.

The *necessity* of charity in life is indicated to us in the Scriptures. There we are told, "Thou shalt love the Lord Thy God with all thy heart, with all thy soul and all thy strength, and thy neighbor as thyself . . . in this commandment is contained ALL the law and the prophets."

The more we analyze this commandment, the more easily can we understand that if we love God above all things and our neighbor as ourselves, we would not need any other law. For if we truly loved God we would not need a commandment to tell us that He is to be worshiped above all else; we would not need a commandment to tell us not to take His name in vain; and we would not need a commandment to tell us to keep holy the one day of seven that is dedicated to Him. If we love our neighbor as much as we love ourselves, we would not need to be told not to kill or injure our neighbor; not to break the bounds of modesty and purity; not to steal, not to lie about our neighbor; not to think evil of or to wish harm to our neighbor.

If we carry this point a bit further and if we really and fully acknowledge that ALL men are our brothers under one common Father, Who is God, it will not make any difference whether they are black or white; whether they are Christian, Pagan or Jew; whether they are rich or poor; whether they are learned or ignorant; whether they are Protestant or Catholic; whether they are a success in life or a failure; whether they are drunk or sober yes, whether they are slipping or staying on the program. No longer would there be unjust criticism, intolerances, bigotry, prejudice, dissensions (group or otherwise), rash judgment, contentions. *Love* would cause all friction to vanish. For if we loved our neighbors as ourselves, we certainly would harbor no attitude nor take any action against any of our fellowmen that we would not take against ourselves.

Now let us analyze some of the difficulties that we find on occasion in our groups that stem from, and are fed by the lack of charity.

I. *TOLERANCE.*

1. *Tolerance In General.*

We hear very much discussion on all sides of the question of tolerance. And we find two questions that are most frequently asked in this matter, viz., "What is tolerance?" and "How far must one go in showing and practicing tolerance?"

Like humility, the question of tolerance and intolerance is elusive. At the same time a precise understanding of it is necessary for a true conception of charity, for TOLERANCE MIGHT BE DEFINED AS THE MINIMUM FULFILLMENT OF THE LAW OF CHARITY. The word itself is derived from the Latin "tolerare" which means "to permit." Therefore we tolerate people, circumstances, etc., even though we do not accept or condone qualities or conditions of these people or circumstances. We must do this either because we *must* which oftentimes is difficult; or we may do this because WE LOVE the PERSON connected with, or who is responsible for, or who permits those qualities or conditions, thereby recognizing and beginning to practice charity which makes tolerance easy. It is thus that God TOLERATES, i.e., permits sin because HE LOVES THE SINNER. He does not WILL evil but tolerates it in order that ultimate GOOD may come to the PERSON of the sinner because He LOVES him. It is true that in human judgment we often confuse what is really good and evil. And what often seems evil to us is in the eyes of God good. This is often true in times of sickness, loss, etc. We deem these circumstances as evil, whereas in reality the only evil is sin—a thought or an action contrary to the Will of God. It is because we so often judge as evil only those things that irritate US, which is not motivated by charity but by self-love, that so often it becomes difficult for us to be tolerant. And thus we become intolerant because we love ourselves and our own opinions (which we soothingly refer to as convictions) more than the basic fact of all human relationship which tells us that ALL human beings are children of the same Father and equal one to another; and that we must love THEM as ourselves; and in doing so we TOLERATE their qualities, circumstances, opinions, etc., because we DO LOVE

THEM. An in all circumstances of life we are TOLERANT because God either wills or permits them to exist. In this way TOLERANCE becomes easy and desirable because we "love God above all things and our neighbor as ourselves."

The more we grow along the path of charity the more we want TO GIVE for God and our neighbor. Mere tolerance ceases to be a problem—it gradually becomes a habit—a product of love. For the minimum of love is tolerance; the perfection of love is WILLING SACRIFICE. "Greater love than this no man has, than he willingly give his life for his friend." That is why Christ so willingly embraced Calvary—His was perfect love.

We find many instances in various groups of the lack of knowledge of or the practice of the law of charity. There are groups here and there who will not accept a new "prospect" without previous investigation into his background! There are other groups who will only accept prospects of their own social standing! Some will not TOLERATE the presence of Negroes, persons of certain denominations, neurotics, unfortunates, drug addicts, etc., etc.! In an odd instance a group will not accept a person unless he or she adheres strictly to a long list of rules and regulations which are of their own making and are nowhere to be found in the twelve steps! Here and there we find groups of the same city or town who will not interassociate with each other! Could they be forgetting: "There but for the grace of God go I"? Or could they be forgetting that A.A. is for ALL who have an alcoholic problem? Or could they be forgetting what is so admirably pointed out in the "big book," "We should never look down upon the lowliest of God's creatures or the worst of man's mistakes"? Could they be forgetting the law of charity? But just a minute—could WE be forgetting it—in condemning them? Should we not TOLERATE these circumstances?

2. *Tolerance of Circumstances.*

a. *External.* We often will not tolerate circumstances connected with our job, superiors, family, associates, etc., because we have not a true concept of the law of charity. If we did we would realize that all the circumstances we cannot change, whether good or evil, are either willed or tolerated by God for our neighbor's or our own good—and that thus in loving God and His Will above all things and our neighbor as ourselves it would become an easy matter to tolerate them.

b. *Internal.* We are agitated because of nervous tension, sickness, sleeplessness, etc., etc., because in failing to see God's Will in these circumstances or in failing to accept God's Will in them we have become intolerant. Contentment is possible under such conditions only by accepting them as God's Will, i.e., IF we love God.

3. *Tolerance of Religion.*

When we are tolerant of the religious views of others it does not imply that we accept their views. We simply PERMIT them to hold their views thereby admitting the right to follow the dictates of their conscience—a right guaranteed to all by the Constitution of the United States.

People who are intolerant are generally referred to as "bigots." They often excuse themselves with the assertation that they have a right to defend their "convictions." But one writer very succinctly points out the difference between "bigotry" and "conviction" by defining "conviction" as "a knowledge which one can explain without getting angry."

Bigotry often stems from prejudice, which according to Webster is "judgment without previous investigation." That is why openmindedness and the willingness to learn often removes bigotry. Over and above this the true understanding and practice of the law of charity would eliminate all bigotry. Fortunately, in A.A. we find less bigotry than in most groups of men, but here and there it does crop up. Are such looking for denominations in A.A. or for sobriety and happiness which later is impossible without tolerance.

II. *CRITICISM, GOSSIP, TALEBEARING.*

One of the most damaging habits that a person can acquire is the habit of uncharitable talk. It is amazing how widespread this practice is and we often wonder whether such people ever could possibly realize the almost diabolical damage that can ultimately stem from a single unkind remark. The great poet, Horace, wrote the much quoted line: "Fama quae crescit eundo" —which, translated, means: "gossip which so grows as it goes." He was expressing the well-known fact that all uncharitable talk in growing does more and more damage as it is related from mouth to mouth. How many wrecks of life there are and have ever been because someone so forgot the law of charity as to slander and ruin his neighbor's good name! Such a person seems to have never realized the fact that all men are equal and that in loving our neighbor as ourselves we would never say anything about someone else which we would not say about ourselves.

Why do we criticize and slander and detract and gossip? Is it not because we look down upon the victims of our tirades? Certainly we could hardly love them, could we? If we did we would be very busy saying good things about them; praying for them; helping them, because to us they are always our equals before God and, hence, if we love God above all things and our neighbor as ourselves we would never use the tongue God gave us to praise Him to destroy the lives of others. If we could but *understand* the law of *love!*

"Not Understood! We move along asunder,
Our paths grow wider as the seasons creep
Along the years; We marvel and we wonder
Why life is life: We drink to fall asleep —
Not Understood!

"Not understood! We gather false impressions,
And hug them closer as the years go by,
Till virtues often seem to us transgressions,
And thus men rise and fall and live and die —
Not Understood!

"Not understood! The secret springs of action
Which lie beneath the surface and the show,
Are disregarded; with self-satisfaction
We judge our neighbor—and then often go—
Not Understood!

"Not understood! How trifles often change us!
The thoughtless sentence, or the fancied slight—
Destroy long years of friendship and estrange us;
And o'er our souls there falls a freezing blight;
Not Understood!

"Not understood! How many hearts are aching!
For lack of sympathy! Oh, day by day—
How many cheerless, lonely hearts are breaking!
How many noble spirits pass away!
Not Understood!

"Not understood! How oft' we deem our own life purer
Than that of him or her—(we judge like gods!)
Whereas, alas, our own soul's surer
To stumble and to totter 'gainst life's odds!
Not Understood!

"O God! That men would see a little clearer!
Or judge less harshly where they cannot see!
O God! That men would draw a little nearer
To one another; they'd be nearer Thee
AND understood!"

III. *IRRESPONSIBILITY OF SPONSORSHIP.*

Many times an individual neglects the responsibilities of sponsorship in helping a new member because the new member is not an attractive personality, because he doesn't LIKE certain qualities in him; or because the new member is not quite equal in his social, financial or religious circumstances. Love, on the other hand, would dictate that we GIVE to all irrespective of such circumstances. It is true that the time that would have to be given to the new prospect would demand sacrifice—but after all, what is love but sacrifice?

IV. *MONEY DIFFICULTIES.*

The everlasting excuses to avoid financial donations to the various projects of the groups often arise from the lack of charity. People who make excuses have never learned the true meaning of love, which means *giving,* not hoarding.

V. *FAMILY DIFFICULTIES.*

It is hardly necessary to go into detail in regard to the various difficulties that are always proving to be an obstacle to many members, i.e., family conflicts. Suffice it to say that whenever *both* man and wife have learned what true love means there can be no serious conflict because love is GIVING. Where both man and wife consistently want to *give* and *sacrifice* for the *other,* there must be serenity and contentment because, after all, it is very easy to *receive.*

VI. *RESENTMENTS.*

Most resentments have their origin in self-love which is nothing more nor less than the absence of true love for either God or our neighbor. If we truly love God and our neighbor nothing that happens would irritate us because we would *want* it—thus *loving* the will of God. For we know that the extreme of resentment is hatred, and hatred is the direct opposite of love.

We have a very detailed explanation of this law of charity in St. Paul's letter to the Corinthians. He tells us, "if I speak with the tongues of men and of angels and have not charity, I am become as a sounding brass or a tinkling cymbal. And if I should have prophecy and know all mysteries, and all knowledge, and if I should have all faith, so that I could move mountains, and have not charity, I am nothing. And if I should distribute all my goods to the poor, and if I should deliver my body to be burned, and have not charity,[1] it profiteth me nothing.... Charity is *patient,* charity is *kind,* charity *envieth* not, dealeth not perversely; is *not puffed up;* is not *ambitious,* seeketh not *her own,* is not provoked to *anger;* thinketh no *evil;* rejoiceth not in iniquity, but rejoiceth with the *truth"* (I Cor., viii. 1-6).

[1] Many people do these things from a motive of vanity, to gtain the world's applause. They have no charity. It profits them nothing before God.

Let us analyze this beautiful exposition of charity:

Patient. One who has charity and loves God and his neighbor is never over-zealous to reform for he knows that ALL evil is transitory, that evil has its day and that God in His own time will eliminate it. He realizes that his is merely the foot-work, serving God and his neighbors. Thus, when actions by members of the group seem to us unsound, it is not for us to impatiently assume the role of reformer, but to patiently bide our time, loving above all things God and His will.

Kind. The most persistent action of Christ's entire life was the fact that "He went about doing good"—doing good TO ALL because ALL men were children of His Father.

Envieth not. (Dealeth not perversely.) Jealousy and envy are the tributes which mediocrity niggardly pays to success. The charitable person is never competitive; never looks for reciprocity; he gives for the joy of giving, the joy of sacrifice—he "envieth not" nor does he ever deal perversely.

Not puffed up. The charitable person is never "puffed up" because his deep realization that all men are equal under God makes him humble, and, looking upon all men as his equals he never in his mind raises himself above them. In reality affectation, and vanity show a true need.

Not ambitious. Ambition is often indicative of deep pride and the lack of charity. Such people love the glory of men more than the glory of God and they become ambitious to strive for the front seat, no matter who may be hurt in the process.

Seeketh not her own. The true master is the servant, and since love is but the "willingness to serve" therefore the one who loves God and his neighbor seeketh not his own but always the good of God and his neighbor. We can rest assured that no one has ever, or can ever, love himself too little.

Not provoked to anger. Too often individuals attempt to avoid resentment and hatred, seeming to forget the fact that we cannot merely *eliminate hatred or resentment*—we *substitute love.* Too many of us try to avoid or to wish away resentments and hatred. This cannot be done. Unless we *practice* charity the very vacuum in our personality will itself become a source of irritation. When someone irritates us or causes us to be angry, there is only one way to eliminate it. We must *do good* to that individual. This *act of love* will automatically eliminate the resentment.

Thinketh no evil. We so readily think evil of others and fallaciously attribute evil to others because we are, through our lack of charity, so prone to look down upon our neighbor as someone below us. Charity on the other hand, never judges by externals but searches for the good motive that may, through no fault of the individuals themselves, have caused the evil acts. Many times we think evil of others because we have such an excess of self-love that the very thought of others' evil doings pacifies our own unacknowledged errant conscience.

Rejoiceth with the truth. Charity doth not look for excuses; it does not attempt to make right out of wrong; nor does it make wrong out of right. Being humble it always searches for the truth—for humility is truth. Again St. Paul tells us that "there remain faith, hope and charity, these three, but the greatest of these is charity." This fact is borne out very dramatically in Christ's description of the Judgment. In describing the judgment of the condemned soul He does not say: "Depart from me because you have sinned through weakness," but He explicitly states: "Depart from me . . . because I was hungry and you gave Me not to eat; I was thirsty and you gave Me not to drink; I was a stranger and you took Me not in; I was naked and you clothed Me not; I was sick and you did not visit Me; I was in prison and you came not to see Me." Interesting, isn't it?

THE WILL OF GOD

"Sought through prayer and meditation to improve our conscious contact with God as we understood Him, praying only from knowledge of His Will for us and the power to carry that out."

We often hear the expression in many group discussions that the twelve steps are a way of life. On analysis we find that this is very true. In fact, the twelve steps point the way to a perfect life because they are a means whereby we adjust our will to the known Will of God—and that is perfection. Throughout the entire program runs the golden theme, "Thy Will be done." We pray thus in the Lord's prayer at the close of every meeting and in the eleventh step it is suggested that we pray "only for knowledge of God's Will for us and the power to carry that out." All this is subsequent to a decision we made in the third step, "to turn our will and our life over to the Will of God."

As we have seen in our discussions on Charity, in loving God and our neighbor the inevitable sequence is to *want* the Will of God—expressed by Him, and in our neighbor. We might say that the daily endeavor to adjust our will to the Will of God is nothing more nor less than the *practice* of Charity.

We also hear many times in the meetings the statement: "There is nothing really new in the twelve steps." Again, on analysis, we find that this is very true—for centuries ago we were told by God Himself, that "This is your sanctification, the Will of God."

We read in The Imitation of Christ, "O, Lord, if only my will remains firm and right toward Thee! Do with me whatsoever it shall please Thee, for it cannot be anything but good." From this we can easily see that the formula for a perfect life, for perfect contentment, for perfect happiness—yes, for true serenity—is the daily seeking to do the Will of God.

This formula for human happiness is so simple that even the most uneducated can easily grasp its meaning. At the same time it is so rich in import that the most profound intellect can never fully plumb its depth. It is the solution to every so-called riddle of life, for their is no problem in human relationship that cannot be solved by that simple statement, "It is God's Will—God's Will be done." It is the answer to all of life's inequalities and in its perfection becomes so sublime that the mystic holds it as the primary object of meditation.

The dramatic example of the working of this formula is brought before our eyes by Christ Himself in The Garden of Gethsemane. There we see a Man bathed in the sweat of His Own Blood, filled with fear, conflict, sorrow, pain—both physical and mental. And then, as we listen to His petition that God remove the cross, and as we hear those sublime words follow that petition, "Not My will but Thine be done," we see solved all the apparent human misery that was placed upon His shoulders—because in wanting God's Will He accepted the cross in peace of mind and contentment.

Now the question arises "How may we *practically* apply this formula to our own lives?" Let us analyze some of the difficulties we meet and see how the acceptance of God's Will in all things becomes the only true solution of life's problems.

1. *FEAR OF FUTURE EVIL, HARM, SUFFERING, ETC.*

How many people in this world, especially the alcoholics, are more or less burdened with fear? The psychiatrist will tell us that the solution for such a condition is to ignore the fear. But if the impending evil is *real,* how unreasonable becomes this advice! If I am to undergo an operation; if I suffer from constant sleeplessness, pain or mental anguish; if I have suffered loss and fear obligations I must meet—how foolish to be told to ignore these facts! If the impending evil is *unreal,* as is often the case in a neurotic individual, how vain is such advice! On the other hand, how quickly fear vanishes when it is replaced by an honest conviction that all that is, is God's Will, supplemented by an honest desire that His Will be done. The scriptures tell that "Good things and evil, life and death, poverty and riches, all things are from God" (Ecclus.). It is this knowledge and the applying of this knowledge to their daily lives that enabled great men not only to bear great crosses but to even become happy under them.

2. *WORRY.*

Worry is a side effect of fear and it is usually indicative of a lack of habitual abandonment to God's Will. Such people have never understood or have never had sufficient faith to accept the assurance of Christ, "Consider the birds of the air, they neither sow nor reap, nor do they gather into barns, your Heavenly Father feedeth them." The oft-repeated exclamation of Christ: "O ye of little faith" was aimed at worry. For when we come to the point that we *know* that God's Will for us is and always will be for the best, then we can be sure not only of the present but of whatever the future may bring because all of our life is in God's hands and His Will will always be done—for our ultimate good.

3. *GIVING UP PRAYER.*

Many people become discouraged in their prayers because seemingly their prayers are not answered and, forgetful of the fact that all prayers are always answered, they cease to pray and even many times become resentful towards Almighty God —all because they have forgotten or have never known that *every* prayer must be qualified with the humble acknowledgment, "if it be God's Will." The mother who really loves her child would never give that child anything which might hurt it no matter how long or how loud the child clamored for it. Likewise God often seemingly does not hear or answer our prayers because the object of them would be harmful. In reality He does answer them but the answer is often "No."[1]

4. *CONSOLATION IN SUFFERING.*

When suffering comes to our lives as it must for all, there is nothing else in this world that will make it more bearable than the acceptance of it as the Will of God. Philosophers tell us that "suffering is the human lot and we must bear it." But that does not make it more desirable. Only seing in it the Will of God and wanting God's Will to be done to us can make it bearable—

---

[1] Cf. p. 29.

yes, even desirable. Others will give the advice that in suffering we should always bear in mind that "there are others who have it worse than we," but we often think when hearing this advice, "What are we going to tell the guy who has it worst?"

One time we were giving a talk to an A.A. group in the State prison. In the middle of the talk one of the prisoners interrupted with the question, "Do you mean to tell me that it is God's Will that I am in this joint?" We asked the questioner whether he believed in God. He said that he did. We asked if he believed that God could do all things. He answered in the affirmative. Then was pointed out to him that since God could do all things He evidently could, if He willed it, get him out of prison. He admitted this was logical. "But," we told him, "He hasn't." He sat down.

In order to be able to apply this formula to our daily problems, we must have *knowledge* of God's Will. That is the reason it is suggested in the eleventh step that we "pray only for knowledge of His Will." Many of the problems of life might be compared to the music of the masters which, to the uneducated, are but a conglomeration of disagreeable sounds, but to the composer—perfect harmony. So with life's sufferings and sorrows. To the atheist, the prayerless, etc., sufferings and sorrows are but evidence of lamentable disorder, but to the one who sees all things as the Will of The Divine Master, everything is perfect harmony and order. It is only by praying for and acquiring knowledge of this Will that we are gradually able to understand and appreciate the "music of the Master."

To the Christian the simplest and the quickest way to gain a complete understanding of suffering in human life is to gaze upon the crucifix. Then slowly it will dawn upon our souls that as God in the beginning created our souls to His image and likeness, so likewise, when He sends suffering to us He is *re-creating* our bodies to the image and likeness of His Son upon the cross. And then, realizing that all this was fully accepted by Him because it was His Father's Will, we, with renewed faith and understanding, can go forward amid sorrow, having learned the lesson of love, of sacrifice, of suffering—that all suffering is for our ultimate perfection—that perfection is submission to the

Will of God. Suffering is no longer a burden but a "yoke," and a "yoke" is something that is carried not by one but by two—Christ and me.

5. *SERENITY.*

The dictionary defines "serenity" or "peace" as "the absence of conflict." And the more we analyze it, the more we realize that all of life's conflicts are, in plain language "kicking against the Will of God." As the child who screams and twists to get out of its mother's arms is more irritated or may even be hurt by so doing, so we, in attempting to free ourselves of God's will in circumstances we cannot change, find more irritation, more conflict, more suffering.

It is very interesting to note how a cross is made. It is done by placing two pieces of wood "contrary" to each other. But as soon as the same two pieces of wood are placed side by side, no cross!

We rebel against the Will of God because of our pride and selfishness we think that we could handle the circumstances of our life better than God. And this very rebellion becomes the source of our unhappiness and discontentment—our lack of serenity and peace. That is the reason that the message of Christmas tells us, "Peace on earth to men OF GOOD WILL," i.e., to those who are submissive to the Will of God. That is also the reason that St. Augustine finally concluded, after years of rebellion against God's Will, "Our hearts are ever restless until they rest in Thee, O God." Ultimately the Will of God is but a hub in life's wheel for the spokes of human relationships, and serenity is God's gift to those who are submissive to His Will. This is the end purpose of the twelve steps, and when we have achieved adjustment (and to achieve this we must practice it) to the Will of God as a matter of *habit,* then and then only shall we have serenity and peace, for then only will be gone the source of conflict—rebellion against the Will of God.

There are many times that we are convinced that something else than that which we have would be better for us, but were we able to *understand* God's Will in the matter we would readily see that it *is* best for us. A classic example of this is the life story of Gerard Grote who wrote "The Imitation of Christ," a spiritual book which is acknowledged as second only to the Scriptures. Gerard Grote was a Religious, and had become an accomplished preacher. However, his superiors forbade him to preach and indicated that instead he should take up writing. For a long time he rebelled against this order, but in the end, having submitted finally to the Will of God, God enabled him to write "The Imitation of Christ" which never would have been written had he been permitted to follow his own will.

There are many times when we too would rather change the circumstances of our lives, but if we want peace and serenity we shall acquire it only by "accepting the things we cannot change" *as the Will of God.* Therefore, no matter what our troubles, problems, difficulties, or circumstances of life may be, we can convert all of them into peace and serenity—yes, and sanctity—*by seeking knowledge of and accepting in all things the Will of God.* Even our sins may be converted into a source of peace of mind if we accept the fact that as far as our past is concerned God permitted sin that through the burden of sin we finally were enabled to return to Him and His security. In fine, if we want not only sobriety, but serenity, all we have to do is to change our heart, and by heart we mean "will."

Are you willing?

THE TWELVE STEPS
AND
THE LOVE OF GOD

"Thou shalt love the Lord thy God with all thy heart... and thy neighbor as thyself." In this law is contained the twelve steps and the program.

In previous discussions we have analyzed the twelve steps of the program and also discussed the necessity of the love of God and our neighbor. Now let us attempt to apply this love of God and love of our neighbor to the analysis of the twelve steps. In doing so we shall see that these steps are all aimed at giving us the knowledge of and the practice of this law of love.

1. *WE ADMITTED WE WERE POWERLESS OVER ALCOHOL—THAT OUR LIVES HAD BECOME UNMANAGEABLE.*

In this first step of the program we make an act of humility. We open the door and perhaps for the first time in our lives become qualified to visualize truth. Unless we take this step it would be utterly impossible to ever gain a knowledge of God and His Love. It would be impossible to have faith in God, it would be impossible to love God or our neighbor. It is our opinion that the ultimate reason behind most slips is the refusal to make full admission in this first step, but having done so, we immediately *want* the knowledge and the practice that the other eleven steps will give us. This step is to be taken once and for all and in taking it we open the door to a new life, and as we enter its threshold we find laid out for us to use the eleven steps that will teach us and enable us to acquire the love of God and the love of our neighbor.

2. *CAME TO BELIEVE THAT A POWER GREATER THAN OURSELVES COULD RESTORE US TO SANITY.*

In this step we are introduced to the existence of a God. We are initiated into the realm of faith, which means acceptance, not necessarily understanding. As we noted in a previous discussion, full understanding of God is not necessary in this step. The only thing that is necessary is to be willing, with an open mind, to accept the existence of a Power and to be willing to learn more about that Power. Having made our initial act of faith, we then shall go on to learn our relationship with God and our neighbor as He wills it. We shall learn God's love for us in His forgiveness and we shall also learn our obligation in turn of returning love for love in order that this mutual giving will retain the sanity of normal living. In the second step we *accept* God in order that subsequently we may *love* Him.

3. *MADE A DECISION TO TURN OUR WILL AND OUR LIFE OVER TO THE CARE OF GOD AS WE UNDERSTOOD HIM.*

In this step we have the beginning of charity, the beginning of the love of God. We "*surrender* our will and our life to the care of God." In this we learn that giving is the essence of charity and we begin to realize that true love is nothing else but sacrifice. Having endeavored for years to run our own lives by our own wills and finding that in so doing our lives had become unmanageable, we now learn that if we love God, if we give our will over to the care of God, that again our lives not only will become manageable but happy and serene.

4. *MADE A SEARCHING AND FEARLESS MORAL INVENTORY OF OURSELVES.*

Here we learn what the love of God demands on our part and how we have failed to return love in the past. Christ has told us: "If you love Me, keep My commandments." The commandments are the basis of the moral law, so in taking a moral inventory of ourselves, we learn wherein we have failed to love Him and our neighbor.

5. *ADMITTED TO GOD, TO OURSELVES AND TO ANOTHER HUMAN BEING THE EXACT NATURE OF OUR WRONGS.*

In this step our inventory becomes operative. In making this admission we begin to take responsibility for our failings and admit the necessity of loving God and our neighbor. Having *acted* upon our inventory, we are given conviction in order that the admission might not remain sterile but become productive in our lives. We see our true relationship with God. His love becomes manifest to us when we ask His forgiveness and receive it. In turn we sacrifice our pride by humbly admitting to another human being our wrongs and herein we begin to practice charity. In this way we are put in the proper perspective.

6. *WERE ENTIRELY READY TO HAVE GOD REMOVE THESE DEFECTS OF CHARACTER.*

This is the continuation of the attitude of love and trust in God that we made in step three. In being ready to let God take over the job of renovating our character we begin to realize that the only security in life is the trusting in His Divine Providence. As the poet tells us, "The test of love is trust." Hence in this step we admit God's love for us and His power to demonstrate that love in our lives, and to show in return our love for Him we in detail again place our will in the hands of His Providence. We are ready to accept all the circumstances of our daily lives as a manifestation of God's love for us in rebuilding our shattered lives. We know that in order to love someone we must believe beyond doubt that he or she is the best. What lover ever thought differently of his beloved. It is true that in human life such a trust is often misplaced. It is because of this that what so often begins apparently as love ends in disappointment. On the other hand, this attitude of love and trust of God can never lead to disappointment because, being God, He always knows best; He is Infinite; and He is infinitely capable of giving absolute security in return for our trust. Humans change; God cannot change. A human who loves can cease to love, but God, being unchangeable, infinitely loves us and shall always infinitely love us. Therefore, with this realization comes the willing readiness to have God in the Providence of His Love, remove all the defects of our character.

7. *HUMBLY ASKED HIM TO REMOVE OUR SHORTCOMINGS.*

We now *use* the attitude that we acquired in the sixth step. Here we prove our trust and our love; we act on it. We want to show God that our readiness and our decision to turn our will and our life over to Him were not mere empty words but that we meant them. In proving our love for God we are not like the lover who is very adept and verbose in avowing his love, but in reality becomes unwilling to prove his love in action by sacrifice.

8. *MADE A LIST OF ALL THE PERSONS WE HAD HARMED AND BECAME WILLING TO MAKE AMENDS TO THEM ALL.*

Having come to a knowledge of God's love for us and the necessity of our love for Him, we now learn that His Will is that we also love our neighbor as ourselves. In this step we made a list of all of the times that we have failed to love our neighbor and we endeavored to find out our true relationship with him. For years we had gone on with the false attitude that our neighbor existed for our benefit—that we were the one to whom all owed homage. Now we learn that we have obligations to our neighbor and that all of these obligations are based on the primary law of all human relationships which tells us that we must love our neighbor as ourselves.

9. *MADE DIRECT AMENDS TO SUCH PEOPLE WHEREVER POSSIBLE, EXCEPT WHEN TO DO SO WOULD INJURE THEM OR OTHERS.*

In the ninth step we begin to practice the love of our neighbor. We admitted the necessity in the eighth step and now we put this into practice. Herein we try to make up for our neglect of the past "except when to do so would injure them or others." The reason for this is that injury to our neighbor would be but a continued breach of the law of love.

10. *CONTINUED TO TAKE PERSONAL INVENTORY AND WHEN WE WERE WRONG, PROMPTLY ADMITTED IT.*

Now we come to the three steps that are the continuing of

the application of the love of God and the love of our neighbor in our daily lives.

The first step puts us on the program. Steps two to nine ready us for the program. In steps ten, eleven and twelve we adjust ourselves to our daily relationship with God and our fellowmen. *It is the program.* We might compare this to the giving of a banquet. We first accept the invitation (1); we then get ready for the dinner (2 to 9); at the banquet we practice the niceties of the social life to the host and the guests. So in the tenth, eleventh and twelfth steps of the program we reap the happiness that comes with living with God and our fellowmen according to the law of charity.

The practice of the tenth step is to insure us against possible recurrence of the neglect of loving our neighbor. This continued inventory *keeps us* in the proper perspective. If we habitually omit this inventory it is impossible to have a true knowledge of what the love of God and our neighbor daily demands of us. It is possible that many who have come on the program have actually "slipped" not realizing the attitudes and actions that really caused it. In such way it is possible that responsibility was lacking in the "slip," but there was responsibility *in having omitted the inventory.*

11. *SOUGHT THROUGH PRAYER AND MEDITATION TO IMPROVE OUR CONSCIOUS CONTACT WITH GOD AS WE UNDERSTOOD HIM, PRAYING ONLY FOR KNOWLEDGE OF HIS WILL FOR US AND THE POWER TO CARRY THAT OUT.*

In the two previous discussions we saw in detail how in this step we practice the love of God. We try daily to know God better because the more we know God the more we will love Him, for He is all lovable. In this daily prayer we turn each twenty-four hours over to His loving care in the morning. In the evening we again demonstrate our love for God by a prayer of gratitude, thanking Him for the blessings of the day. We ask forgiveness for our failings, knowing that He will forgive them all because He loves us. Throughout the day we often turn our thoughts towards God as the lover so often thinks upon his beloved, even while busy at his daily tasks. In our meditation we endeavor to make the thoughts of God's Providence and Love a powerful motivating factor in our daily living. From time to time we leave daily tasks to go to the quiet sojourn of a retreat—a vacation with God. In all this we visualize God as our loving Father, realizing that we are all equally His children.

And, having learned through prayer and meditation to love Him and our fellowmen, we won't be in much need of detailed directives, for he who truly loves God and his neighbor constantly thinks of giving, of ever seeking His Will, and is forever freed of conflict, discontent and unhappiness.

12. *HAVING HAD A SPIRITUAL AWAKENING (EXPERIENCE) AS A RESULT OF THESE STEPS, WE TRIED TO CARRY THIS MESSAGE TO ALCOHOLICS, AND TO PRACTICE THESE PRINCIPLES IN ALL OUR AFFAIRS.*

Having learned and experienced God's love for us, we now in our gratitude return that love in the person of our neighbor. We are told in the big book that all our twelfth step work is for the purpose of "disciplining ourselves into habits of unselfishness and love." When we go to the meeting we *give,* by our very presence, encouragement to our neighbor. In speaking we *give* the benefit of our experiences to him. In making calls and in sponsoring new prospects we *give* of our patience, talent and time. By our financial contributions we *give* of our material goods. In every act of our twelfth step work we are *giving* which simply means we are loving. That is the reason that the twelve steps are so often referred to as a "give" program, for it is nothing more nor less than the practice of the love of God and the love of our neighbor, for what is love but *giving?*

"THOU SHALT LOVE THE LORD THY GOD WITH ALL THY HEART AND THY NEIGHBOR AS THYSELF." IN THIS COMMANDMENT IS CONTAINED ALL THE TWELVE STEPS AND THE PROGRAM.

SPEAKING OF LOVE

LOVE IS CONFIDENCE

We should never look upon God as a HARD man. Most of the difficulties that good people have with being confident in God stems from an internal feeling that God is a hard, grasping man who wants to get everything out of us and give nothing in return. We should try always to realize that above everything else God wants our LOVE, and with love comes happiness and contentment in serving God. But we must keep ever in mind the loving Father that God really is. We must always remember that as long as we tread this earthly sphere, God is our FATHER, only in eternity is He our Judge. Realizing how much God really does love us and how lovable He is will go far to make it easy to love Him and to have great confidence in His Providence for us.

FIRST THINGS FIRST

From our childhood many of us have been told more of the punishments God has in store for us if we fail to please Him than of the rewards HE WANTS to give us when we do please Him. Let's put "first things first." The first thing necessary in loving God is to believe Him lovable. What kind of people do we love? First, they must be easy to get on with. Do we really think in our hearts that God is really easy to get on with? Rather do we not think Him touchy, unapproachable, easily annoyed or offended? Would our father wish us to hang our heads, be shy and shrinking in his presence? How much less so our Heavenly Father? Didn't He tell us that even if a parent would forget its child, He would NEVER forget us? He has an almost foolish love for us. LOVE is first; fear a poor second.

TWENTY-FOUR HOURS

We should never cry over spilt milk. Nor should we dwell on the faults of the past. Leave them alone; leave them to God.

Often the despondence caused by mulling over past wrongs keeps one away from God more than the wrong itself. Don't waste time being discouraged. Go to God. No matter how horrible seems the past, He LOVES us.

Keep both eyes on the present. Twenty-four hours—TODAY. Some people always have one eye on the past and the other on the future, instead of both on the present. We should never waste time deploring the past and being apprehensive of the future. GRACE WILL BE GIVEN TO MEET EACH DAY THE DIFFICULTIES OF THAT DAY—TWENTY-FOUR HOURS AT A TIME. It brings life down to our size. We leave the past to God's mercy, the future to His providence—to His LOVE.

EASY DOES IT

One of the greatest mistakes in life and especially the spiritual life is hurry. We are always in such a hurry to reach the end, to be perfect. We are perfectionists, but perfection takes time Half the secret of success in learning consists in repetition, yet no one wants to repeat. Thus in the spiritual life we want to skip declensions, genders, verbs, and syntax. We want to be better IN A HURRY. We want to read God's secrets before we can spell. We don't prepare ourselves for God's inspiration with ground-work, foot-work, above all, HUMILITY. We often wonder, after the way we have tried, that we are not better. How different from the saints who were always amazed and grateful that they were not worse. When we are going forward we probably think we are going backward. If one opens the door of a dark room he cannot see the dust or dirt in it. But if even a ray of light is let in the dust becomes very noticeable. The more light, the more the dust is seen. So with God's grace and light. The more we have the more we notice our faults. And the cleaning job is a LIFE-TIME work. EASY does it.

GOD'S WILL

The primary condition for doing God's Will in our regard —our growth in the spiritual life—is to BELIEVE we can do it. Let's remember:

1. God is much more interested in our sanctification than we ourselves. "This is the Will of God—your sanctification." Man does not go to God, it is God who comes to man. His infinite LOVE for us impels Him to constantly seek us.

2. We sometimes think past sins may make it hopeless for us ever to come close to God. On the contrary—we are forgiven in such a way that they no longer raise any obstacles between us and God. "Even though your sins be as scarlet, they shall be as white as snow." It is a false idea to think that God bears us a grudge on account of the past.

3. God has personal and special love for us against which no argument can stand. He realizes our weaknesses more than we do ourselves, pities us and gives us any amount of time to correct our faults. Go back over your life—doesn't it become apparent that He has taken infinite pains to seek and to help us?

STEP NUMBER SEVEN

"We humbly asked HIM to remove our shortcomings." He often uses our neighbor as the instrument. Most of us have a good deal to put up with from our neighbor. We even have difficulties with very good people. They are not omniscient, they often make mistakes, and they treat us according to their ideas. BUT that is a part of the way in which God wishes to remove our own shortcomings.

Conceited as we are, we should be much worse if we were not corrected by others. There are some dreadful gaps in our character. We are like trees that have not grown straight. If we really mean the seventh step and would let God have His way, and bear with what He does for us through our neighbor, we would grow much more symmetrical—and quick. We "humbly asked Him" to do it—why not accept His way? Why form such harsh judgments and blame our neighbor?

MORE OF THE SAME

"We HUMBLY asked. . . ." The only class of people who can hear themselves praised without satisfaction or blamed without displeasure, are the saints. A saint with the HABIT of humility doesn't look upon a slight with distress. But we, who are not yet saints when we receive a snub are disappointed; we feel sore; that is inevitable and we should accept it as our normal condition.

We make a resolution never to be proud again—and then become miserable at the thought of vanity. Why are we so stupid? Of course our resolution vanishes. There is no recipe to think ourselves into humility. The quiet acceptance of our feelings in this regard means recognition of our pride and paradoxically is the beginning of humility. If we pretend we have no jealous, hurt, angry, etc., feelings we are rebelling against facts, and that is only a continuance of pride. We are on the high road to humility when we bear these proud feelings quietly, admitting their presence. This will gradually make us humble.

STILL MORE

There is nothing that God does or permits while we are in this life, the object of which is not to bring us to love Him more. It is true that He allows trials, misfortunes, set-backs, etc., to come upon us—but they are always for our greater perfection. We shall get a lot of comfort from the realization that the circumstances—all of them—in which we are placed are just those circumstances in which, God, in His Wisdom, knows are BEST for us.

PRACTICALLY SPEAKING

THE ORDER OF CHARITY

Some years ago a very sincere member of A.A. and a founder of his group came to us in a very upset state of mind. It seems that what promised to be very serious conflicts were creeping into his life. His wife was becoming very resentful of his A.A. work in so far that it deprived her and their family of his presence and companionship on such frequent occasions. Yet, he told her and me, "we are told in A.A. that we are to put A.A. before all else; it should be the most important thing in our life; and unless I do I fear I shall not retain my sobriety; and if I don't I fear that I shall not retain my wife and family."

It did not take much analysis to get to the core of this man's problem. In fact it is a frequent cause of family conflict, and stems from a lack of understanding of what "Put A.A. first" means and a lack of knowledge of the law of charity.

When it is suggested to us that we place A.A. first in our lives, it means that we should make the TWELVE STEPS primary in our living. It does NOT mean that we should make our TWELFTH STEP work primary. The twelve steps themselves teach us to practice charity; charity demands that we love our neighbor AS ourselves. This gives us an indication that in practice, in the law of charity there exists a certain order of love: God, ourselves, our neighbor. Hence our primary concern is the welfare of God, i.e., His Will as we learned in two of the previous chapters.

Next in the order of charity comes OURSELVES. Because unless we are concerned with and seek first our own welfare, we shall not for long be of any good to either God or our neighbor. Failure to realize this one factor is also often the cause of difficulty when individuals, although very sincere, practice twelfth step work to their own detriment. We have had contact with many who had slipped merely because AN OVERDOING OF TWELFTH STEP WORK brought about a case of overtired nerves, irritations, conflicting thinking, wrong thinking, and—as a result—drinking again. Such individuals had confused the twelfth step with the twelve steps. Practicing the twelfth step work is necessary for complete sobriety and happiness, but practicing it to the detriment of oneself causes the loss of sobriety and much unhappiness. We must ever regulate such by following the true order of charity. God first; then ourselves.

And then OUR NEIGHBORS. And even in the doing of good to our neighbor we must follow the order of charity which dictates that OUR FAMILY COMES FIRST; then our friends, then all the rest—our enemies. It was the failure to recognize this order that caused the difficulty of our friend we mentioned in the beginning. He too was confusing the issue. He was confusing the twelfth step with the twelve steps which teach us the practice of charity IN ITS PROPER ORDER. And this means that if there is a question of family or twelfth step, we must, if we want to follow the order of charity, choose our family's welfare before that of our neighbor in general. How many A.A. "widows" do we find because of such misunderstandings even in sincere members! To say nothing of the many who deliberately use it as an excuse!

SPIRITUALITY VS. PRACTICALITY

One often hears the remark, is disCUSSING the spiritual side, "That's all very fine, but after all we must be practical." What a confused idea of spirituality such a one must have! How he must have ignored or misunderstood two very patent phrases in the A.A. program! He is still relegating the spiritual life to the realm of theory! and as a result is missing the PRACTICAL benefits that accrue therefrom. He has failed to read or has ignored the implications of the very concise statement in the A.A. Book: "This spiritual life is NOT a theory, we must LIVE IT." And he has evidently missed the end phrase of the twelfth step which reads: "And practice these principles IN ALL OUR AFFAIRS." What he really fails to realize or understand is that the spiritual life IS VERY PRACTICAL.

As we saw in our discussion on Prayer and Meditation in volume one the living of a spiritual life is merely the daily attempt to honestly adjust our wills to the Will of God. And we are being very practical when we do this "in ALL of our affairs," whether it is prayer, business, finance, home-life, social-life, sleeping, eating, etc., etc. No problem or action of life is too "practical" to bring God into the picture, and that is being very spiritual.

Why can't God help us meet a financial obligation? Why can't God help solve a group problem? Why can't God guide our thinking, our conversation, our journey, our working, our playing, our business, our decisions, our family welfare, our Clubs, our EVERYthing? Didn't we come to believe that He was "all-powerful"? Then why should we limit the realm of His influence?

Which means why can't we become God-conscious AT ALL TIMES? We believe that, if we but pause a moment to analyze it, we would find that is what we mean by the much used phrase "get OUT of the driver's seat," not just move over and let God squeeze in for the "prayer curves." There would be much less swerving, and skidding, AND SLIPPING.

HUMILITY THROUGH LOVE

We do not believe that we can ever discuss humility too often; We are positive we can never acquire too much true humility. So in a discussion on charity or love, it is significant to note that true humility only comes through true love. Confidence and humility always go together. And confidence is begotten only of love. We shall place complete confidence only in one we love. One of the reasons why men are so anxious to exalt themselves —to overestimate their own value and their own powers—to resent anything that would tend to lower themselves in their own esteem or in that of others—is because they see no other hope for their happinesse SAVE IN THEMSELVES. That is often why they are so "touchy," so insistent on getting their own way, so eager to be known, so anxious for praise, so determined on ruling their surroundings. They clutch at themselves like drowning men clutch at a straw. And as life goes on they are never at peace having found nothing at the end of every road but SELF.

But when one begins to seek God, and to love God, and to love others, he of necessity begins to see the inadequacy of himself—he begins to become humble. His hope then is placed in God alone; for he sees no hope in himself. He no longer has to worry about getting his own way; all that matters is that God should get His way. He knows that the LESS he has to do with the arranging of his own life, the more likely is it that things will turn out always for the best. He is by no means spineless or inert. On the contrary, let him once be certain that God wills something he will tackle it with joy and confidence, because he knows his sufficiency is from God and not in himself. He now knows life is a partnership based on love; and whether he acts, or whether he lets God—or even others—act, he trusts with unshaken confidence in God Whom he loves "above all things." And God never refuses to aid him, because He in turn infinitely loves him. It is all but a return to the simplicity of childhood based upon the realization of the Fatherhood of God and the brotherhood of man which has its origin and roots in LOVE.

Now to become practical. Many have asked for a "practical guide" to humility, a guage whereby one may "test" oneself. The following are safe indications of practical humility and are a digest of the voluminous writings on the subject:

To speak as little of one's own self or affairs as possible; to mind one's own business; to avoid curiosity; not to want to manage other people's affairs; to accept contradition or justice require it, and then only moderately and with simplicity; to pass over the mistakes of others, to cover them up, even where prudent, to accept them; to yield to the will of others, where neither duty nor charity is involved; to hide one's own ability or talent (but to use it); to avoid ostentation; all of these are in the powers of all of us.

But one can go further. To accept blame when innocent; to accept insults or injuries; to accept being disliked; not to seek especially to be loved; not to be put out at one's own mistakes; to be kind and gentle even under provocation; to accept correction gladly; to yield in discussion even when right; not to be self-opinionated or self-assertive. And if we fully understand that the perfection of humility is the perfection of loving God, we may even desire to go still further.

To rejoice when despised; to thank God when one is humiliated; to be glad of one's lowliness; to be patient with one's own failings; to meet failure with a ready smile; to even glory in one's own infirmities. Then it is that love is becoming ardent and true and constant.

How far have YOU come, chum?

"CAME TO BELIEVE ..."

Go to God; but go to Him not only as to one who has a human heart, but who is capable of INFINITE love.

Go to Him as to one who loves us, and if only we understand that a little better, it will explain everything and make everything easy.

Don't think that God requires us to stand on ceremony with Him. We can never be too childlike, too simple, too direct.

Why do we not believe His own words? Why would He say He loves us if He does not do so in fact?

The shortest way to the mind and heart of God is to take Him at His words. A saint is a person who believes God literally, and trusts His promises entirely and always.

What is the explanation of all this?

God Who framed the heavens, has chosen to dwell with man on earth. "God so loved the world...."

Why was His infinite Power attracted by our weakness? Why was His Pity greater than our willfulness? Why was it that the Creator and the creature, Perfection and imperfection, Light and darkness, were thus brought together?

Not by constraint, because no one can constrain God. Not in His Wisdom, nor in His Greatness, nor in His Justice, nor in His Power, will we find written the secret—why God created us, and dwells amongst us.

One little word holds it all: The highest, dearest, best of all words; another word for God Himself—LOVE! GOD IS LOVE.

Let's approach Him by love; abide with Him in love. The LOVE of God can FILL our hearts!

"And human love needs meriting;
How hast thou merited
Of all man's clotted clay the dingiest clot?
Alack, thou knowest not
How little worthy of any love thou art!
Whom wilt thou find to love ignoble thee,
Save only Me, save only Me?
All which I took from thee I did but take
Not for thy harms,
But just that thou might'st seek it in My arms.
All which thy child's mistake
Fancies as lost, I have stored for thee at home;
Rise, Clasp My hand, and come."
—Francis Thompson

Let nothing disturb thee,
Nothing affright thee;
All things are passing;
God never changeth;
Patient endurance
Attaineth to all things;
Who God possesseth
In nothing is wanting;
Alone God sufficeth.
—S. Teresa

ATTITUDES

"Within this earthly temple there's
a crowd:
There's one of us that's humble, one
that's proud;
There's one that's broken-hearted
for his sins,
And one who unrepentant sits and
grins;
There's one who loves his neighbor
as himself,
And one who cares for naught but
fame and self.
From much corroding care I should
be free,
If once I could determine WHICH
IS ME!"

Once upon a time a stranger lost his way and seeing a farmer plowing in a nearby field stopped and asked what road he was on.

"I dunno," the farmer replied lackadaisically.

"Well, where does it lead to?" queried the stranger.

"I dunno," the farmer repeated.

"What's the name of the nearest town?" the stranger again asked.

"I dunno," came the staccato reply.

"You certainly are dumb, aren't you," the inquirer said in exasperation.

"Mebbe so," mused the farmer, "but I'm not lost!"

One of the most important things to do in preparing for a long automobile trip is to find out the best roads leading to our ultimate destination. If we are not sure of our road, if we do not have certitude as to our direction, if we take the chance of driving on an uncharted highway, we may ultimately be in the same predicament as the stranger in the little story just related.

He knew his destination, but, having lost direction and the proper road, he was lost. He did not get lost because he did not keep moving, but because he kept moving along the wrong road.

Now let us carry this thought over to the A.A. Program. Many individuals become "lost" along the way of A.A. because they are attempting to follow the wrong directives. They work A.A. to their own destruction, not because they are not active in A.A., but because they have acquired, willingly or otherwise, the wrong viewpoint towards A.A., either in general or in relation to some of its parts. In other words they are on the wrong road because they are working with the wrong *attitudes.*

In general we find three classes of A.A.'s three over-all attitudes, which in turn give us the good, the bad and the indifferent A.A.

In the first of these classes we have the members who have acquired a *completely spiritual attitude* toward the program. They have become convinced of the primacy of the spiritual, and all of their A.A. activity and their entire lives are regulated and directed by spiritual values. To them material prosperity, etc., are only secondary and ever dependent upon the Will of God which to them has become their unfailing "road map." They never slip. They are the ones who display in their every action, in their countenances, in their every word—peace, contentment, serenity. They are the ones who are always doing so much, yet unseen. They are the ones who have fully experienced the "expulsion of the compulsion to drink." To them liquor is no longer a problem, no longer a temptation, no longer even a matter of much thought. They are the truly *spiritual* men, and the *spiritual* women. And far from being morose, apart, and alone, they are the very backbone of every A.A. group. They are the ones who have acquired a *completely spiritual attitude.*

The second class of A.A.'s are the indifferent ones. They are the ones who have a half-and-half point of view, a *partly spiritual, partly material attitude.* They are the ones who have a spiritual attitude in some phases of A.A. and their lives, but who still in many things put *material values* above the ultimate spiritual values. They are victims again and again of that time-worn rationalization: "You gotta be practical." They have never really taken the time to think through the ultimate road, and often turn off because the pavements "look very smooth." They are often victims of the "squirrel cage"—drink cravings, resentments, etc., etc., because they are more or less often determinedly seeking material advancements and ending in conflicts. Many slip, many stay sober—but all of these will never know the meaning of serenity. Fortunately many ultimately acquire the spiritual attitude and come to realize the primacy of the spiritual—the hard way. They are the bulk of the A.A.'s.

In the third class we find the A.A. members, if they can be called such, who have a *completely material attitude.* They are the no-God individuals, the "no-spiritual-angle" boys and girls, the "first-step Johns." They have come to the point of being convinced that they are alcoholic, but not unmanageable. They know liquor has them whipped, and how they hate it—the "being whipped," not the liquor. Their every striving and longing and determination is for material advancement, material pleasure, material well-being. And withal they expect to stay sober! They don't. Even their weeks, or months, or even in odd cases their years of sobriety are a constant struggle against a drink. They are the "dry-drunks"—dry and very unhappy. But ultimately the first drink comes along and they slip. A few come back not only sobered, but finally convinced of the primacy of the spiritual. Many of them slip and never come back. We would like to say that they in reality had never came in—for they really hadn't.

Oftentimes it is difficult to ascertain the proper attitude in regard to the many phases of the A.A. program. Lack of understanding at times proves a stumbling block to some in their endeavor to acquire the correct attitudes. It is with the hope of clarifying these misunderstandings that we analyze the various *wrong* attitudes so often found in A.A. and then give in each instance what in our humble opinion is the correct attitude. They are given as a result of years of observation of hundreds of groups and thousands of individual members throughout the country. Let's take a look around.

1. *ATTITUDE TOWARD THE TWELVE STEPS*

a. *The "1st and 12th step man."* This one tries to maintain sobriety by using only the first and the twelfth step. It may be very well in the beginning, but unless such a man endeavors to use all of the steps for himself, he probably won't stay sober, and he certainly won't be happy. Such individuals should realize that the A.A. program is a twelve-step, not a two step.

b. *The "no spiritual angle man."* We have analyzed him above. He seldom stays sober long, never permanently, and when he slips often never returns.

c. *The "careless man."* He has "looked over" the twelve steps. He admits their necessity, practices most of them "once in awhile," but is in constant trouble—mental, nervous, tempted, etc. He has never taken the time to carefully understand and use *all* of the steps consistently as best he can. He often stays sober, is seldom happy, and quite often slips.

d. *The "rationalizing man."* He has been told that he must place A.A. first in his life. Confusing the twelfth step with the *twelve steps,* he works the twelfth step day and night to his own ultimate destruction. He seemingly is not aware that if he would work all of the twelve steps he would learn the two great virtues of prudence and charity which in turn would tell him that if *twelfth* step work interferes with the well-being of himself, or his family or his neighbor he had best let up a bit on his twelfth step work. Many have slipped because they so overworked the twelfth step that, because of over-tiredness, or family conflicts, or dissension with one's neighbor, they reverted, perhaps imperceptibly, to their old ways of thinking and drinking.

The correct attitude: The one who has the conviction that *all of the twelve steps* are necessary for sobriety and happiness, and who *tries* to the best of his ability to learn more about them *all,* and who honestly endeavors to practice them *in all his affairs.* Such a man doesn't slip, and he's happy, and he's secure.

2. *ATTITUDE TOWARD THE A.A. BOOK.*

a. *The "re-write specialist."* Here we have the man who always finds new ways, new rules, new therapies, new what-have-you's—everything but the honest attempt to follow the suggested way that has written as a *result of experience.* His attitude stems from a deep-seated pride—that he knows a *better* way dictated by his own egotism and desire for his way of thinking. Such thinking has produced the many "rule-groups" here and there in the country. One such group has twenty-five pages of *their* way of doing it! We in no way want to deny whatever of good many be in any of these procedures, but we do maintain *it is not A.A.* For A.A. is written very explicitly as to suggested procedure in the Alcoholics Anonymous Book.

b. *The "non-reader."* A gentlemen who (and their number is amazing) has never done more than skip through the A.A. Book and who often parades as one who knows *all* the answers. It is amusing to experiment at times by using something verbatim from the A.A. Book in a talk and then to note how many tell you what a "wonderful idea that was in your talk"! And it was all taken from the Book!

c. *The "one-timer."* These are the ones who have read the A.A. Book *once*—in the initial stage of their sobriety. Usually their sponsor loaned it to them. They never have bought one of their own. Not realizing that even the most intelligent of men must read and re-read the book to fully digest it, they read it once, in many cases very cursorily, and as the months and years pass they wonder why they never seem to get a solid understanding of the whole program.

d. *The "own-but-no-loaner."* He has bought a book—and he hangs on to it. He is too "tight" to take a chance on loaning it to a newcomer who perhaps can ill afford to buy one in his present financial circumstances. His lack of charity is an obstacle to much happiness—if he should be fortunate enough to maintain sobriety.

The correct attitude: The one who reads the A.A. book *carefully and thoughtfully,* and then *re-reads* it *carefully and thoughtfully,* and who perhaps re-reads it a third or a fourth time; who afterwards again reads it from time to time to refuel; and who, when occasion demands it, loans it to others. Such a one eventually knows *most* of the answers, but he doesn't brag about it, for one of the answers is the necessity of humility.

3. *ATTITUDE TOWARD THE TWELVE TRADITIONS.*

a. *The "tain't necessary for my sobriety guy."* He cares little or nothing for the welfare of A.A. as a whole. He has attained a modicum of sobriety, and to satisfy his selfishness in a rationalizing manner without twinges of conscience, he is always saying, "I came into this for my own sobriety and that's all I care about." In reality he doesn't, because he often loses it!

b. *The "Club-A.A."* It is amazing how many of these individuals are extant and who seem determined to bump their own heads before realizing that the Tradition as to Clubs was written like all the rest, *as a result of experience!* And this tradition states that A.A. Clubs should be *outside* the A.A. group and incorporate and separate therefrom. Yet it is a fact in the writer's experience that *most* groups still persist in tying the Group and Club together *as one entity* and only learn the hard way—after a lot of dissension and slips! Their name is legion.

c. *The "non-anonymi."* The one who disregarding the common good of A.A. and the security of the prospective members, shout to the world that they are members of A.A.—*for their own material advancement.* And the pity is that when they slip, they not alone are hurt, but others, not yet reached, put off their recovery.

The correct attitude: The twelve traditions, like the twelve steps, are suggested *as a result of experience* and for the general good we, both as individuals and groups, should try our best to adjust.

4. *ATTITUDE TOWARD THE GROUP.*

a. *The "I-don't-care-what-the-group-does-man."* He *never* helps with group activities, never offers to take part in constructive ideas, seldom contributes toward the "kitty" without a "creak." He smugly sits behind a cloak of clever selfishness and misses very much of the happiness that the group-participant enjoys. If he should slip he is the first one to yell loudest and longest for the group for assistance!

b. *The "group-must-do-it-my-way-fellow."* He is on the opposite extreme of pride and selfishness. He is very active, always offering *destructive* criticism, and always contributes to the "kitty"—with a grand show and splurge! Like buttons, he is always "popping off." Any idea offered by anyone else besides himself can't possibly work. His ideas are always the best and sure to work. He takes part in every discussion—to knock. And there is always at least one in every group! Sometimes we feel that God permits this—so the rest can have a chance to practice tolerance and patience. And strange to say, they usually stay sober! They are drunks—not alcoholics. Frequent resentments do not throw them.

c. *The "new idea man."* Unlike the one above, he is seldom cantankerous, but he is always working on a new idea for the group. A social project, an athletic project, a mass drying-up scheme, a new jail-approach and others—mostly unworkable—ad nauseam. He's harmless, but a bit irritating at times. His sincerity keeps him sober—and he is probably enjoying it!

d. *The "reformer."* He is a rabid prohibitionist at heart—now that he *can't drink*. So he is determined to dry everyone else up—not from an honest desire to help the sick alcoholic, but from a perverse jealousy arising from his own hurt pride which has its origin in the fact that he is very irritated over the realization that he can't drink. So he doesn't want his wife, nor his family, nor his friends, nor anyone to drink. Of course he gives as his excuse that it is a temptation to him! Every day he is plagued by the desire to drink, but he is afraid to. He is an outgrowth of the "first-step-man." Usually such a one slips—over the first step!

e. *The "view-with-alarmer."* He is the individual who is always ranting about so-and-so or such-and-such hurting A.A. and who always ends his every spell of ranting with "we ought to do something about it." He is usually the self-appointed protector of A.A. It is a lovely rationalization for his own deep-seated pride. He has failed to realize the evil, if the object of his alarm be evil, has its day and that God in His own time and way will eventually eliminate it, and that not being a superior, one should watch the most dangerous situation of all—*oneself!*

f. *The "closed-group-fanaticist."* He is against and strenuously opposes any open meetings in his area, meetings to which the wives may come. We often wonder if such individuals have ever analyzed the A.A. Book and asked themselves: "If the wives were not in need of the A.A. help and therapy why should the writers of the book give an entire chapter the wives?"

The correct attitude: The conviction that the group welfare comes first, that the group *conscience* (not the group-knockers who though few in numbers always make a lot of noise) should dictate group procedure: that personal welfare is a close second; that one should work conscientiously and quietly for the good of the group in order that both the group as a whole and the individual may eventually benefit.

5. *ATTITUDE TOWARD GOD AND PRAYER.*

a. *The "atheist."* The "no-God-man" in person. It is amusing to see these individuals in their feeble attempts to stay sober. Can you imagine trying to take the twelve steps without God? It's impossible. For these individuals it is one of two choices —God or the bottle. And the few who ultimately make it—the hard way—usually find the latter several times first.

b. *The "agnostic."* He doesn't deny God—nor does he admit Him. Usually a sincere but confused individual. Most of them eventually make it—hand and hand with God. He needs help and encouragement, not condemnation.

c. *The "on-occasion man."* He believes in God, and he believes in prayer—on occasion. In between these occasions he slips—often. His faith in God may eventually bring him back —to a consistent belief and to consistent and persistent daily dependence and prayer.

d. *The "giver-upper."* He comes to A.A. He gets sober. He prays daily—for a while. Then he rationalizes (often subconsciously), "I'm well now—I don't need God." So he quits his daily prayers, he forgets God's goodness to him, he takes all the credit. Then the day comes when he looks in the mirror and glories in what a swell job that fellow in the mirror has done. Then he invites the gentleman in the mirror out for a drink!

e. *The "prayer-mechanic."* Here we have an individual who realizes the necessity of prayer, but who in such realization evaluates his prayers according to their number. He prays and prays and prays and prays—verbally. And his actions are so often so contrary to God's Will—especially in matters of charity and tolerance—that his prayers are practically futile. He prays much with his lips, but his heart and his will are far away from God. He is usually loaded with pride and selfishness and intolerance. He many times slips—and wonders why!

f. *The "after-pray-er."* He prays, perhaps daily, *after* the day is finished. He wonders why he so often falls into so many difficulties each day. Instead of turning each twenty-four hours over to the care of God and asking for the strength of sobriety *at the beginning* of each day, thus assuring himself of God's grace, blessing and guidance for that day, he lazily puts off his prayers until evening. It takes less effort. It produces less results. Seemingly forgetting that he is "powerless over alcohol," he goes through each day on his own. Such individuals usually stay sober but seldom progress in the spiritual life. A few slip—God permits it to draw them nearer to Himself. The rest remain sober, but forfeit much of the happiness that would be theirs if they approached *God in the morning.* They miss the security that would result from daily dependence on God *through* the day. They can never know the real joy that would be theirs if they worked along *with God* each day "in all their affairs."

The correct attitude: The man who has the conviction that there is a God; that He is all-powerful; that He loves us infinitely. Pursuant of this he is also convinced that *daily* prayer is absolutely necessary for *permanent* sobriety; and that dependence on God *throughout* each day is necessary for permanent happiness.

6. *ATTITUDE TOWARD THE INVENTORY.*

a. *The "tain't necessary man."* Here we have the man who by pure chance has retained sobriety for a period of time, and who tells the newcomers: "Tain't necessary to take an inventory. Look at me, I'm sober and I never took an inventory!" Deluded soul! Sad to say, he hasn't slipped—yet. He is usually the type that only slips after a year, or two or three—and never returns. The lack of an inventory has caused all of his past wrongs and wrong thinking to be merely buried in his subconscious. Never having obtained a *true* picture of himself and his faults and failings, his mind and soul are fertile ground for his already firmly entrenched pride, which in itself strange to say, often enables him to retain a long period of sobriety—negative brand. Usually an extrovert, he seldom thinks about himself inside—he is afraid to do so lest he must leave his pedestal of self-opinionated vanity. Often a good speaker—and frequent—he does not realize that his speaking is a subconscious attempt to feed that vanity. He is often referred to as a fine A.A., for indeed he is—*on the outside.* He is the one who evokes the remark "And to think John slipped—and after four years on the program!" Whereas in truth he was never *on the program.*

b. *The "careless man."* He has taken a general inventory. He may even on occasion continue to take an inventory—very carelessly. These inventories are neither "fearless" nor "searching." Rather they have been *fearful,* lest he has to do something about his biggest faults, and *hiding* them to himself. He forgets that his faults are never hidden from God, and seldom from his fellowman. He has achieved a modicum of honesty, but is burdened with his basic fear or pride—oftentimes laziness. If his carelessness stems from fear or laziness, he usually stays sober, is not very happy, and through God's grace ultimately recognizes his difficulty, does something about it, and then and then only achieves happiness with his sobriety. If his carelessness on the other hand stems from pride he usually only learns the hard way—through a slip. Pride is the chief obstacle to the Grace of God.

c. *The "scrupulous man."* "Scrupulous" comes from the Latin "scrupula"—a term used by the Romans to denote the pebbles that so often found their way into their sandals. We can imagine the result—afraid to take a solid step and constantly irritated and held back in desired progress. A similar situation has been set up in the scrupulous individual. He doesn't have pebbles in his sole, but his *soul* is loaded with imaginary pebbles of sin and wrong. He sees sin in everything. His inventory is a nightmare. He takes it over and over again and is never satisfied. He pays much attention to details and is extremely frightened by his more serious wrongs of the past. He becomes the most unhappy of men and usually ends up with a lovely anxiety-neurosis or guilt-complex. There are many such in A.A. What such a one doesn't recognize is that his basic trouble too is pride, and that pride is behind his stubborn refusal to admit that he is little different from the rest of men. He doesn't seem to understand that God knows his weaknesses—both past and present—much better than the individual himself, and that all that God asks is an *humble* admission, a sincere good will, and an unwavering dependence upon His Grace instead of upon one's own unaided strength. Cure of such a condition comes only with much meditation on the mercy and love of God and by blindly following *competent* advice and direction. These individuals must give unswerving obedience to the directives and judgment of another—and that other should be one who is qualified to give direction in such cases—a clergyman or a good psychiatrist. Many times much harm results from well-meaning members giving advice to such people as: "Forget it!" or "Let yourself go!" or "You're not an alcoholic, you're a neurotic!" Others do even greater harm by making fun of such unfortunate individuals. The proper handling of such individuals is to encourage them to seek competent psychiatric or spiritual help from one who is qualified to give it.

d. *The "general but not regular man."* This person has

taken the general inventory, perhaps even very conscientiously. But that ends it. He achieves a good quality of sobriety in the beginning. And usually he retains it—for a time. However either through lack of realizing the need, or poor advice, or sheer carelessness, he does not take the tenth step—the inventory—regularly. As a result he makes progress—backwards. Old faults, wrongs, wrong-thinking, and ultimately "drinking-thinking," creep unrecognized back into his personality and he slips. And to his amazement and chagrin he finds that he has made much progress—in his drinking!

e. *The "procrastinator."* He has been taking his inventory for months or years—tomorrow. He has sincerity of a sort but his fear or laziness keeps that sincerity merely mental. Action never follows, for tomorrow never seems to come. Procrastination aided by rationalizations keeps such a person from making any progress in his spiritual life, and keeps any progress or success in his life at a minimum. The majority of these members stay sober; are seldom happy; and are always wondering why. Some slip and find out.

f. *The "hurry-it-up speedster."* This gentleman takes his inventory—and quick. He takes his general inventory in his first days of sobriety. This factor alone prevents him from getting a clear picture of himself. Subconsciously at least that is exactly what he is after. Suspecting that he is morally bankrupt, he fears to bring this out in the open and so hurries to list a few "usual" faults and personality defects. The quicker this is done the better, so that he can again parade about as the person he would have everybody believe he is. Such an individual may even take a regular inventory once in awhile—in a hurry. So he fools nobody but himself. He is subject to frequent inner conflicts, he is seldom happy, and is subject to recurrent nervous spells. His entire living is hurried. He has never learned the value of "easy does it." About the only time he ever stops is to look at a bottle—or to get one.

The correct attitude: The conviction that *serenity is impossible* and that *sobriety is at most, doubtful* without a sensible general and faithful regular inventory taken carefully and not hurried.

7. ATTITUDE TOWARD DISCUSSION OF OUR FAULTS WITH ANOTHER HUMAN BEING.

a. *The "distributor."* The discussion of his faults is distributed to dozens of individuals. One to this person and another to that. A few of the ones he can boast about, he saves for his talks to the group in general—especially his "marvelous" feats of drinking. His telling of his misdeeds to so many others and his detailing his drinking experiences to the group is done with no idea of obtaining help and advice. It is done from a motive of pride. He tells others what he has done—to top them. The entire process is but a series of boasts. He gets nothing from it unless it be a building up of his own hurt pride. He has never really taken the fifth step.

b. *The "confession man."* This individual is the Catholic who hurries to confession merely hurriedly telling his more serious sins. He takes no time to discuss the basic causes of his defects. He indeed gets the benefits of confession—forgiveness. But he does not get a true picture of himself. Such an individual is usually the one who is constantly falling into the same serious sins—he has never tried to eliminate the causes of them because he has never taken the time to find them. What he has never realized is that although Confession is necessary for the Catholic—it is only *part* of the fifth step. He must take the time to discuss the circumstances, etc., that are behind his wrong thinking and doing.

c. *The "testimonial-giver."* This person details all the wrongs of his past *publicly*. For some misguided reason he thinks this is how A.A. works. He has missed two things in the A.A. procedure: 1. Only those things should be related publicly that will identify an individual as an alcoholic. This certainly calls for no gruesome details. 2. Any detail of one's past should be related *only* when it is deemed necessary to help someone else. This latter usually only occurs when in private discussion one endeavors to lead another to realize that he is not worse than every one else. The one great virtue necessary here is prudence.

In this classification we also find the "tain't necessary man," the "careless man," the "speedster," the "procrastinator," and the "scrupulous man" (Cf. above).

The correct attitude: The fifth step aims above all at honesty. One of its chief purposes is to obtain a true and honest picture of one's self according to the judgment of another human being in order to avoid the extremes that self-adjudication often leads to.

8. *ATTITUDE TOWARD RELIGION.*

a. *The "bigot."* He has no use for anyone who believes contrary to what he does. Often it stems from ignorance. Sometimes it is malicious and diabolical. The latter are few, but do come along in A.A. They do untold harm. They give scandal to the newcomer. They are responsible for much dissension in A.A. Strange to say they often stay sober for a long time, sometimes for years. But when they slip they not only hit bottom, they go through it and do not return. For after all one cannot mock God for long.

b. *The "fanatic."* Often a very religious man in his own way, he becomes an "apostolic zealot" and tries to convert everyone he meets in A.A. to his form of Religion. His zeal may even be praiseworthy—outside of A.A. However, such an individual is usually suffering from spiritual pride—looking down on anyone who is not as good as he is. What he certainly seems to miss is that *formal* Religion has no place in A.A. Any zeal for such that one might have should be expended *outside A.A.* Religions, creeds, dogmas, etc., should never even be brought up in an A.A. group or meeting. And when such a "fanatic" insists on doing so, he causes much harm to the newcomers, much irritation to everyone else, and much unhappiness and disappointment to himself.

c. *The "A.A.-is-my-Religion-guy."* This very philosophical appearing individual is always sure to bring out in all of his talks and discussions: "A.A. is my Religion." Such a person fails to understand that A.A. is not Religion—has no connection with Religion. He would be much more honest if he would say: "A.A. is my way of life; I have no Religion." For in reality he hasn't.

Most of these men are sincere. A few are not. The latter have a very fine excuse—to *them*—for having no Religion. They say Religion is for hypocrites. What they don't seem to know is that there is always room for one more!

The correct attitude: A.A. is not concerned with denominations or formal Religion. Everyone has the *right* to follow the dictates of his own conscience but that very right *imposes* upon him the *obligation to respect this right in others.*

9. *ATTITUDE TOWARD OUR NEIGHBOR.*

a. *The "excepter."* He is able to forgive everybody *except* so-and-so; he is willing to associate with everybody *except* this one and that one; he is willing for anybody to come to A.A. *except* this type and that type. And since "so-and-so or "this one and that one" or this type and that type" seem to always be around, he is not very happy, frequently irritated and resentful, and often upset emotionally and mentally. Not having charity enough in his soul to bring *all* within its scope, he seldom is able to eliminate these persistent upsets. And lo and behold he suddenly realizes that he is powerless over alcohol, all alcohol *except*—a little beer, or wine, or what have you. And he is soon on his way—out.

b. *The "criticizer."* He is an expert with the sling-shot, the hammer, and the loudspeaker. Everything that is brought up he destructively criticizes. He never has gotten far enough in solid thinking to offer anything constructive, so he tells everyone what is wrong with them, with their suggestions, with their speaking. Usually his severest criticisms are done *about* someone to someone else. Very maladjusted and unhappy inside, he takes devilish delight in pointing out the faults of everything and everyone. Nothing has ever been done in the group by anyone that has quite suited him. Actually nothing *he* has ever done has suited him so he projects this inner disappointment upon everybody else. Before long he criticizes his own sobriety —this first honest and constructive criticism he has ever made —and then he endeavors to tear it to pieces—and usually succeeds!

c. *The "gossiper."* Here we have one of the greatest contributory factors in A.A. group troubles. His neighbor's name means nothing to him. Everybody is to him just another object which his glib and malicious tongue may bandy about in his gossiping tales. He usually prefaces his stories with: "Did you hear"—and then follows any and all the dirt that he has been able to dig up in the last twenty-four hours. He knows everyone who has slipped and is determined that everybody else find it out. He is conversant with every family difficulty of everyone in the group and is determined to converse very glibly about it to all. He rationalizes and excuses himself with that age-old excuse for uncharitable talk and gossip: "Well, it's true!" He has never learned that true charity demands that we have our neighbor, not be an inane loudspeaker for all of our neighbor's faults and wrongs. Nor could he possibly understand in his stunted mind the tremendous damage that is done as gossip grows as it goes from mouth to mouth. "Fama quae crescit eundo!" ("Gossip which so grows as it goes.")

d. *The "slanderer."* The most diabolical of all! And sad to say frequently found among the A.A. ranks. They seldom stay sober long, but they hang around like leeches "seeking whom they may devour." A thousand times worse than the "gossiper," this individual takes hellish delight in spreading lies about other members. He usually picks out the more active members, the more successful and capable ones. Raging inside with jealousy and bigotry, he endeavors by his diatribes to unseat them from the so-called place of "honor" which he so frustratedly envies in his own emptiness and malice. Judas-like he seldom shows his malice to the object of his venom, but, with a kiss of pretended friendship, spreads the vilest of rumors behind their backs. The writer could mention many, many such instances, but charity forbids. Suffice it to say that almost everyone who has been very active in furthering the A.A. program has felt the sting of such a one's twisted and demented mentality. And along the path of A.A. the writer has met many a one who is drinking again because of unbearable circumstances brought about by someone's diabolical and slanderous tongue. As mentioned above, such an individual frequently slips and shows his true colors. But the bottle again is too good for such unless it be over the head.

e. *The "letter-writer."* The Grapevine is full of letters. Mostly fine, constructive and informative. But the gentleman here referred to as the "letter-writer" shows himself by the personalities in his letters. They very adroitly make a show at protecting their victim's anonymity by simply referring to "a certain member" in a "certain locality." How clever! Anyone who gets around knows exactly to whom he refers. Everyone in that locality knows—but that is exactly what he wants. What such a person does not seem to know is that many know who is the writer of the letter. And prudent men know the personal malice that dictated it. We can always be fairly certain that every letter of a critical personal nature was written from a vindictive motive. Such never write their criticisms to the individual who is its object. It would take courage to do that. Real men honestly criticizing another will do so to the person; cowards write about him to someone else—to the Central Office, to the Grapevine, to superiors, to families, etc., etc. Poor, unhappy, dry-drunk souls!

f. *The "classifier."* In this category we have the originators of 'silk-stockings' groups. These are the groups open only to certain types of people—the so-called better class. If you are from the other side of the tracks you just don't belong. They do twelfth step work—provided the prospect is from the same side of the tracks. There are always many slips in these groups. It seems that too much pride mixed with their so-called charity is too "intoxicating"!

The correct attitude: The man who realizes that the sobriety that has been given to him is to be given to *all* irrespective of race, creed, color or class. Charity to be true must embrace *all men.* His twelfth step is a labor of love—a love of God and of all men as equally the children of God. Their number are few, but their happiness is unfathomable.

10. *ATTITUDE TOWARD SEX.*

a. *The "sex substituter."* To justify his irregularities he has formed for himself a "psychiatric excuse" justifying his actions by the phrase "one must substitute one passion for another." His prospects in A.A. are usually women and he preys upon their emotional difficulties with his pet phrase. And the sad part of it is that he usually succeeds—until they both are drinking again. After his debauch he sobers up again and is ready for his next victim. It is difficult to tell how much grave harm these unscrupulous individuals do to the lives of others. It would be better that "a millstone be tied around their necks and they be drowned in the depths of the sea."

b. *The "impossibilist."* "Continency is impossible" is this one's stock cry. What such a one little realizes in his conscience-soothing is that if he would add one word to his excuses it would be very true. For continency is *humanly* impossible. What he does seem to have overlooked is that with God *all* things are possible. We say the same thing about sobriety. Sobriety for the alcoholic is impossible—without the grace of God. The alcoholic, if he really practices the A.A. program, admits this basic fact in the very first step: "We admitted we were *powerless* over alcohol. . . ." Not only the alcoholic, but *all* men must admit this same powerlessness over sex—but must follow up with, as the alcoholic does in relation to alcohol—"admit that God can" give one continency, purity and chastity. Wise Old Solomon knew this very realistically—wherefore "he besought God" for the gift of continency. A very important truth that our "impossibilist" has seemingly not as yet learned is that "*nothing* is impossible with God." Of course he really doesn't want to know this—his attitude is too handy for an excuse. In practice he soon carries his rationalization over into his sobriety —and it becomes impossible, so he drinks again. For we know from experience that such never remain sober very long.

c. *The "you-have-to-have-companionshipist."* Enlarging upon the statement which he has picked up in A.A., that "an alcoholic should not be alone too much," this individual twists its true meaning and surrounds himself with many companions—one at a time and women! Again we have one whose sex-excuses lead inevitably to the bottle again.

d. *The "sympathizer."* This A.A. is always feeling sorry for and filled with sympathy for the newcomers—if they are women. His rationalization is "what she needs is sympathy." And he figures that he is one of the best little sympathizers in all the world with a thorough knowledge of women—how to get them. He does, and she does, and they do—drink again!

e. *The "Mr.-fixit."* The self-appointed marriage counselor. This is his entree into apparent family friendship. In his own egotistical pride he deems himself tops as a marriage counselor. Of course it is always the wife who needs counseling. So he manages to "fix" everything—for himself. The next thing he realizes is that he is "fixing" himself—a drink!

f. *The down-right "chiseler."* He has a bit of honesty, if it can be called that. His great fallacy is that he deludes himself by thinking that he can carry on as he does and remain sober. He has that very far-fetched attitude that he can break one of God's laws willfully and flagrantly, and then expect the grace of sobriety at the same time. The writer has come into contact with many of these contradictory personalities, but has never seen one that has remained permanently sober. On rare occasions, one or the other has been so "unfortunate" as to retain a sort of dry sobriety for a period of years, but when the toll is finally taken, the results are terrific. They seldom return. We can't mock God.

g. *The "as-long-as-you-don't-do-iter."* This individual has never come to a realization of the importance of "right-thinking" as well as right living. He doesn't seem to be aware of the very basic fact, that *as we think we ultimately live.* Furthermore he seems unaware that this principle is doubly true in this matter we are discussing. He goes along—for awhile—on the fallacy that "as long as you don't *do* wrong in this matter, it is perfectly o.k. to think as you wish." But then the day comes when thinking leads to doing. The bottle is not far behind.

h. *The "necessityite."* A very peculiar individual. Some crackpot nominal psychiatrist or psychoanalyst has told him that "such things are necessary for good health, etc., etc." He believes it, and with a very normal desire for health, he rationalizes his wrong-doing—and then soon proceeds to damage his health very drastically on his next binge. One person very blatantly told the writer: "My doctor told me I'd die without such things!" He's not dead yet—and of course he's not sober.

i. *The "Club-sheik (or sheba)."* One shows up in every A.A. Club on occasion, in some groups, frequently. Such do much damage and often give our A.A. Clubs a "black-eye." He (or she) frequents the Club for one reason—to ensnare someone. The fact that the someone is somebody else's husband or wife seems to make no difference. Using A.A. as a front and a sham, he (or she) just loves to sit around with one of the opposite sex to have "private" discussions. It is not long until things begin to happen. A family is often broken up—others are hurt—then come the binges, with their resultant messes. The sad part of it is that almost always innocent people are hurt, badly and permanently.

j. *The "story-teller."* There is always one of these in every group. He has a morbid hobby of telling "dirty" stories. To everyone and everywhere and all the time. He hasn't the intelligence to enjoy or give a witty clean story—he has lost that type of thinking long ago. Humor and dirt are synonymous to his warped mentality. The pity of it is that he goes about presuming that everybody else has the same mentality. Little does he realize how much most of the members detest his rantings. He is a frequent "slipper," but doesn't seem to have sufficient intelligence upon which to ever build permanent sobriety and happiness.

k. *The "platonite."* We do not believe that this person is ever very sincere in his attitude. He only is trying to fool others by his ever ready excuse, "It's only platonic." But he really convinces nobody, merely kidding himself that others believe him. They don't. One married man tried to convince the other members of a certain group that his week-end excursions with his beautiful secretary were "platonic." It wasn't long until he married her. Did he "slip"?—and how!

The correct attitude: The knowledge and conviction that God is the Author of sex and therefore that it is something good in itself. When used in accordance with God's laws and plans, man becomes in a way "co-creator" with God in the procreation of the human race. Self-control outside of marriage is possible but only with the assistance of God's grace. This one must ask for—regularly. *Willful* abuse of God's law in this regard, without exception, makes permanent sobriety *impossible.*

11. *ATTITUDE TOWARD THE FAMILY.*

a. *The "change-my-wifer."* This attitude keeps many out of A.A. It fools them into believing that they are not alcoholic. Such a person blames all of his drinking difficulties on his wife, always coming back with the reply to anyone who might criticize his drinking, "If you would only change my wife, I'd be all right." What such an individual doesn't seem to have learned is that there is only one person we can change—that is ourselves. We also find many members who still go about with this false attitude. They always blame others, or circumstances—everything but themselves. So they are always endeavoring to change others, and circumstances, etc. As a result they seldom work on themselves, seldom try to change themselves, seldom remain sober for long—and are never happy.

b. *The "twelfth-stepper" outer.* Doing twelfth step work enables this party to have a lovely excuse for something he has long desired—to get away from his family or wife. He gives to A.A. the many A.A. "widows" who are so numerous in many groups. He never misses a meeting—so he won't have to stay home or take the wife out. He is always around the Club—but never in company with his wife. He makes many calls on new prospects, and many 'pseudo-calls,' for it fools his wife. Eventually he returns home and wants his wife very much—to sober him up!

c. *The "instructor."* Having gotten a lot from A.A. he is determined that his whole family get it too. So he "instructs" them ad nauseam on A.A. Instead of leading them, he insists that they do as he does. The result is much fallacious knowledge of A.A. for the family, frequent conflicts, and family dissensions. Finally, in a morass of self-pity, he feels unappreciated at home and seeks the bottle again "for a bit of consolation"—and ultimate desolation.

d. *The "she-should-be-glad-I'm-soberer."* After innumerable years of excessive drinking and neglect of his wife and family, this person, having achieved a few *months* of sobriety, is always telling about how "unappreciative " his wife and family are, and after all, he tells you, "she should be glad I'm sober"! Seemingly having conveniently and quickly forgotten all *his* past wrongs and drinking, he egotistically expects all to bow and scrape to *his* marvelous accomplishment—a few months of sobriety! "A one-eyed man is king among the blind!" Usually the constant family dissensions caused by his self-justification leads to much unhappiness, and he, too, often returns to the only close friend he ever had—his only true love—the bottle!

The correct attitude: The individual who is very conscious that, for most of his past, *he* was to blame; that *he* has very often *wronged* his family; that a lifetime is all too short to try to make up for these past wrongs. He daily endeavors to lead his family—by example. He daily attempts to learn and practice true love for them which means *giving* not expecting. He and his family ultimately become very happy—and he stays sober.

12. *ATTITUDE TOWARD ONE'S JOB.*

a. *The "I-should-be-the-bosser."* Somewhere in A.A. he has heard that all alcoholics are very capable people. Stretching this a bit, he figures that he is the most capable. So he is never satisfied with a position of inferiority. His egotistical rationalizing convinces him that he knows more than the "boss." Accomplishments fail to justify his attitude. He becomes very unhappy in his work, frequently indulges in resentments and self-pity, and every alcoholic in A.A. knows what that means—the bottle.

b. *The "always-anxious-for-a-raiser."* No matter how much this person makes, he always thinks he should have "another raise." Never quite satisfied with his job, and never too efficient in his work, he still is always looking for more—and more—and more—and more. The constant anxiety and dissatisfaction that is a result of this attitude usually causes loss of many jobs, and he wonders why. If this anxiety is carried over into other phases of his living, (and it usually is), he encounters trouble with his sobriety—and wonders why.

c. *The "over-timer."* Here we have a very sincere person, but very imprudent. Typically alcoholic he is an extremist. But the two things he seems never to learn is that our slogan, "easy does it" applies to *all* activities of an alcoholic; and that one of the basic circumstances which an alcoholic must avoid is "over-tiredness." So he works ten, fifteen, even eighteen hours a day. He kids himself that he *must* do it, failing to realize that if he slips, which he will if he continues his imprudent over-work, it will never be done. Many otherwise excellent members of A.A. have slipped simply by over-tiring their minds, bodies and nerves by excessive time given to work. There is an old Latin axiom: "In medio stat virtus," i.e., virtue is always in the middle course. Extreme action of any sort is never virtuous. Easy does it!

d. *The "loafer."* Someone in A.A. has told this individual to "avoid to much pressure." He also has heard "easy does it" —so he follows them literally. He has gone off the other end. Many times without a job, when he is working he takes every possible opportunity to dodge his duties. He is determined not to work himself into a slip—so he "eases" himself into one! Easy does it but *honest* labor, within reason, never harmed any one.

e. *The "wife-worker."* Every once in awhile one of these comes along. "Why should I work," he will exclaim, "my wife's got a good job!" Then he will follow up with, "And further-more it gives me a better chance to do A.A. work." What he really means is that he has more time to "loaf" with his A.A. buddies. He works—on everyone but himself. He slips frequently. In reality that is why his wife hangs on to her job—she knows!

The correct attitude: The one who does his work, whatever it may be, conscientiously and without anxiety. He tries to better himself in his job, but is not too eager. He returns solid work for his pay. Such a one is usually happy in his job no matter what it may be. He is also happy in his home, in his A.A. activity—and he stays sober.

13. *ATTITUDE TOWARD MONEY.*

a. *The "make-a-million-fellow."* He seldom has a solid job, because he is always waiting for the one to come along wherein he can "make a million." His alcoholic "big-shotitis" has been accentuated in the financial angle. His dreams are to some day have lots of money so he can spend his days in rest and relaxation. The only thing that is not quite apparent in his "dreams" is that there is usually a bottle therein. One often wonders whether someone hasn't told him to lay up a lot for a rainy day—and that he is expecting another deluge!

b. *The "spendthrift."* Another form of "big-shotitis." His careless spending on everything and everyone is in no way motivated by charity, but by vanity, as were the average alcoholic's spending-sprees in his drinking days. He is always in debt and wonders why he "can't make ends meet." His spending often ends in another kind of a "spree." Such a man needs badly: humility, prudence and planning.

c. *The "A.A.-don't-cost-nothing" fellow.* Having heard the over-worked, over-emphasized "there are no dues, no money needed, etc., in A.A.," he has taken it literally and squawks at every "kitty," every request for financial help, every mention of money. Just how such an individual figures that a group of people can meet in a rented hall, have coffee and do-nuts, etc., for free is beyond comprehension. He in reality knows better, but the above quoted remark is an excellent salve and excuse for his "tightness." We have often wondered whether the constant emphasis on "no dues, etc.," is not a little bit over done.

It provides such a beautiful excuse for these misers—who are also usually the biggest critics of how things are run. We are of the opinion that we should begin to change our approach and clearly specify that *information and help on how to stay sober* costs nothing, *but* meetings, Clubs, group activities *do* cost and should be supported *by the members* who can afford to do so. Or perhaps is the constant "money-squawking" a product of an innate miserly nature?

d. *The "horder."* He has done very well financially since coming into A.A. And now he holds on to his money. His stock excuse is "I worked for what I got." How little does his selfish mentality realize that his ability to work, his job, all the circumstances that have enabled him to do well is *a gift* of God! For it is from Him that we get both the will to do and to accomplish. Such a person, being so unappreciative and ungrateful for those things given to him, often eventually loses them —and then some—on the next binge which usually sooner or later follows.

e. *The "expecter."* This person comes to A.A. not so much for sobriety, but "expecting" material gain and fortune. And when he doesn't get it, as often happens, he is disappointed. He hears members relate how much financial and material success they have had since coming to A.A. and he puts this as his goal. When it doesn't come along, he becomes more disappointed. Then comes resentments, self-pity—and the inevitable slip. What he has completely missed (and the writer feels that this point is not emphasized enough) is that A.A. promises *only* sobriety and happiness *inside,* not material happiness, to those who sincerely work the program.

The correct attitude: The one who realizes that A.A. is a means to achieve *personal sobriety and happiness,* not *material* nor *financial gain.* He makes an honest effort to make money, to save it, to plan prudently for the future—*all subject to the will of God.* And if he should be blessed with a material superabundance he is willing to gratefully share it with those who have it not. Such a one remains happy and sober whether he makes and has little or much.

14. *ATTITUDE TOWARD THE FUTURE.*

a. *The "worrier."* He is always worrying and wondering about what *might* happen, how long he will stay sober, how he will meet the morrow. He is always asking "what if... ?" The ultimate result is conflicts, nervousness—the bottle. He needs badly to *practice* the twenty-four-hour program, to live *one* day at a time, to put *all* the future into the hands of God's Providence. He should remind himself over and over again that *grace will be given for each day when it comes* and that grace is never given today *for tomorrow.*

b. *The "determined-planner."* He does very well in planning for the future but he is *determined* to push his plans through no matter what may come up to change them. Caring little for the Will of God and pushed along by his own egotistical pride, he attempts to run rough-shod over all obstacles. He little realizes that obstacles will come along which he cannot change or push aside; that his frustration at these points will but plant and cultivate deep resentments or self-pity; that these two little gentlemen will show him the door—the "swinging one"!

c. *The "if-I-only-knewer."* This one is quite willing to follow the program "if he only knew" what tomorrow would bring. He doesn't exactly worry about the future, he in reality is doubting the efficacy of today. The old reliable and wise advice is, "If you did know that all will be well, what would you do today? That do and all *will* be well."

d. *The "expect-the-worst."* This individual doesn't "wonder" what may happen, he *knows* that the worst will always happen to him. It is a form of self-degradation often stemming from a lack of knowledge and conviction of God's mercy and forgiveness. It inevitably leads to self-pity—often to despair. He also needs the twenty-four-hour program and frequent meditation on the mercy, love and goodness of God.

The correct attitude: The one who relies *implicitly* upon Divine Providence for tomorrow and concentrates on the task at hand, *today.* He does the foot-work and leaves all the rest in the hands of God knowing that He will, in His time and ways, crown his every effort with success. This attitude is basic for living one day at a time.

15. *ATTITUDE TOWARD THE PAST.*

a. *The "insincere."* This one's sorrow is surface. It does not contain an honest decision and desire to do better. He is sorry for his past because *he* has been hurt, not because he has sinned against God and others. It is the self-sorrow of Judas, and usually ends the same way either actually or by the bottle.

b. *The "built-complexist."* This one's past constantly hangs heavy upon his mind and soul, not as a salutary motive of penance, but as an obstacle to progress and present activity. It is based on an over-exaggerated fear of God. It in practice denies His Mercy. It often leads to bad nervous conditions, conflicts, and always keeps one away from God Whom he so much fears. Scrupulosity is also a by-product of such attitudes. What such a person needs is encouragement and *action in the present* coupled with frequent, sane meditation on the innumerable instances of God's Mercy and forgiveness. He should try to more and more strive for the conviction that God asks only present good will. Having this, the past, no matter how terrible, is no obstacle to His grace. "Action is the magic word."

c. *The others-were-to-blamer."* Here we have one who has been led to believe by some crack-pot psychoanalyst that some past environment led to his alcoholism and wrong actions, such as an over-indulgent parent, circumstances, etc. So now he blames *them* for his present condition. The resultant self-pity, resentments, and rationalizations stymie present honesty, minimize present responsibility, and become wonderful excuses for the first drink. He doesn't need an excuse for the second!

d. *The "dreamer."* This individual frequently indulges in recall of the past apparent good times associated with drink. He is adept at suppressing, consciously or otherwise, the sufferings attached inevitably thereto. Such "stinking" thinking always leads to try it again. He does and his former "dreams" are very quickly and surely replaced by the stark reality—"nightmares"!

e. *The "bragger."* Still loaded with pride, this misled individual, with the excuse of identifying himself as an alcoholic, delights in *bragging* about his past drinking escapades and wrong doings. He is the "quart-a-day" man. "I'm a *real* alcoholic, I drank a quart a day for forty years!" And as he details all the gruesome experiences of his past he is inwardly patting himself on the back as one of the greatest guys that ever lived—an evil life. Little does he realize that his bragging is motivated by pride which failing to find anything good in his makeup must use his wrongs to place him above his fellowmen. He doesn't usually stay long on his false pedestal—eventually he "slips" off.

The correct attitude: The man who has the conviction that *he* has been responsible for most of his past and that *he* can, with God's help, make up for it; that, presuming true contrition, God has forgiven those wrongs and asks only present goodwill; that in A.A. one's past is to be brought up *only* when one feels it is necessary to help somebody else and that even then the details are usually not needed. Such a one seldom thinks of his past except to urge himself on to penance and better living. He leaves it all to God's infinite Mercy, and lives today—twenty-four hours at a time—so as never again to return to his former way of living.

16. *ATTITUDE TOWARD SPONSORSHIP.*

a. *The "one-call-that's-all-fellow."* When this person calls on a new prospect, he merely invites him to a meeting—that's all. He offers no real help, no follow-up, no initial props. He makes one call and that is all. His stock excuse is "well, after all, you shouldn't spoil them!" His real reason, perhaps hidden from himself, is his lack of charity and his laziness. Usually he himself is one who had to be carried around in a "plush basket" for months before he was able to follow part of the program on his own. He doesn't seem to understand, or he doesn't want to understand, that the average newcomer needs a lot of help and daily contact until he is thinking clearly enough to continue on his own. A very selfish person, he never has heeded that important statement in the A.A. Book: "We do these things with a conscious effort to discipline ourselves into habits of unselfishness and love." So he remains selfish—he won't even share his next bottle!

b. *The "zealot."* He comes into A.A. with vim, vigor and vitality. He "devours" the program. Then he sets out with a determination to dry up every drunk in town. To the jail, the asylums, the hospitals he goes. He searches out "skid row," the taverns and the courts. He tries to bring them all to A.A. He only learns by much experience that A.A. only works for those who *want* it. Many, many new A.A.s go through this stage of learning. It is all part of their education. They are not hurt by it. Before long they settle down and realize that in A.A. we should work for our own sobriety and happiness and be *ready to be a dependable source of information for those who ask for it.*

c. *The "100%-expecter."* In his twelfth-step calls he expects *all* that he calls upon to make it. Forgetting that he is merely the instrument and that it is God who gives the success, he is discouraged and worried when one of his prospects does not make the program. Often a sincere person, he begins to chastise himself, thinking that perhaps he is at fault and didn't do all he could for the new fellow. He should realize, if he does what he can in all prudence, that even if *all* of his prospects fail, he has by his efforts *insured* his own sobriety and practiced charity. Success with prospects, or the lack of it, *is in no way indicative of the quality of one's own A.A.* The success is God's business, ours only the foot-work.

d. *The "Mr.-big-shot-sponsor."* Here we have a follow-up attitude of the above—when the sponsor happens to be successful with most of his prospects. Taking the credit unto himself, he swells with pride and becomes the "best little sponsor in the group." If anyone doubts this they need only to ask him. He will tell you, "Look at me, I have more men sober than any other member. My approach must be the best, etc., etc." Feeding his pride and failing to give credit where credit is due—to Almighty God—he grows into a very dangerous trend of thought. And if continued it isn't long before he needs a better sponsor—for himself.

e. *The "butter."* He would like to make calls, and go to meetings more regularly, and do all the rest of the twelfth step work *but*—he is too busy, too tired, or any of a dozen excuses which he calls reasons. And then, as usually happens, he is the one who cries the loudest when all the group don't run frantically in response to his call when he slips.

f. *The "pill-man."* Behold the self-appointed M.D.! His pocket is always loaded with barbitals, benzydrine, bromides, paraldehyde or what have you. He gives some to every new man he calls on. And then comes a prospect upon whom several of these "doctors" call. They all give him pills. He is lucky if he doesn't die as a result. Some have here and there! We wonder how such a dangerous person has failed to realize that his practice is contrary to very serious laws which forbid a layman to prescribe and administer drugs! We very definitely feel that *no drug should ever be given to anyone unless it is expressly ordered by a qualified doctor. Many* are seriously hurt by such self-appointed "pill-men." And, at times, these walking dispensers end up taking their own medicine. It is a wonderful substitute for alcohol!

g. *The "hospitalizer."* Accentuating the fact that alcoholics are sick people, he insists that *all* should be hospitalized. He even takes all of his prospects to the hospital—drunk, sober or coming off. Very often he imprudently signs them in himself—and then wonders when the hospital bills *him* for the costs! Behind his inane actions is a hidden desire to get the new prospect off his hands and still retain his "good" name as an ardent sponsor.

h. *The "de-hospitalizer."* Here is the direct opposite of the one above. He doesn't think anyone needs to be hospitalized. And, judging everybody by himself, he will stoutly aver, "Look at me, *I shook it out.*" This one and the one above both need a bit more objective judgment. The sincere and prudent man knows that *some* do need hospitalization and *some* do not need hospitalization, and in the ordinary course of events the one to decide this question is a doctor not a layman. Hospitalization is needed when lack of it may damage the physical or nervous system of the prospect coming off of one. *Only a doctor* can give the correct decision from his examination. We should never ourselves simulate this ability to diagnose.

i. *The "go-buy-yourself-a-booker."* A very selfish individual. Too parsimonious to ever give or loan an A.A. book to the new man, he excuses himself of this responsibility by telling all of his prospects, "go buy yourself a book." And the poor nervous, confused, "broke" new man wonders what it is all about. And we wonder if perhaps this factor isn't responsible for so many in A.A. who *have never read the A.A. book.* Their name is legion.

j. *The "what-am-I-to-sayer."* He is very adept at excusing himself from making twelfth step calls by pleading that he hasn't the slightest idea what to say to the new prospects. He leads himself to believe that the approach to such must be "learned." He's never listening when others discuss the approach—for if he did listen he would know that all anyone has to say on such a call is to tell the new man about one-self. So he goes merrily on his way with a lovely excuse for not doing twelfth step work. What he is really doing is hanging on to his selfishness and pride —or just plain laziness. He takes out no insurance—and "accidents" do happen.

k. *The "amateur."* A bit different fellow from the "pill-man" above. He doesn't administer pills—just advice. All sorts of advice and as the gospel truth. Advice on medicine, psychiatry and theology. He, in his egotism, has become doctor, psychiatrist and clergyman. Seeming to forget that we are competent to offer advice and suggestions *only* on how to stay sober and on the alcoholic problem itself as handled in A.A., he has taken unto himself a M.D., Psc.D., and a D.D. And when he finds members who have other basic problems that need *competent* medical, psychiatric or spiritual guidance, he proceeds to solve them himself for the poor "guinea pig" instead of directing him to one who is qualified in such matters. As a result, the poor fellow seeking help gets more confused and often slips.

We believe that it is very important to always remember that *medical problems are for doctors, mental problems are for psychiatrists, religious and spiritual problems are for the clergy*—we are *not* competent in such matters. Much harm is done on occasion to the newcomers by such "amateurs."

l. *"The-female-sponsor."* Perhaps we should have classified this fellow under number 10. He also belongs there. He is always willing to make a twelfth-step call—if the one asking for help is a woman! This peculiar type of individual also comes into the picture in the "slippee." Every time they slip they call for help but insist on having a sponsor of the opposite sex. And we know from experience that as long as this mentality persists in the person they will remain "among the slippees"!

m. *The "screener."* We find this pride-infected individual frequently here and there. He will call on a new prospect after he has first ascertained that the one needing help is in his social or professional circle. All others are screened or relayed to someone else. He thinks he is practicing charity on his calls whereas in reality he is feeding his pride. When he slips, as he usually does, he insists that one from his "social strata" call on him. He wonders why he never permanently makes the program!

n. *The "graduate."* Here we have an A.A. "elder," one of the "old-timers." He has now been sober for a few years, knows all the answers and has become rather smug in his sobriety. So he rationalizes that some of the "young fellers" in A.A. need the experience and should make the twelfth step calls. The only thing he hangs on to in twelfth step work is going to meetings—to give his sagacious advice to the "young-uns"! Behold the long-dry slippee! But then what else could one expect. All of his crutches have one by one left him since his "graduation" day—charity, humility, prayer and insurance. The old-time crutch soon begins to hover in the background. Before long he reaches for it—the bottle.

o. *The "spoiler."* The opposite of the "one-call-that's-all guy." He merely substitutes for an over-indulgent parent or wife or husband of the past. He coaxes and cajoles; he "takes" the new fellow to many meetings; he gets him a job; he pampers him by minimizing the truth—his most solid help that is offered is a pat on the back and a "push." Then he wonders why his prospects slip so often. If he would only know the truth—they love it! "In medio stat virtus."

p. *The "preacher."* A very spiritual minded person. He is a cousin to the "religious-fanatic" above. His initial approach is through the entire spiritual side or religion. He takes the newcomer to his priest or minister before the poor fellow is able to even read the *first* step. He tries to make the poor fellow run before he is able to crawl. He tries to make the befuddled prospect into a saint before he is even able to realize that he is a sinner. He is simply repeating a mistake that has been made for years—attempting conversion before conviction.

q. *The "never-mention-God-man."* This one is one the opposite extreme of the "preacher." He will not even mention God nor prayer to the new prospect lest "he frighten him"! So he apologizes for God and as a result gives the new fellow nothing really secure to hang onto. What both he and the "preacher" should learn is that we should never apologize for the One upon Whom the entire program depends and on the other hand that we should not "pour" it on such a confused brain. Let's stay with step one and two on such calls, but let's keep them *both. No one* has ever been frightened away from A.A. by the *suggestion* of dependence upon God.

The correct attitude: We cannot keep that which has been given to us unless we in turn freely give it to *all* who ask without exception. *All* of our twelfth step activities should be accompanied by sincere charity, a deep humility, and prayer for prudent guidance. Such as the really successful sponsors even though they may have never kept *one* prospect sober, for the actual success depends on God.

17. *ATTITUDES TOWARD MEETINGS.*

a. *The "good-chance-to-have-a-card-gamer."* This individual goes to most of the meetings—so he can get into a card game. He hasn't the slightest motive of learning something or of giving something—he goes only for the game. During the meeting he is anxious and jittery for it to be over—so he can play cards. If he would but reminisce a little, he would recall a similar circumstance of his drinking days—when he was always jittery and nervous for everything he had to attend or do to get over—so he could get to a tavern. Soon a few of his cronies get together and hit upon the brilliant idea of "substituting" a card game for the meeting. The card games become their A.A. They return to the meetings *after* their slip!

b. *The "in-and-outer."* This fellow attends the meetings, listens to the speakers, and it all goes in one ear and out the other. They have applied everything they hear—to somebody else. This person progresses very little if at all, often has trouble, and sometimes never returns. He never has learned to listen.

c. *The "bored-to-deather."* One member told the writer, after one of his slips, that the reason he did not attend the meetings much was because he was always "bored to death." What the gentleman in question needed to realize was that one does not go to A.A. meetings primarily to be entertained, but to learn; that there is never a talk so bad that one cannot get some help from it—even if it be only an opportunity to practice patience and tolerance; and that one very important reason one should attend meetings regularly is to *give* encouragement to the newcomer by one's very presence. After all this is primarily a *give* program. We feel sure that the above gentleman would have been very much chagrined, to say the least, if everyone had had his attitude when he went to his first meeting—and found an empty room! Of course, in order to be able to take something home from every meeting one must have an open mind, a bit of charity and humility.

d. *The "meeting-a-day-keeps-the-D-T's-away-fellow."* He has heard that one should go frequently to meetings especially in the beginning. He does—every day. A typical extremist alcoholic, he is always at every meeting of every group. Then he wonders soon why he tires of A.A. and becomes so jittery and nervous, etc., etc. So he tries a little relaxation—in liquid form. Easy does it!

e. *The "socialite."* This individual is always clamoring for more "social" activity for the meetings. He's a first cousin of the "board-to-deather," although a bit more sincere. He usually stays sober and is quite harmless. The others manage to keep him in his place.

f. *The "religion-injector."* He brings the Bible in—and gives the answers. He thinks the Bible should be on the table and that at most meetings a clergyman should speak. Then comes the inevitable sequence—doctrinal subjects and religious discussions. Fortunately, except here and there, he doesn't get that far. The others keep him in his place too. Our good clergy friends also should realize that they or any non-alcoholic should speak at an A.A. meeting only on occasion. *Only "members" of A.A. should do so regularly.*

The correct attitude: The one who looks on the meetings as the greatest source of insurance against a possible slip. He goes to meetings for three primary reasons: to learn, to avail himself of the much needed group therapy of insurance and to *give* by his presence encouragement to all. He enjoys the meetings, no matter how bad the speaker. He is happy and he doesn't slip.

18. *ATTITUDE TOWARD SPEAKING.*

a. *The "I'm-not-a-public-speaker-man."* Motivated either by fear or sheer laziness, this fellow excuses himself from every speaking by the stock phrase above. He doesn't seem to realize that ability to speak well is not a necessary ingredient for leading a meeting. There is only one quality necessary—sincerity. Many a member has plucked the solution of a long-standing problem from a very bad speaker—rhetorically speaking. God by no means chooses the best public speakers as His instruments.

b. *The "actor."* We can always be sure of a good "show" when this person speaks, but we can never be sure of much solid A.A. He is not one of the wonderful humorists whom we find all around the country and who are a blessing to A.A., but he is the individual here and there who is determined to "steal" the show for himself. He will use any type of falsehood if it is necessary to get "top billing." He is often an accomplished speaker—but a poor A.A. which fact he conceals to himself. Wherefore many are surprised when he slips—which he usually does. Without sincerity and humility permanent sobriety is impossible.

c. *The "risque."* He can never give a public talk without injecting dirt into it. The pity of it is that usually he is a very accomplished speaker otherwise. He probably thinks that "humor" comes from "humis"—which means dirt! He gets many invitations to speak at various groups—he seldom is invited back. His filth-filled mind can not seem to grasp the fact that MOST members—both men and women do *not* sanction such tripe in public speaking. One time such an individual, while speaking, began to look around the hall and very naïvely asked, "I'm just looking whether there are any women present before I tell this story." Just then a gentleman jumped up from the audience and caustically remarked, "There are no women, sir, but there *are gentlemen."* He didn't tell the story. These individuals are to be pited—they are psychopathic.

d. *The "my-own-story-in-detailer."* This one believes that in order to identify himself as an alcoholic he must tell all of his past drinking career *in detail.* So he rambles on and on and on—ad nauseam. The writer sat in on a meeting where one of these individuals was holding forth. He had taken two hours and a half to detail all the rottenness of his past when the chairman had to call quits—and he hadn't gotten drunk yet! We should always remember that one's past is to be told *only* when there is a *need* to help someone else.

e. *The "cry-professional."* Here is the one—and there are many—who cry "professional" whenever an out-of-town speaker comes and the group pays his expenses. He is one of the "jealous Johns" who write to the Grapevine about the *many* members who are making a "good living" speaking around the country. The writer has met most of these fine speakers who unselfishly give time and talent to all groups to whom their circumstances permit them to go. He has never yet met one who is making a "good" living therefrom. But he has met many who are having a tough time meeting expenses, and a few whom it is costing quite a bit each year—thanks to the "cry-professional." Of course this latter poor soul of stinted vision has never been invited to speak at other groups, but if he ever were we pity the group who would have to pay his expenses. Envy is the cause of great paradoxes in human nature.

The correct attitude: Speaking at meetings is part of the twelfth step work, and everyone should try to contribute his share regardless of how "poor" a speaker one may be. One's primary endeavor in such should be above all else *sincerity.* No fee should ever be asked, but a group should not invite a speaker from a distance without paying his travelling expenses. Justice demands this. God often has given great talent in speaking to some of our members—but He seldom finances him!

19. *ATTITUDES TOWARD THE MORE ACTIVE MEMBERS.*

a-z. *The "jealous-Johns."* We shall include all under one classification. Among them are the "knifers," the "sling-shot-artists," the "libelers," the "criticizers," the "tale-bearers," the "self-appointed-elders" and many, many other shades of classification. The one term includes them all—the "jealous-Johns" —John Doe by name—and goaded on in their diabolical pursuits by a venomous jealousy of the success of others. The object of their "black" are is every member of A.A. who by circumstances or otherwise has become very active locally or nationally—from Bill on down. Perhaps the less we say about them the better—jealousy is an insidious thing. Experience has accentuated one fact—they seldom stay sober for very long. Once in a while they do. In one or the other case for as long as eight or ten years—but retribution sooner or later comes. On the other hand the "victims" of their tirades are still sober, happy and in time achieve a habit of pitying such unhappy, jealous souls instead of becoming resentful. It's an old adage of human nature—"if you want to be talked about, *do* something."

The correct attitude: The member who is *grateful* that God has placed among our membership many talented, active, self-sacrificing persons through whom we are able to share in the benefits of A.A. as we have it today.

20. *ATTITUDE TOWARD ALCOHOL.*

a. *The "dry-drunker."* He is dry—and how he hates it. He has decided he is an alcoholic but has never decided to do *all* that is necessary for happy sobriety. Still on the negative side, he is a frequent subject of conflict, nervousness, resentment and unhappiness. He becomes more unhappy dry than he was drinking, so he does—drink again.

b. *The "prohibitionist."* This is the "dry-drunker," who has managed to stay sober for awhile and has come not only to hate his sobriety and the fact that *he* can't drink, but also has come to hate alcohol and the fact that others *can* drink. So he sets out to dry up everybody and becomes an ardent backer of the prohibition movement. But after awhile hate gives way to first love. He and his old love meet again—"the bottle and he, and the tavern makes three."

c. *The "beer-experimenter."* The age-old advice—all wrong —becomes a lovely rationalization. This time he will stay away from the hard stuff—just stick to a little beer! And he does— for awhile. Then he is convinced that he is not an alcoholic, so he concludes: "Bring on the liquor—cases of it!"

d. *The "temptation-courter."* There's a tavern in the town, and every day he goes down—to the tavern to drink a "coke" to prove to himself he doesn't have to take a drink of liquor. His admission of "powerlessness over alcohol" was merely verbal—he didn't really mean it. So he is trying to build up *his* strength of avoiding that first drink. Eventually he does—drink the liquor.

e. *The "prude."* This individual has developed an abnormal *fear* of liquor. He won't go near it and usually won't tolerate people who do. Ordinarily he is a very sincere man and stays sober, but bordering on the scrupulous, he has stymied much happiness for himself. Another alcoholic extremist, he has overemphasized his "powerlessness." He seems to forget that when *necessity* demands that one be around liquor or places where liquor is server, God will provide the strength. In some instances, where this fear becomes excessive, the very fact of frantically trying to avoid liquor will paradoxically impel one to seek it. One should not fight anything nor anybody. Easy does it. The above mentioned person, too, is the one who will refuse to take medicine if it has alcohol in it! He provides an excuse for the one who slips and then blames his slip on the medicine the doctor ordered. After such latter become honest, they will tell you that they not only took the teaspoon the doctor ordered—they took the whole bottle!

f. *The "reservationist."* He has taken the first step "with reservations." He hopes that the day will come when he can drink normally. It does—but *not normally. Most slips stem eventually from some sort of mental reservation in taking the first step—in admitting:* I am *powerless* over alcohol. Any of a hundred things might *occasion* a slip, but the usual *cause* is such mental reservation. That is in reality why such a one does not use this, that or the other part of the program. He is not convinced he needs it. And without the program there is no lasting and happy sobriety.

g. *The "man-of-indecision."* This party is convinced he is an alcoholic "at times." At other times he thinks that maybe he isn't. He is constantly in the middle thinking "maybe I am, and maybe I'm not." And the day soon comes when he definitely finds out—the hard way. One should remember the reply given the founder of one of the A.A. groups when an out-of-town A.A. came to give him information about the program. He told his caller that he wasn't sure he was an alcoholic. Came the blunt reply. "Make up your mind, man, you either are or you aren't!"

The correct attitude: The one who is convinced, once and for all, that *he is powerless over alcohol* and therefore sincerely practices *all* of the twelve steps to the best of his ability as a means of attaining *both* sobriety and happiness. Such a one stops fighting anything or anybody. He stays sober and happy. He has realized in his own self the meaning of the phrase "the expulsion of a compulsion by a Higher Power." His complete humility has enabled God to expel his former compulsion to drink.

21. *ATTITUDE TOWARD THE BASIC VIRTUE OF HUMILITY.*

a. *The "since-I've-become humbler."* This misguided person believes that one can think oneself into humility. So he is always talking about how humble he has become. He is "proud of his humility." And it isn't long before he becomes proud of all of *his* accomplishments. Then one day he too sees that "great humble" man in the mirror—and he invites him out for a drink!

b. *The "elder."* He has been sober now and in the group for a long time. He knows all the answers. The need of humility has long been forgotten. He inwardly pats himself on the back that he has achieved a *habit* of sobriety. He figures that is all he needs. And soon we have another long time sober slippee.

The correct attitude: Humility is the most basic of all the virtues. Any other virtue is impossible without it. For the alcoholic, sobriety is impossible without humility. It is acquired not by talk but by action, with a deep conviction that *all* depends on God—all that we are, all that we have, all that we ever hope to be, has been *given* to us by *Almighty God.*

And so:

"Within this earthly temple there's a
crowd. . . ."

THE GRACE OF GOD

(A Meditation)

One of the most frequently heard phrases in A.A. discussion is "but for the grace of God." It is used over and over again because we realize that the entire recovery of the alcoholic in A.A. has been by the grace of God. From the second step on through the entire program every success of the alcoholic, his every activity, his every victory is the result of God's guiding and helping grace. Yet in spite of this factor, we find that many members neglect this need in one of the most important parts of the twelve steps—in meditation.

As we saw in a former discussion, meditation is "thinking about truth." In this activity there are two kinds of "thinking." First to think about and seek truth in its relation to ourselves and our lives—that is NATURAL meditation. Secondly to think about and seek truth in its relation to God and ourselves, asking His guidance and help in doing so—that is SUPERNATURAL meditation. This is what is meant in the eleventh step when we "seek through prayer and meditation." Natural meditation is helpful—but we must meditate on a supernatural basis if we ever hope to find the full truth and the true attitudes in all of our affairs. For without the light of God's grace there will always be much self-deception, much surface thinking, much error in our seeking for proper attitudes.

We can see an excellent analogy of this fact in the world around us. In contemplating the works of nature we gaze with admiration upon the greater things of creation. We admire the sun, the moon and the countless stars which shine in the firmament. We behold with ceaseless wonder the limitless expanse of the heavens, the boundless ocean, the lofty mountains. All of this objects fill us with awe and are easily brought to our attention because of their very vastness.

The same thing is true in the works of man. In the great metropolitan centers we marvel at the huge skyscrapers, the mechanical perfection of the great bridges, the engineering accomplishments in the large underground tunnels and the magnificent highways. The very size of the giant airplanes that soar in the skies fills us with awe. Their magnitude alone arrests our attention.

Likewise in the physical order. The serious disease, the broken bone, the maimed back all make themselves known without searching.

But there are other works of nature, infinitesimal in size, that escape our notice and are only known as a result of long scientific research and seeking. Such are the atom, the neutron, and the electrons.

In man's work too we find delicate and perfect feats of manufacture, many of which are hidden from the naked eye. Such are the masterpieces of the craftsmen who fashion tiny watches whose parts and mechanisms keep the time, but which are hardly visible to unaided vision.

In the physical order we find like phenomena. For deeply hidden behind every disease lie the invisible bacteria and the infinitesimal virus.

All of these we must search for. Not being apparent to normal human vision, we must use the magnifying glass and the miscroscope. And even then, we know there are forces, etc., which escape human attempts at identification.

And yet we know from experimentation and research that these small minute parts of nature and of man's handiwork are in truth responsible for all of the resultant great forces—both for destruction and perfection in nature and manufacture. For it is the infinitesimal atom, and neutron and electron and their exact juxtaposition that make possible the skyscraper, the bridges, the highways, the airplanes, etc. We know too that the atom, the neutron and the electron are the greatest forces in the world for destruction as exemplified in the atom bomb. It was the hair-like guide on the bomb-sight that made possible the accuracy of the bombing mission in the past war. And it is the bacteria and the virus that cause all the diseases and disintegration that man's physical self is heir to.

Now let us carry these thoughts over into the moral and the spiritual order. It isn't difficult to see and know the great sins, and conflicts, and problems. But behind these problems most times hidden from view, are the real causes of the problems themselves. There we find WITH THE HELP OF GOD'S GRACE the insidious labyrinth of pride, the indiscernible taints of self-pit, the unapparent motives of uncharitableness—the incessant and invisible self-seeking in most of our actions and thinking. It is only the microscope of God's grace that will bring these damaging causes of our difficulties into focus. It is only with the help of His grace that we may ever hope to find ultimate truth. It is only with the grace of God as a guide that we may ever achieve the really proper and correct attitude "in all of our affairs." This is accomplished only by sincere seeking "in prayer and meditation"—meditation in the presence of God, having sincerely asked the help of His grace. For it is only through such meditation that we can ever find the right vaccine for all of our spiritual ills. It is only then that we can finally truthfully say that we have joined the ranks of the 'good' A.A.'s —BY THE GRACE OF GOD.

ACTION

In the May 1949 issue of the Reader's Digest under the title, "Whose Business Was It?" Fulton Oursler told the following true story.*

—When a woman jumped, one summer's day, from a high window of the Russian consulate in New York, the crash of her body on the pavement was heard around the world. But at that time the world heard only a part of the truth.

No outsider knew that Madame Oksana Stepanovna Kasenkina would never have taken that spectacular leap if a young Connecticut farm wife and her brother, a novice lawyer, had not first intervened in an affair that seemed to be no business of theirs. This brother and sister set in motion a chain of events whose climax did more than anything else, before or since, to bring home to Americans the reality of Soviet duplicity and ruthlessness.

Now, with their permission, the story can be told.

It begins in a farmhouse at Ridgefield, Conn., on August 8, 1948, a sultry Sabbath morning.

Home from early church, the family surrounded the breakfast table, where Daniel McKeon was dividing Sunday comics among the children. Louise, blonde young wife and mother, scanned the New York Times. "A terrible thing is happening!" she suddenly exclaimed, and read aloud from the front page. On Sunday a 52-year-old widow had been kidnaped by Soviet officials from an estate near Nyack.

"Just listen to what went on!!" gasped Louise.

Ten days before, Madame Kasenkina, in this country to teach the children of Russian delegates to the United Nations, had been ordered to return to Moscow. Her passage was arranged on the Soviet steamship *Pobeda.* Instead of going aboard, she hid herself. When the vessel sailed without her, she fled for protection to Valley Cottage, home of the anti-Communist Countess Alexandra Tolstoy, aging daughter of the great novelist. Madame Kasenkina's purpose was to remain in the United States

---

*** Reprinted with permission of the Reader's Digest.**

and become a citizen. But Soviet raiders pounced on her sanctuary, and now it is fear she was being shanghaied to Russia, to be liquidated.

These accusations were denied. According to Jacob M. Lomakin, Soviet Consul General, who now was holding the woman under "protection" in his New York house, he had merely "rescued" her from the bondage in the household of Countess Tolstoy. Known to newsmen as a churlish fellow, the dour-faced Lomakin was today all smiles. He protested that he wanted everybody to know the whole truth.

Reporters crowding his office were introduced to a pale-faced woman garbed in black, with red rings around her brown eyes. Lomakin said:

"Here is Madame Oksana Stepanovna Kasenkina. She came with us willingly. She wants to go to Russia."

These assertions were obsequiously confirmed by the woman herself. To experienced newspapermen, however, her assent seemed only an act of terrified obedience; they noticed her uneasy glances, her frightened air and plucking hands.

On that humid Sunday morning, this same ugly news story was being read in millions of safe American homes, yet it did not occur to any of us that we should or could do anything about it.

But Louise McKeon, looking across at her husband, was deeply moved:

"Prisoners of Russian officials always agree with their jailers. There are horrible ways of making people do that. I believe that woman is really going to her death."

"Probably!" agreed her husband.

"Won't anything be done about it?"

"Well, after all, that consulate is technically Soviet territory—"

"Why don't *we* do something about it?" blazed Louise.

Dan McKeon blinked in astonishment. A new light was shining in his wife's eyes, a glow of dedication. With all her duties as mistress of a large house, mother of six children, and with club and church duties besides, why was Louise McKeon thus suddenly on fire? As the explanation dawned on him, Dan smiled. This was what came of talking recently to one of their oldest friends—Father James Keller, founder of the Christophers, who goes about inspiring ordinary people with his belief that they can by selfless acts bring about extraordinary changes in the world.

"But what can I do?" Louise had asked Father Keller. "A busy housewife, buried in Connecticut, can't help change the world."

"I don't care if you are buried in Alaska," Keller had replied. "Drop that feeling of personal futility and just try something sometime. When you do you will not be alone; the Good Lord will be right there helping you."

And now, on this Sunday morning, Dan McKeon realized that for his wife this moment was her *"something"* and she was going to try something!

"But what can you or I possibly do in a case like this?" he argued. "Only the State Department can deal with Soviet Russia."

"Just the same, I'm going to do *something!"* cried Louise. Dan McKeon rose and put his arms around her. "All right, darling, I'm with you," he said. "Now let's see—what could we do?... Why not talk with your brother about it? Pete's a lawyer. And he's coming up from New York today."

Now Peter W. Hoguet was a very new lawyer; only a year out of law school, he had just recently passed the state bar examinations. When he arrived at the McKeons' home they found that he was as indignant as they about the Kasenkina case. However, he didn't see that there was anything he could do.

"But no American could kidnap another American and get away with it, could he?" Louise argued. "Are Russians allowed to break our laws?"

"Sis, it's not our business."

Louise McKeon's retort was a searching question: "Well, if it's not our business, whose business is it?"

Peter Hoguet shrugged and gave no answer—then.

But on Monday night as he rode the train back to Manhattan, the question would give him no peace: "If it's not our business, then whose business is it?" Tuesday morning he dropped in on a friend, an experienced attorney.

"Women get queer ideas, don't they?" Peter began offhandedly, and told of his sister's excitement. But the other man exclaimed: "She's right. Whose business is it—if not yours?"

From that moment young Peter Hoguet found his days a living melodrama.

First he decided to rely on a principle in law older than Magna Carta—habeas corpus ("That you have the body"), which is the right of any citizen believing that another is illegally detained to bring that person into a court of justice where the facts may be ascertained.

Rather than sue alone for such a writ, it would be more impressive, Peter felt, for him to appear as representative of some patriotic organization. Accordingly, he went to Christopher Emmet, a Common Cause, Inc. With Mr. Emmet's cooperation, the application was drawn, and on Wednesday afternoon Peter Hoguet held his first professional conversation with a judge in chambers; to Justice Samuel Dickstein of the New York Supreme Court he offered papers alleging that a woman was being held against her will in the Russian Consulate "through power, deceit and terror being exercised upon her."

So cogent were his arguments that when he left he clutched a document commanding Jacob M. Lomakin, Soviet Consul General, to be in Manhattan Supreme Court at Foley Square at 10 a.m. the following morning, Thursday, and to have with him "the body of Oksana Stepanovna Kasenkina by your detained and imprisoned, as it is said."

Now all Peter had to do was to lay hands on Lomakin, one of the most elusive men in New York. He studied newspaper photographs, to fix in memory the image of his quarry—lean, pale face; jutting, cliff-like brow; eyes like deep cisterns, almost empty of light.

In legal protocol a lawyer of record does not serve his own summons. So Peter called a friend, another young lawyer,

Hugh Donohue, New York Commander of the Veterans of Foreign Wars.

Their rendezvous was the lobby of the Hotel Pierre at Fifth and 61st Street, across the street from the stately marble-front mansion occupied by the Soviet consular staff. Almost at the instant of their arrival, as if unseen forces were already helping, a black limousine drew up before the consulate, and a lean, pale man with jutting forehead sprang to the sidewalk.

"Lomakin!" cried Peter. The writ was in his pocket; no time now to pass it to Donohue; legal etiquette would have to go hang. Peter ran across the street as a cluster of reporters deployed around the Russian consul. Furious at the ambuscade, Lomakin raked his pockets and belabored his own doorbell; lucklessly for him he was without a key. Peter sprang up the marble steps, brandishing his paper.

"Mr. Lomakin? This is a writ of habeas corpus for Mrs. Kasenkina."

Lomakin locked his hands behind his back. But Peter pushed the court summons down inside the consul's buttoned coat. Lomakin seized the detested thing to throw it into the street, and that angry act betrayed him; the order of the court was in his hands.

"Mr. Lomakin," exclaimed Peter, mopping his face, "you are now served. I'll see you in court."

At ten o'clock next morning the youthful attorney appeared in Foley Square. He, who had never before had a case, found himself surrounded by cameramen. In the courtroom he assembled his witnesses, Countess Tolstoy and her associates from Valley Cottage. But where was Lomakin and Madame Kasenkina? Would the Russian official disregard an order of the New York Supreme Court?

When Justice Dickstein appeared on the bench, Peter Hoguet arose and announced: "Your Honor, I am ready to proceed."

But Russia was not ready. Indeed, it looked as if Peter Hoguet was beating his head against an iron curtain. In Washington the Russian Ambassador, Alexander S. Panyushkin, had declared that the "entirely inadmissable assumption" that Lomakin could forcibly detain Madame Kasenkina was "incompatible with the dignity" of the consular office. And the U.S. Department of State had telegraphed Governor Thomas E. Dewey, suggesting that Justice Dickstein defer further action. To this plea Justice Dickstein agreed for two wholly sensible reasons:

1. Word had been received from Lomakin that he needed time to consult with his embassy. Under the fair play to American courts he was to be given that time.

2. There was need to consult with the State Department on whether Madame Kasenkina had been brought to this country under diplomatic privileges, or as a mere consular employee. That technical point might determine the whole issue.

What the Judge did not know, nor did Hoguet, was that a Soviet ship was to sail at midnight of this same Thursday; within a few hours, Madame Kasenkina was to be shipped out. Then the habeas corpus writ could never be enforced.

Madame Kasenkina knew that she was to be a passenger on that ship. While Peter Hoguet stood glum and forlorn in court, the pallid woman in the case was being held in a third-floor room of the house on 61st Street.

Through an open window came the noises of the city: cars, trucks, the shrill voices of children in Central Park nearby. Fantail pigeons fluttered on her window sill, but Stepanovna did not see. Overcome with lassitude, lost in a mental cloud land, she slumped in a rocking chair. She had told friends that she scarcely heard the music coming from a portable radio on the bureau. If guards had suspected that Madame Kasenkina understood a little English there would, of course, have been no radio in the room.

Madame Kasenkina's mind had gone back to the year 1937. In those days she was a teacher in a biological institute in Moscow and her husband was also a science teacher. In the middle of night, heavy blows on the front door aroused them from sleep; Soviet troopers broke in, seized her husband and dragged him off. She never saw him again; never even learned his offense.

From that moment Madame Kasenkina dreamed of escape from the Soviet Union. But she had guilefully concealed her hope as she played the role of a frantic servant of the totalitarian state. At last she had been brought to the United States. She had determined never to go back to Russia. Yet there she was, trapped like an animal—and, so she believed, no one, anywhere, cared what happened to her.

Presently she stood up and walked to the window. Looking out toward the street, she saw a sight that startled her, even in her misty state of mind. A crowd was staring at the front of her prison house. Police had to hold them back. What had brought all those people here? She must try to understand, try to clear her head. Last night a nurse had come to her bedside, thrust a needle into her arm, spurting into her veins the narcotic often used by Soviet police. Under its influence the mind of the drugged person becomes a dream world and all resolution fails; it was the purpose of the drug, Madame Kasenkina has stated, to break her will.

Still bleary-eyed from the dose, confused when she was desperately wanting to think, Madame Kasenkina swayed dizzily toward the bathroom. She fumbled with the cold water spigot, bent over and splashed the chilly stream over head and cheeks. Now she began to think more clearly. Again she started toward the window, when she heard a voice from the radio uttering her name! What was the man saying, the newscaster with the excited voice? Intently she listened, hearing her name repeatedly mispronounced but unmistakable. She was overpowered with emotion. A little part, at least, of what she heard she could translate.

There had been court action on her behalf! This news rekindled her mind and soul. Now she knew why crowds filled the street below. She was not abandoned; the fate of an individual still meant something in America. Somebody had tried; somebody did care! All those people cared!

In that ineffable moment of realization, Madame Kasenkina was inspired to any sacrifice that might blazon the truth unmistakably to the people. She turned resolutely to the open window. Leaning far out on the projecting ledge she looked down three stories to the concrete pavement of a walled-in yard. It was a moment of Gethesmane. Two floors below she saw a telephone line strung across the court. She aimed her body at that wire, and jumped. The wire, though it nearly severed her hand, broke her fall and saved her life.

All America knows the rest of the story. From a bed in Roosevelt Hospital, the crippled Madame Kasenkina was a more effective witness against tyranny than she ever could have been on the witness stand. And with what world-stirring results!

Consul General Lomakin had to leave this country in disgrace. Other officials were also called home. In the pillory of international news they, and the mighty Molotov with them had been exposed as arrant liars. Not only in the United States but throughout Europe the Kasenkina case galvanized public opinion against Soviet lawlessness.—

The dramatic story just quoted is very illustrative of the proven, but strangely seldom used, fact: MOST problems of life and living could be solved if one would only DO something about them instead of thinking, worrying and debating about them.

This is especially true of the alcoholic. How many times have we not solved ALL of our problems MENTALLY, but actually they seemed to keep multiplying. That is why we were dreamers, perfectionists and procrastinators. We thought a lot, we did little. And when alcohol lent its charm to our imaginations, we not only solved our own, but all of the world's problems—MENTALLY. And when liquor itself came to be a problem, we solved it—every time—in our minds. "Never again," we vowed, but we DID little or nothing about it.

That is the reason the Alcoholics Anonymous book stresses that there should be a "minimum of analysis, and a maximum of ACTION," for "action is the magic word."

That is the reason why psycho-analysis is so dangerous and often so damaging particularly to the alcoholic. Most alcoholics have little difficulty analyzing their personalities. They have torn themselves apart for years, and DID little or nothing about what they saw. And because of this they became loaded with fears, phobias and what have you. ACTION alone will eliminate such from the personality.

That is the reason why so many apparently on the A.A. program slip: because they have taken all of the steps and eliminated all of their problems MENTALLY, but they have taken NO ACTION to *practice* the steps or to *solve* their problems.

That is the reason the twelve steps are written in the PAST tense—they PRESUME action. "We admitted . . ." "Came to believe . . ." "Made a searching . . ." "Admitted to God . . ." "Humbly asked . . ." "Were entirely ready . . ." "Made a list . . ." "Made direct amends . . ." "Continued to take . . ." "Sought through prayer . . ." "Having had . . . we tried to carry. . . ." We also note in the twelfth step that it tells us that we "TRIED," not necessarily that we SUCCEEDED. In other words as long as there has been ACTION in the twelfth step.

That is the reason so many conflicts, problems, etc., still remain with many of us, because there has been much thinking our way out, BUT NO ACTION. It is something like the story of the gentleman who failed to show up at his office for a few days. A friend, thinking he might be ill, went to his home and found him sitting in a littered room, hollow-eyed and gaunt.

"What's wrong with you? Sick?" the friend inquired.

"Not sick, just problems."

"What have you been doing to solve them?" the friend asked.

"I have spent three days just sitting here THINKING my way out of all my problems," he said.

"And have you found it?"

"I'm worse off than I was before."

He didn't seem to know that the only way to solve a problem is with action—"a minimum of analysis, a maximum of action."

Finally, that is the reason we have A.A. today; because BILL ACTED IN AKRON.

Now let us take a look at the twelve steps of the program and see practically how this works:

1. *WE ADMITTED WE WERE POWERLESS OVER ALCOHOL—THAT OUR LIVES HAD BECOME UNMANAGEABLE.*

Many a one had taken this step MENTALLY years ago. But there never had been any action, and so the drinking continued—to get worse. Such admission entailed no follow-up, so it but fed our self-pity and resentments. "I am powerless, POOR ME," or "I'm powerless, and it's YOUR fault. . . ." But in A.A. we make this admission with a POSITIVE attitude that we can and will do something about it. Hence (paradoxical as it may seem) the ACTION of one step is the looking to and using the solution in the subsequent steps ONE AT A TIME AND IN PROPER SEQUENCE so that we find THE ACTION OF EACH STEP IS CONTAINED IN THE FOLLOWING ONE. So, if we are POWERLESS, in order to DO something about it we must seek power somewhere. This we do in the second step, "a Power greater than ourselves."

We find in A.A. many who still have made their admission only mentally. They are the "first-step Johns," the "no-God-guys" who have admitted they are powerless, and how they hate it! In reality they haven't admitted it to themselves deep inside, for if they had, only fools would hesitate to seek, "a Power to restore them to sanity"—or maybe that IS the reason they hesitate!

So we ADMITTED that we are powerless over alcohol, and what are we DOING about it? ACTION demands that we

2. *CAME TO BELIEVE THAT A POWER GREATER THAN OURSELVES COULD RESTORE US TO SANITY.*

And here again the step often remains in the mind. There is no action, and "faith without works is dead." This need of action in the matter of faith is very clearly explained in the Alcoholics Anonymous book in the chapter "Into Action." And we feel that every new member (yes, and every old member) should thoroughly digest this chapter of the big book. No other phase of the A.A. program is so vital; no other step in the achieving and maintaining of sobriety is so necessary; and no other factor comes into play in our everyday living in A.A. For it is here that the entire working of the twelve steps evolves —from ACTION; God's and ours.

Lack of concerted action in step two denotes a weakness of faith. Such hesitancy may be very much present in the early days of every A.A., but eventually, in God's time and way (with our willingness) there must be ACTION. And again the action of step two is contained in step number three.

Here we find how illogical is the practice of the first and twelfth steppers—the "guys" and "gals" who proclaim loudly and long "I stay sober by only the first and the twelfth steps." Maybe so. So did we stay sober—many times—on sheer will power. But for how long? And how happy were we? And what eventually happened? So too with the dyed in the wool first and twelfth steppers. They MUST eventually get the other steps and use them or else . . . because it is our sincere conviction that permanent sobriety and happiness is impossible without ALL of the steps. Not perfectly—no one achieves that—but in the best way each can in her or his own way. For, again, the ACTION of one step is the taking of the next. Nor let us forget that the twelfth step itself clearly states that "having HAD a spiritual awakening as a RESULT of these STEPS"—plural!

So having taken the second step—its action takes place in step number three. For, if we truly believe that a "Power greater than ourselves can restore us to sanity" the only logical practice of that faith would be when we

3. *MADE A DECISION TO TURN OUR WILL AND OUR LIFE OVER TO THE CARE OF GOD AS WE UNDERSTOOD HIM.*

This of necessity presumes that we have reached some concrete form of belief, in God as we understand Him. As far as A.A. is concerned and as far as the achieving and the maintaining of sobriety is concerned, it matters little what our belief is—BUT IT IS PARAMOUNT THAT WE ACT ON IT regardless of what it may be. For in the realm of faith—above all else —ACTION IS THE MAGIC WORD. As a spiritual writer of old tells us: "ACT as if everything depended on yourself; BELIEVE and trust as if everything depended upon God."

Now if the decision in the third step is sincere, if it is not only mental, if it does not remain sterile, then we must necessarily take step number four. Why? Because how could we honestly turn our will and our life over to the care of God unless we KNOW what our life consists of? Or unless we make some sort of inventory to find out just what we are turning over to Him? So therefore we

4. *MADE A SEARCHING AND FEARLESS MORAL INVENTORY OF OURSELVES.*

The Alcoholics Anonymous book suggests that the inventory be written—again indicating the value of ACTION. And if there be sincerity in the making of our list, then the action takes place in the next step wherin we

5. *ADMITTED TO GOD, TO OURSELVES AND TO ANOTHER HUMAN BEING THE EXACT NATURE OF OUR WRONGS.*

Many of us have admitted our wrongs "to God and to ourselves" for years. That is easy—it entailed no action, no change, no effort. It remained merely mental—and clogged the mind the more. But ACTION takes place when we admit our wrongs "to another human being." Otherwise there could be no true mental catharsis, no improvement, no relief. And although many balk at this particular phase of the fifth step, it is precisely the most important phase, for it is ACTION—and ACTION IS THE MAGIC WORD.

If we are honest in taking this fifth step, again its action flows into the demands the subsequent step. For if we have sincerely admitted our wrongs, our faults and our failures—we certainly must take step six and

6. *WERE ENTIRELY READY TO HAVE GOD REMOVE THESE DEFECTS OF CHARACTER.*

Here we are entirely ready and willing to accept all that happens each day as God working on our character. We try to fit in with all the circumstances of our life as best we can. Each day we ACT, saying in effect: "You arrange my life, God, we'll do our best each day to FIT in." And here again sincerity in this step finds its expression and action in the next step. For if we honestly want God to "remove our defects" we logically

7. *HUMBLY ASKED HIM TO REMOVE OUR SHORTCOMINGS.*

Here again many fail to get past the mental or vocal stage. They ask God to remove this and that fault, but they expect Him to do ALL of the job. They themselves do no FOOTWORK, take no action. In other words, there are many who spend much time and futile energy in "wishing away their faults" without taking any practical steps to PRACTICE virtue. Loudly they petition God to take away their pride, etc., but they make no concerted effort to PRACTICE humility. On the other hand the sincere person takes ACTION—and in order to intelligently begin the practice of humility, etc.

8. *MADE A LIST OF ALL THE PERSONS WE HAD HARMED AND BECAME WILLING TO MAKE AMENDS TO THEM ALL.*

Many of us even went so far in our endeavor to achieve and maintain sobriety in the past as to make such a list as suggested in the eighth step—but only MENTALLY and it remained in the mind in fear and trembling or was frantically pushed back into the subconscious there but to add fuel to the conflicts that the alcoholic knows so well. But in A.A. we write it out and in sincere—we USE this list, we DO something about it in the next step wherein

9. *WE MADE DIRECT AMENDS TO SUCH PEOPLE WHEREVER POSSIBLE, EXCEPT WHEN TO DO SO WOULD INJURE THEM OR OTHERS.*

DIRECT amends. For that is true ACTION; the sort of action that gives the practice of humility, the one virtue that the alcoholic needs above all the rest. For "thinking" sorrow is really no sorrow—true sorrow demands ACTION. Not merely we "wish" we hadn't done this, we "wish" we hadn't done that, but we didn't do this or that, we did do this or that—we are sorry and are GOING TO DO PRECISELY THIS AND THAT TO MAKE UP FOR IT. That is ACTION!

Now for a moment let us recapitulate. Let us look closely at steps one to nine, and then to the three last steps ten to twelve. On analysis we find that there are three definite sections to the twelve steps:

1—Here in the admission we have the "door" to A.A. And **since we are speaking of ACTION** we find that many merely **"open" the door but do not go in** because there is no action. As **we mentioned above**, they merely came to the point of admitting that they were powerless and then instead of ACTING and looking to the next step they immediately turned their gaze in—"I am powerless—poor ME" and the door was closed again.

2-9—In these eight steps we have the program of readjustment. It is through them that we "get on the program." And we find that action throughout these steps gives a new personality, but a personality which demands constant ACTION to insure progress, and that action takes place in the DAILY or REGULAR follow-up in steps

10-12—So we find that steps one to nine are TAKEN ONLY ONCE. But action demands that we continue to use what these steps have given us and we find the "continued" action of the first nine steps in steps ten, eleven and twelve. And unless there be this action, we shall find ourselves sooner or later going BACK over the other steps and OUT the door again.

It is very amusing to hear speakers make the remark, "I use all the twelve steps every day." That is impossible. The daily program is in the last three steps. In them are contained the ACTION in the daily life of the good A.A. So we

10. *CONTINUED TO TAKE PERSONAL INVENTORY AND WHEN WE WERE WRONG, PROMPTLY ADMITTED IT.*

Here again we should not be deceived by thinking that this is a mental affair, that it is sufficient to "admit it" in the secrecy of our heart and room. We must ACT on it. If we have "blown our top" we must go to the person involved and admit we were wrong. Even though we may have been right in our contentions, we were wrong "BLOWING OUR TOP." And unless we rid ourselves of it by the EXTERNAL admission, we as alcoholics are in danger of ultimately blowing another top—the bottle's! It is true that the nature of many wrongs we may be guilty of are such that public admission would be neither necessary nor advisable—but we should admit them to SOMEONE. And for this purpose we should seek for someone in whom we have absolute trust.

In the regular taking of our inventory and attempting to eliminate the wrongs from our lives, we shall soon find how impotent we are of ourselves and we shall soon find out that for success we must REGULARLY seek for assistance from a higher Power, from God. So in order that HE may ACT on our characters we

11. *SOUGHT THROUGH PRAYER AND MEDITATION TO IMPROVE OUR CONSCIOUS CONTACT WITH GOD AS WE UNDERSTOOD HIM, PRAYING ONLY FOR KNOWLEDGE OF HIS WILL FOR US AND THE POWER TO CARRY THAT OUT.*

In prayer perhaps more so than in the other phases of our living, we find that ACTION IS THE MAGIC WORD. It is not sufficient to merely VERBALLY or MENTALLY seek help from God, and to find out His Will for us—we MUST ACT ON IT. Centuries ago we were told that "He who cries Lord, Lord, will not enter into the kingdom of Heaven, but he who DOES the Will of My Father, he will enter the Kingdom of Heaven." Action is the magic word! Or as one writer puts it "When you pray for potatoes, reach for a hoe!" We must do the footwork and then and then only will the "power" of God flow through us to give us not only sobriety, but contented sobriety. We ASK for God's Will for us by VERBAL prayer; we LEARN God's Will for us through MEDITATION; we DO the Will of God by ACTION.

In seeking the Will of God, we have It very clearly outlined for us in the subsequent step. So in order to ACT upon it we

12. *HAVING HAD A SPIRITUAL AWAKENING AS THE RESULT OF THESE STEPS, WE TRIED TO CARRY THIS MESSAGE TO ALCOHOLICS AND PRACTICE THESE PRINCIPLES IN ALL OF OUR AFFAIRS.*

First of all in the twelfth step, we find that God has ACTED upon us. And as a result of our ACTING upon the first eleven steps, He has given to us a "spiritual awakening"—an entirely new outlook toward God, toward our lives, toward our neighbor and toward ourselves. So now we continue to go into action to insure our sobriety and our new-found happiness by

1. "*Trying* (action) to carry this message to other alcoholics" and by

2. "*Practicing* (action) these principles in all of our affairs."

First of all we notice that we "TRIED" to carry this message to other alcoholics. As was noted above it is NOT NECESSARY THAT WE SUCCEED in doing so. ACTION is the magic word, and if there be ACTION, i.e., if we TRY, we are practicing the twelfth step regardless of whether we succeed or not. We have ACTED in doing God's Will—the rest, the sobriety of the "prospect" is in God's Hands.

So many become confused in this phase of the program. And many slip as a result of gauging this twelfth step work not by their ATTEMPTS but by their SUCCESSES. They either become depressed and full of self-pity by their lack of success; or they become elated and proud because of their success. What they fail to realize is that the ATTEMPT is action and all that is necessary; the SUCCESS is God's action, not ours.

Secondly, the action in the twelfth step also necessitates our "PRACTICING these principles (i.e., all that we have learned in the first eleven steps) in ALL of our affairs."

Many in A.A. seem never to have noticed this second half of the twelfth step. They have action galore in carrying the message to other alcoholics, BUT THEY DO NOT ACT ON THEMSELVES, they do not practice the principles of A.A.

in their own lives—in their prayers, in their homes, in their business, in their social lives. We don't like to say that these individuals get too much twelfth step action, but that their action in the twelfth step is lopsided, is not balanced. As a result we have another slip and hear the remark "and he was such an ACTIVE A.A. too!" It is precisely because of the importance of the action in the second half of the twelfth step and because it is action that others do not see, that we can never judge who is and who is not making the program. Remember? ACTION IS THE MAGIC WORD—ACTION ON ALL OF THE STEPS and ALL OF THEIR PARTS.

Since we feel that the second half of the twelfth step is so all-important, and since so many seem to miss this import, let us take a few "practical" examples of "practicing these principles in all of our affairs" and endeavor to see just how ACTION plays such an important role "in ALL of our affairs."

1. *RESENTMENTS.*

There is only one way to rid ourselves of resentments and that is by ACTION. Many A.A.'s spend time and waste energy in "wishing away" their resentments. How often one hears "I WISH I liked John," "I WISH I didn't resent Mary," "I WISH I liked my boss, my job, etc." But they take no ACTION and of course they continue to resent John, or Mary, or their boss, or their job. etc. Resentments simply will not be WISHED away. There must be POSITIVE ACTION. If someone irritates us we must DO some positive good to or for them; we must speak well of them, or speak cordially to them, or help them, or pray for them, and so forth. For it is only by a POSITIVE ACT of charity that we can replace resentment. Difficult? Sure, but very effective. ACTION IS THE MAGIC WORD.

Some time ago while visiting and speaking in a distant city, we were informed by the chairman of our visit that he would not accompany us to the meeting of "Blank" group that evening. Since he had been doing so to the other groups, we asked why.

"Oh, the chairman of 'Blank' group and I aren't speaking," came his reply.

"We thought you were a member of A.A.," we exclaimed in astonishment.

"We are," he hastened to assure us.

"And still you refuse to attend a meeting because you and the chairman are not speaking?"

"Well—yes," he hesitantly answered.

"Now look here, John" (his name was John Doe), we insisted, "you are not only going to the meeting with us tonight, but you are going to shake hands with the chairman of 'Blank' group."

"I just couldn't do that," he exploded, "never."

"OK," we replied, "if you don't go, we don't go. And there will be no talk."

"But you must go," he insisted, "it is already arranged."

We stuck fast. "You don't go, we don't go and that is final."

He finally agreed very hesitantly to go with me. As we entered the foyer of the auditorium in which the meeting was to be held whom did we see standing in front of the inner door but the chairman of "Blank" group.

"All right, John, let's see some action," he whispered.

With a supreme effort John edged over to the door and slowly held out his hand. It will never be known just which of the two was the most astonished, for both almost automatically responded to each other with friendly banter.

We remained in that area three weeks. During that time the chairman of "Blank" group and John talked to each other on the phone daily and now are close friends. ACTION IS THE MAGIC WORD. It works, it really does!

2. *SELF-PITY.*

In the matter of self-pity ACTION is of paramount importance. THINKING and TALKING about OUR condition but adds fuel and nurtures the self-pity to grow at an amazing pace. ACTION alone will stifle it and replace it. We must DO SOMETHING, anything—so that we may move away from ourselves as it were. And the most effective action is the doing for and with others. Twelfth step work is particularly intended to help allay the self-pity which has in the past so saturated the alcoholic's personality and now tries to wedge itself into our thinking so frequently. Many A.A.'s have slipped because they tried to talk or wish away their thoughts and attitudes of self-pity—and found only a bottle at the end of their "dream." ACTION IS THE MAGIC WORD.

3. *TEMPTATIONS.*

God will always "lead us not into temptation" and give us the strength to overcome them no matter how strong and persistent they may be PROVIDED there be ACTION on our part, provided we do the foot-work. It is not sufficient merely to pray for strength or for removal of a temptation! We must DO our part to remove ourselves from the temptation!

The writer remembers an instance in one of the groups some years ago which is very illustrative of this fact. John (his name was also John Doe), a member of the group, was always "crying" about how hard it was for him to stay sober—so much harder than any of the rest (poor fellow!) because there was liquor around him all day in the place where he worked; of course John made no effort, took no ACTION to remove this occasion of a slip nor did he seem interested in finding another place to work which would have been easy in his type of work at that time. He merely spent time and energy WISHING away his temptation. Perhaps he even prayed that it be removed—but HE took no ACTION and he continued to be tempted and he continued to slip—until he got another job.

Especially in the matter of sex—which incidentally is so often the prelude to a slip—is ACTION absolutely necessary for safety. Every writer of the spiritual life down through the ages has emphasized the fact that flight alone is the conqueror of sexual temptations—and that means taking ACTION to REMOVE the occasion. Prayer is necessary, that is true, BUT prayer alone is not enough. Again, we must do the foot-work, we must take ACTION.

And so on with all temptations—we must pray to God for the strength BUT WE must also ACT for ACTION IS THE MAGIC WORD.

4. *NERVOUSNESS.*

How often one hears the following remarks among A.A. members (and others too!): "Gosh, but I'm jittery lately. "Gee, but I get mad easily. Must be something wrong with my spiritual life. I seem to 'blow up' on the slightest provocation." "My nerves are getting jagged again. I wonder what's the matter with me?"

What really is the matter in so many of such individuals? There is nothing wrong with their soul, nor mind—their nerves are simply crying out for them to ACT by getting to bed earlier, by taking time out each day for rest, by DOING something about their overloaded schedule or routine of living. It is not sufficient —as so many seem to think—to wish their nerves were stronger. All alcoholics must accept the fact that their nervous systems are not and will never be as strong as one would want them to be and therefore must ACT to arrange their mode of living accordingly. Otherwise they may be reaching for something to "quiet" their nerves—a bottle—of liquor or pills. Nervousness is eliminated only by ACTING to remove the cause. ACTION IS THE MAGIC WORD.

5. *NEUROSIS.*

Most neuroses begin with too much analysis and too little action. When we turn the mind in upon ourselves and permit it to stay that way too long it acts like a magnifying glass. It both magnifies and burns! And since an alcoholic by nature is often an introvert self-analysis simply accentuates the problems.

There are very few types of neurosis that would not be cured by ACTION. Even if what we do turns out to be a mistake, it is by far better to ACT than to analyze. We should keep in mind when fear of making a mistake haunts us, as it so often does in the case of the neurotic, that a worm is the only creature that can't stumble!

Eevery neurotic should bear in mind that it makes little difference as to the how, what or the why of the present state of mind, ACTION is the cure—ACTION IS THE MAGIC WORD.

6. *FEAR.*

The emotion of fear is something good. It is a natural and unavoidable reaction, a safety measure. It is the commonest trait in life. When normal it goads the individual into ACTION as a safety measure against some real danger. It becomes abnormal when it is turned not against the danger that EXISTS but against the imaginary danger of what MAY happen or exist. As a result there is no action—there is stasis. The individual refuses to act because he is AFRAID of what MIGHT result. Such a person with his mind split between the past and the future is loaded with all kinds of fear "feelings" which stem not from reality but from imagination. ACTION alone will gradually eliminate these fears which every alcoholic has often experienced.

Many A.A.'s "even after they have adopted the 24-hour program and have taken action" are still dogged by fears of various sorts. They are afraid of places, people, circumstances, etc. Now it is not in the province of the present booklet to examine into and try to ascertain what might be the psychological cause of such fears. Most times it makes little difference. That is why writers have taught us in the matter of such fears to "ACT contrary" to them. Again it is ACTION that will eliminate them.*

In A.A. we find many who are afraid to speak publicly. The cure lies in their acting contrary to this negative fear BY SPEAKING. In time they will find that the fear has dissolved itself in the action of speaking.

There are others who fear making a "twelfth step" call. These find out how amazingly quick such fear disappears after making such calls.

The same is true of fear of crowds, and a host of other phobias that so often exist in the "negative" mentality of the average alcoholic. And in the case of most alcoholics, fear has been the one thing that has more than anything else saturated his thinking through the years of his drinking. When he comes

***In many abnormal fears the help of a competent psychiatrist may be needed.**

to A.A. he learns that most of them can and will be eliminated if they are brought out into the open and ACTED on. ACTION IS THE MAGIC WORD.

7. *SCRUPULOSITY.*

Scrupulosity is a by-product of fear. An exaggerated fear of God and hence an exaggerated fear of doing wrong, or committing sin.

The term "scrupulous" as mentioned in our chapter on Attitudes, comes from the Latin "scrupula"—a term used by the ancient Romans to denote the pebbles which so often found their way into their sandals. We can imagine the result—afraid to take a step forward and constantly held back in desired progress. Every step "hurts." A similar situation has been set up in the scrupulous individual. He doesn't have pebbles in his "sole" but his "soul" is loaded with imaginary pebbles of sin and wrong. He sees sin in everything. His inventory is a nightmare. He takes it over and over again and is never satisfied. He pays much attention to details and is extremely frightened by the more serious sins of his past. Oftentimes he ends up with a lovely anxiety-neurosis or guilt-complex. There are many such in A.A. The cure of such condition is achieved by ACTING blindly on the advice of a COMPETENT director—preferably a clergyman or psychiatrist. They should add to this close association and activity with the group or groups. Gradually such a person will realize that he is little different from the rest of men; his gaze will turn outward; and finally his scruples will in time vanish. The biggest obstacle a scrupulous individual has to overcome is his INACTIVITY which has been brought about by fear of doing wrong. He simply must ACT—for ACTION IS THE MAGIC WORD.

8. *AVARICE.*

Avarice is nothing more nor less than plain "stinginess." And it is amazing and amusing to see how many A.A.'s dry up as far as liquor is concerned but then become "tight" as they ever were in the matter of charity. This phenomenon is so frequent that we find many of these individuals honestly chagrined at their avariciousness, fully realizing that it is dangerous to their sobriety. What many do not realize is that talking about it and wishing it away will do no good. They must ACT by GIVING especially at times when perhaps they would otherwise not be expected to give. Thus acquiring a positive HABIT of charity and generosity the negative habit of avarice is eliminated. Charitable ACTIONS alone will cure avarice—ACTION IS THE MAGIC WORD.

9. *CONFLICTS (Family, job, etc.)*

In the A.A. prayer we ask for the "serenity to accept the things we cannot change, to change the things we can and the wisdom to know the difference." In the matter of conflicts (and their name is usually legion) the mistake is often made in thinking that "accepting the things we cannot change" is a PASSIVE matter. Many do not realize that to accept something that conflicts with our desires we must ACT by CHANGING OURSELVES. Otherwise the conflict will only continue. There must be ACTION either on the source of the conflict by changing or removing such circumstances or there must be action on ourselves by changing our attitudes, desires and so forth.

A.A.'s have slipped because they ignored the necessity of ACTION in the matter of the conflicts in the circumstances of their life. Instead of ACTING either by changing the circumstances or themselves, they tried to ignore the conflict. This passive approach accomplished nothing. In fact it only aggravated the circumstances—the conflict actually grew and finally was solved "for a little while" by the bottle.

In dealing with conflicts of all types, it is paramount that we ACT "to CHANGE the things we can"—or to "ACCEPT (by CHANGING ourselves) the things we cannot change." There must be action—for ACTION IS THE MAGIC WORD.

10. *HUMILITY.*

We all realize that an alcoholic needs humility more than any other virtue. It is the foundation of all spiritual living—and for the alcoholic a deep humility is a paramount necessity. Yet how many make the mistake of believing they can "think" or "talk" themselves into humility. Or there are some who think that they can become humble by ACTING humble. One becomes humble not by THINKING or TALKING or ACTING humble but only by ACTS of humility.

An excellent example of this is indicated in the ninth step of the A.A. program. In this step we are advised to make "DIRECT amends" for the injustices and injuries to others of which we have been guilty. This is advised because of both the necessity of humility for the alcoholic and because of the NECESSITY OF ACTION in the acquiring of it. Neither justice nor charity would demand that we make DIRECT amends—as long as the amends are made; but to acquire humility the ACTION required in the DIRECT making of amends carries the A.A. far along the path of humility.

Likewise, after we have made all these direct amends—and it may take a long time to accomplish this—we must still continue to PRACTICE humility not by ACTING but by ACTIONS for ACTION IS THE MAGIC WORD.

11. *PRAYER.*

We all know that continued and sincere prayer is necessary for the maintaining of sobriety. But what many seem to forget is that prayer in order to be sincere must be accompanied by ACTION on our part. We must, as we mentioned above in the eleventh step, do the foot-work.

Some time ago a member of an out-of-town group came to us seeking help in solving his "problem." His difficulty seemed to be in finding a suitable job. And what confused him was the fact that he "had prayed and prayed for months for a job" but still had not obtained one.

Sensing something wrong in his approach, we happened to ask, "You, of course, have looked around for a job during this time?"

"Oh no," came his reply, "but I have prayed so hard that I thought one would show up!"

We would not have the reader think that we are in any way belittling the power of prayer. Rather on the contrary we sincerely believe prayer is very necessary in all the circumstances in our lives and we have seen many miracles as the result, but we would like to insist that answer to prayer is not ORDINARILY a result of God's action alone, but is the result of OUR action AND God's. God usually works THROUGH us not ON us. We must first be willing. And this good-will and sincerity is usually manifested by ACTION on our part—by OUR foot-work. "When you pray for potatoes, reach for a hoe"—remember?

Sincere prayer and the answer to such ordinarily follows a definite pattern; we pray on our part; we ACT on our part; God ACTS on His part. ACTION IS THE MAGIC WORD.

12. *SLIPS.*

Many members object to the use of the term "slip." They maintain there is no such thing, but that what we call a "slip" is in reality a willful decision to drink again. We neither agree nor disagree with this opinion. The more we see, the less qualified do we feel to judge one way or another. However, we are convinced, after having talked to many such individuals, that the second and subsequent "slips" stem from the fact that THEY DID NOT TAKE ACTION TO REMOVE THE CAUSE OF THE FIRST ONE.

Let us for a moment consider a few of the usual causes of slips:

a. *Mental reservations in taking the first step.* We believe that this is the most widespread of all actual causes of a slip. Such individuals are not FULLY convinced that they are alcoholics. They come to A.A. with the secret hope that some day they will be able to drink again normally. The day—they think—comes; they try it; they slip. Frightened by their experience they return to the group. If they now ACT on the cause of their slip; if they DO something about removing their mental reservations; if they take ACTION instead of continuing merely to HOPE, they will avoid future trouble. But if they they remain inert and again hang on to their reservations they are certain to slip again. ACTION IS THE MAGIC WORD.

b. *Neglecting twelfth step work and meetings.* We like to rate this as the number two cause of most slips. These A.A.'s are usually very enthusiastic in the beginning. But gradually they start missing meetings and avoiding twelfth step calls. They have quit learning and they have quit giving. They seem to ignore the fact that has been proven by experience: an alcoholic must CONTINUE to learn and to give else he will lose what he has—sobriety. Action upon himself and for others must be a continuous process for the maintaining of sobriety and happiness. ACTION IS THE MAGIC WORD.

c. *Neglect of prayer.* Among the three big causes of slips is the neglect of dependence on a Higher Power — the neglect of prayer. It is so easy to come to a stage wherein we again feel self-sufficient. Such condition of affairs precedes a slip by many days—sometimes by months. It is a fairly well established fact that the alcoholic who does not ask for the strength of sobriety each day MAY stay sober, but being on his own again anything might happen and usually does. Such a one having slipped must accept this fact and realize that for ASSURED sobriety one must ACT daily on his knowledge of his own powerlessness by SEEKING it daily from God. ACTION IS THE MAGIC WORD.

The first and most important question a "slipper" should ask himself after a slip, and after he has given his mind a chance to clear a bit, is: "What was I not doing that I should have been doing to prevent a slip?" If he finds that out and removes the cause he will not slip again provided he does not let up on another phase of the program which may cause one. But he must take ACTION for ACTION IS THE MAGIC WORD.

13. *WORRY.*

Worry has been defined by one writer as "too much thought, too little ACTION." The worrier is one who does not seem to realize that THE FUTURE IS DETERMINED NOT SO MUCH BY PLANNING TOMORROW AS BY ACTION TODAY.

Whatever one's problems may be, we all would avoid much worry and trouble if we approached them from the point of

ACTION by asking ourselves, "What can we DO NOW towards their solution?" And then if we ACT NOW and DO NOW what can be done NOW, all problems will eventually be solved. ACTION in the PRESENT determines the future, for ACTION IS THE MAGIC WORD.

14. *IRASCIBILITY—ANGER.*

One of the most common faults of the alcoholic is irritability which so often causes him to become irascible and angry. Although we realize that much of this stems from a poor nervous system which he has inherited or damaged by his drinking, still many A.A.'s achieve gradually a remarkable control of this tendency. But they do not achieve such by talking and wishing and hoping, but by ACTION. Nor do they foolishly take ACTION by endeavoring to "hold it in"—only to lead to a greater explosion. Irascibility and anger, like all of the faults of human nature are negative. But even more so than the rest of the faults the alcoholic is heir to, these two must be controlled by SUBSTITUTION of the OPPOSITE VIRTUE. There is a saying going the rounds today, "Accentuate the positive." We would like to give you a very similar one for the control of the emotions and for the eliminating of faults: "ACTION on the OPPOSITE!"

So in the working toward the control of our irascible, nervous natures we must ACT by PRACTICING the opposite virtue —by performing ACTS of meekness, of kindness, and of gentleness. St. Francis of Assisi, by nature, was one of the most irascible characters in history—but by practice and the grace of God he habitually controlled this tendency and outwardly was known as one of the most gentle of men. He ACTED on the opposite—he consistently and constantly PRACTICED gentleness. This continued ACTION kept his irascible nature completely subjugated. Perhaps we may not hope to achieve such perfection—but ACTION in this regard will take us far—ACTION IS THE MAGIC WORD.

15. *MOODINESS.*

Under the heading of moodiness we shall include depression, self-analysis, "the blues," and all those manifestations in our make-up that make us feel we are "crawling."

Every human being is subject to a cycle of "feeling." The curves of this cycle may reach from the depths of depression to the heights of elation. The length of these cycles varies in every individual. In the alcoholic these curves—partly from an inherent condition of personality and partly as a result of years of excessive drinking—are very much sharper than in the average person. So when it reaches its lower arc a time of moodiness sets in. "Thinking on ourselves" at times like this only accentuates the condition. ACTION is imperative to avoid further descent into the depths and into the realm of "thinking drinking." ANY TYPE OF ACTION is the panacea. And the sooner the ACTION is taken on the advent of these periods of moodiness, the more effective it will be. Too many get the idea of trying to "sweat out" the recurrent cycles. Inactivity only makes them worse. We must bear in mind that much of the cause of these attacks is physical in nature—and therefore physical ACTION is the best preventative. ACTION IS THE MAGIC WORD.

16. *ONE'S JOB.*

There are two circumstances relative to one's job that often cause difficulty to the alcoholic and is contributory to his drinking.

In the first place the new member is often faced with the problem of getting a job. And many make the mistake of holding back until a job completely to their liking comes along (as if there were such!). As a result indecision sets in. This indecision flows into an affects all of the alcoholic's thinking. Nothing is more wearing than indecision. The exhaustion that follows such becomes a lovely excuse for a "lift"—and where could an alcoholic find a "lift"? It won't be long!

In order to illustrate the tiring effect that indecision has on one's nervous system they tell the story of the fellow who went to work assorting tomatoes. His job was to put the good tomatoes into one basket and the spoiled ones into another basket. For several days he worked and then suddenly quit his job. A friend asked him why he had quit.

"Well," he replied, "You see, I just couldn't take it. The work was too much for me."

"What do you mean the work was to much for you?" his friend exclaimed, "It certainly is not hard work putting some tomatoes into one basket and some into another."

"But it wasn't putting them there that was so hard—it was those darned 'decisions' that got me down!"

Indecision is hard on anybody—to the alcoholic it is poison. So again there is one thing to do about getting a job—GET ONE. Take ACTION. Any job—even if it is the simplest of jobs and it is kept only for a few days, GET ONE—and then another and another and so on, if necessary, for that is ACTION and ACTION IS THE MAGIC WORD.

Another difficulty presents itself to the A.A. who has a job but is very discontented with it. He too MUST TAKE ACTION. Otherwise eventually he will become a prey to resentment, self-pity, nervousness and a host of other mental attitudes that to the alcoholic are dynamite—and the bottle will not be far behind.

Such a person has two possible courses of ACTION. Either he must ACT and change his job ("change the things we can"); or he must once and for all accept his job with ALL of its circumstances ("accept the things we cannot change"). But in either instance he must ACT either on his job or himself. ACTION IS THE MAGIC WORD.

17. *SELFISHNESS.*

All human beings are selfish. The alcoholic is pathologically selfish, having become so through his years of "retreat" from reality into the phantasy of alcohol. When he comes to A.A., one of the first things he is told is that A.A. is a "selfish" program. To his "selfish" mentality, this makes sense. So he gets "on" the program. After a time he begins to realize that his "selfishness' in taking A.A. for "his sake" and for no one else's was in reality charity—for "charity starts at home." The "selfishness" in acquiring sobriety for himself was in truth the "giving to himself" so that in turn he might "give" what he acquires to others—and that is charity, GIVING. So he learns that he can't keep what he has received unless he gives it away. It is the old paradox of living. We keep what we give away and we lose what we try to keep for ourselves. Or as we were told centuries ago "he that loses his life shall find it." And here it is that the alcoholic's accentuated selfish nature rebels. He begins to WISH he was not so selfish, but wishes avail him nothing—he IS very selfish. The solution? ACTION. He must DO deeds of unselfishness. And when an A.A. tries this a few times he is amazed at the "happiness" that he gets from his unselfish ACTS. As time goes on and the alcoholic continues that "practice" of doing unselfish acts, he comes to the day when he realizes the fact that he HAS BECOME UNSELFISH—by ACTS of GIVING of himself, for ACTION IS THE MAGIC WORD.

18. *JUDGING OTHERS.*

A very prevalent pastime in A.A.—and in every place where human beings gather—is the habit of judging others, gossiping and criticizing. Without the slightest foundation of fact or reason, how often we freely give to the ears of whomsoever might listen the "facts" about him or her or them! Many A.A.'s feel the "burden" of this bad habit and sincerely are anxious to eliminate it from themselves. But again when there is a gathering, they again sit in judgment. What's the answer? Action in JUDGING OURSELVES HONESTLY.

Many will find that their habit of rash judgment, gossiping, etc., stems from their carelessness or omission of their own inventory. One often wonders at times how many A.A.'s take regularly the tenth step. Those who DO, those who ACT on themselves by a regular personal inventory (and the tenth step does say "CONTINUED to take"), have little difficulty refraining from judging others in their criticisms, gossiping and careless talk about others. They are too busy ACTING on themselves, endeavoring to change their own faults—so much so that they have not much time "searching" for the faults of others. They are busy taking ACTION on THEIR OWN character and thus do not ACT on others' characters.

Wouldn't it be wonderful if every A.A. would honestly "continue to take personal inventory?" If every A.A. REGULARLY took the tenth step? Wouldn't it be heaven in the groups? But wait a minute—typically in alcoholic fashion, there we go "dreaming." For the present we are still very much on earth. And there will always be, in and out of A.A., the guys and gals who judge and gossip and criticize on and on—but how about YOU? Do you regularly take the tenth step? A little ACTION here will do the trick—for ACTION IS THE MAGIC WORD.

19. *THE TENTH STEP.*

Since we are speaking of action on the tenth step relative to the elimination of criticism, etc., it might be well to analyze more in detail how action works on the tenth step in general. Many A.A.'s sincerely take the tenth step mentally and regularly but are stumped as to how to "go about DOING something" toward the control and elimination of the faults they consistently seem to find in their inventory. We already, in speaking of resentments, humility, and so forth, have suggested ACTION to help control these specific difficulties. But we have been asked many times how one is to go about a systematic approach to the problem of the inventory as a whole.

In our booklet, "The Golden Book of the Spiritual Side," in speaking of the general inventory in the fourth step, we mentioned one such method, namely that since our soul is a simple substance and cannot be divided, that the time-honored way of working on one's character is by determining our biggest fault and consistently working on that. In this way each improvement in this one fault would necessitate an improvement in all the rest of our faults. For because of the simplicity of our soul when one fault is made headway with, the rest of our faults simply MUST follow along.

We quote from the Golden Book: "We have the seven fundamental passions of man: The tendency to pride, envy, greed, lust, gluttony, sloth and anger (which includes that A-1 enemy of all alcoholics—resentment). What are we going to do about these? Those who are experienced in such matters tell us that we should 'ACT contrary.' Therefore, if we tend to be angry and resentful, we should practice the contrary positive ACT by speaking kindly and doing good to those against whom we are angry or resentful. . . .

"If we analyze the human being, we shall find that the mind or soul is a simple substance and cannot be divided. This is the reason that in our drinking days we were always so unhappy and so full of conflicts. We were doing things secretly and trying not to do them publicly. This can't be done, for the soul of man is indivisible. We can use this truth to great advantage in fighting against our evil tendencies. If we pick out our biggest failing, our most frequent tendency to evil, and work on that ONE the rest will come along. Therefore, if we DAILY strive with the help of God to control our PREDOMINANT passion, all the other passions will take care of themselves. . . ."

The above method is undoubtedly effective. However many complain that it becomes so very monotonous to each day strive towards the one goal. And many want to know if there is some way in which a bit of variety can be injected into this dull business of the tenth step. Some months ago we heard of a very novel way of doing exactly that. It is called the "Poker-chip Method." And while adding variety to our daily efforts it also can be very effective, for it too is based on ACTION.

This is the way it works: Having through our general inventory discovered and enumerated our faults and tendencies to evil, we print THEIR OPPOSITE virtues on a set of poker chips. For example, if we find (this is only for the sake of example—every alcoholic will surely find many other defects!) six such faults: resentment, pride, greed, dishonesty, laziness and criticism, we simply print their opposites on six poker chips —kindness, humility, generosity, truthfulness, work, speaking-well. Then we place these chips in a box on our dresser or in some handy place. And each morning we take one—without selection—from the box. THAT IS THE VIRTUE WE ARE

GOING TO STRIVE FOR THAT DAY. At evening we replace the chip in the box, mix them up again, and the next morning we take one again without selection. Although it may happen that we get the same one on consecutive days, on the average we shall have constant variety and through the daily ACTS of virtue achieve the same results without so much monotony.

No matter what method we may use in our use of the tenth step, there must be some ACTION or the inventory itself will remain sterile and that means slipping backwards. There simply MUST be action in regard to our faults—ACTION on the opposite, for ACTION IS THE MAGIC WORD.

20. *THE MEETINGS.*

The meetings in A.A. provide a fine social outlet for the members and are a part of the valuable "group therapy" which A.A. brings to bear upon the alcoholic problem. However there is a more important purpose of the meetings—it is there that the members, both new and old, learn and retain the knowledge of and the necessity of practicing the twelve steps of the program. So oftentimes we find members who go to the meetings regularly but only for the social side. They pay little attention to the talks and discussions—except to criticize—and the talks and the discussions themselves are left exactly where they found them—in the meeting hall.

There is a story that has gone the rounds for many years wherever there is public speaking. It tells of a gentleman who was hurrying to church one Sunday morning and evidently was very late for the services. As he neared the church he saw a large crowd of people leaving the edifice. Anxious to learn whether the services were over, he stopped a little old lady coming down he steps.

"Is the sermon over?" he queried.

"No," the lady replied, "the sermon is not over."

"Well then, why are all these people leaving church if the sermon is not over?"

"Because the minister has left the pulpit."

"But I thought you said the sermon was not over: now you tell me the minister has left the pulpit. How is it possible for the minister to have left the pulpit before the sermon is over?"

"The minister has indeed left the pulpit: but still the sermon is not over. For now it is really beginning. The people receive the value of the sermon only if and when they ACT on it in their daily lives!"

This same truth can be applied to the A.A. meetings. The members who ACT on the talks and the discussions in their daily lives are the ones who get the full value from the meetings. On the other hand they who take no such action get from the meetings, exactly what they go to obtain; a social evening. As a result they learn little A.A.; they take home little A.A.; they practice little A.A.—and then the inevitable slip and once again we hear, "And to think John attended meetings so regularly!"

There are many such in A.A.—many who although attending meetings regularly take no ACTION on what they hear there and thus make no progress except backwards—for meetings without ACTION are sterile—ACTION IS THE MAGIC WORD.

21. *LAZINESS.*

One of the paradoxes of the alcoholic problem is the contrary to popular opinion the average alcoholic is lazy by nature. In spite of his seemingly continued frenzied activity, he is goaded on to this only because he has reached a point in wrong living and wrong thinking wherein he dare not stop too long to think. He cannot be alone with his thoughts, so activity distracts.

However, when the alcoholic comes to A.A., sobers up, straightens out his thinking and living, there is grave danger that he might easily drift into his pre-drinking habit of "dreaming"—which is but a by-product of laziness. If he does, his dreams will inevitably comprise the "pleasant" aspects of his former drinking escapades. It is natural for one's mind to avoid the "unpleasant" happenings connected with former actions. And as these past pleasantries become more and more attractive only a miracle will save the individual from "trying to recapture" his dreamworld.

Therefore it is well to keep in mind that continued ACTION, keeping busy with the present, alone will keep us out of this dream stage. Every alcoholic should spend very little time in his "past" or "future"—he should constantly keep busy in the present, he should maintain a concerted and purposeful action in his daily living. And for the alcoholic a hobby of action of some type is paramount for his leisure hours. Idleness is poison to any human being—to the alcoholic it is the doorway to a slip. ACTION IS THE MAGIC WORD.

22. *GOD.*

In many A.A. groups one hears the expression that the "twelve steps tend to orthodoxy." They mean by this that any alcoholic who sincerely takes the twelve steps ultimately seeks a more formal knowledge of God—usually in religion. It is not the intent of the author to give judgment in this matter. Religion as such has no place in the A.A. set-up. It should never be brought in for formal discussion, nor do we feel groups should ever try to inject any such into their meetings. If there are any who feel the need of more formal discussion of God they should do so away from A.A. and should not in any way appropriate the A.A. name for their discussions. That is our opinion. For we all know that religion is one of the three "dangers" to A.A. harmony if injected into its therapy. The other two are politics and money.

However God does come into the A.A. program—very much so. He is mentioned specifically in six of the twelve steps. But He is to be "as each member understands Him." And since this booklet is dealing with ACTION we thought it well to indicate the value of ACTION in our relationship with God—"as we understand Him."

We shall understand God more and more ONLY if we DO something about our knowledge of God, i.e., if we take ACTION in learning more about Him. For we must "improve our conscious contact with Him." Where shall we get this added knowledge? That is beyond A.A. and is entirely up to each individual to do in his or her own way. But we do learn in A.A. here, as in all the other phases, that we shall not improve our knowledge of God unless we DO something about it—for ACTION IS THE MAGIC WORD.

In all of our A.A. and in all of our living—in our thoughts, in our homes, in our jobs, in our prayers, in our social lives—in fine in EVERYTHING we shall achieve happiness and we shall maintain contented sobriety if we, instead of RESOLVING to do it, DO IT! "NOW is the acceptable time" was told to us centuries ago—TODAY—that is all we have for sure. Our ACTIONS today will determine our tomorrow. Let's don't think about it—let's DO IT NOW. If we are really sincere, we will ACT TODAY—for sincerity is ACTION and ACTION is THE MAGIC WORD!

Let's get moving, huh? . . .

THE MAGIC ACTION

"WE MADE A DECISION..."

The following observation is very, very often heard in A.A. circles everywhere:

"There is something missing from my A.A. There's something of the program I can't seem to be able to grasp. Some of the members have a peace of mind and a serenity which I haven't got. What is it? What makes the difference?

The above question is often put by otherwise very sincere members of A.A. It is one of the most common difficulties encountered. It is the "missing link" between mere sobriety and serenity that they are seeking: the difference between the many members who are "dry" and the other many members who have "got the program," who have both sobriety AND serenity.

It is the writer's opinion that the "missing link" so often queried about above is AN ACTION along the twelve steps that flows into and determines ALL the other ACTIONS in the life of the member and gives them their quality: SINCERITY IN TAKING THE THIRD STEP—a one hundred percent decision with no "if's" "and's" nor "but's"—TOTAL SURRENDER. It is in this sincerity or lack of sincerity in taking this step that makes the difference between the serene member and the merely sober member; between the member who has peace, and the member who has problems; between success and failure.

We have already indicated that in the realm of FAITH ABOVE ALL ELSE ACTION IS THE MAGIC WORD. And the more we analyze the third step the greater will be the impact and the import of it upon EVERY ACTION in our lives. For through it WE BECOME ONE WITH GOD—and that demands peace; that necessitates strength; that makes failure impossible. All this will be ours PROVIDED we HONESTLY, ONCE AND FOR ALL—MADE A DECISION TO TURN OUR WILL AND OUR LIFE OVER TO THE CARE OF GOD AS WE UNDERSTAND HIM.

It is in the ACTION in taking this step that we begin to experience peace and serenity. It is another decision—a FULL decision with no reservations, no holding back, no cutting of corners. The more complete and unconditional our admission was in step number one, the more readily and fully will we make this decision to turn our will and our lives over to God. Oftentimes it is the mental reservations in the admission that we are powerless over alcohol and that our lives have become unmanageable that often proves a stumbling block in step number three. Many would like to turn MOST of their lives over to the care of God, but certain associations, practices, and relationships—we don't like to let them go. Thus problems remain—and peace stays away from our minds and hearts. Therefore ALL dishonesty, dishonest practices, illicit relationships, and all the many things in our lives which we know to be contrary to the Will of God must go. For it is here we shall fully understand the meaning of the term "unconditional surrender." BUT having once and for all FULLY made this decision of surrender—having once and for all ACTED without ANY reservation—we shall, perhaps for the first time in our lives, experience true peace and serenity. We shall finally really begin to live. We shall at last understand what Christ meant when He told us that we must first die in order to live—die to all that is of self in order to live to all that is of God—His will, His providence, His love. For we have LET GO—we have LET GOD as the A.A. Book points out, LET GO—LET GOD—ACT. Let go of ALL of self and the circumstances surrounding self—and let God ACT as He sees necessary. ACTION IS THE MAGIC WORD!

Here, again, trouble starts for many. We balk—we doubt—we begin to query to ourselves "Will God?"—"What will God?" etc., etc. We begin to question God's power, His wisdom, His love. Many even go so far as to "fear" Him—as we read in the "Hound of Heaven"—"lest having found Him, we have nothing else besides. . . ." Or like the story about the little old lady in the storm. Seeking reassurance, she anxiously asked the captain: "Are we in any great danger?"

"Don't worry, madam," he answered, "after all, we are in the hands of God."

"Oh," she gasped, terror written on her face, "is it as bad as all that?"

Whereas the attitude should be it "is as GOOD as all that." And "having found Him we shall have ALL else besides"—PEACE, and CONTENTMENT and SERENITY in ALL of our actions. Let us not forget that the twelve steps are written as a result of EXPERIENCE—not as a theory. And all of those who "radiate the program" in their peace of mind—are the ones who HAVE surrendered ALL to God in step number three; they are the ones who have LET GO—and LET GOD; finally, they are the ones who have ACTED on the third step and "made a decision (with NO reservations) to turn their will (ALL of it) and their life (ALL of it) over to the care of God"—ALWAYS. And ACTION is the MAGIC WORD.

If we are not willing as yet to take this step unconditionally, we should, as we are advised in the A.A. book, pray that God will make us willing—praying both for the will to do and the strength to accomplish. We should therefore continue to pray, "God make me willing." For this again is ACTION and ACTION IS THE MAGIC WORD!—if we LET GO—LET GOD.

SERENITY

"God grant us the SERENITY . . ."

Today the world is filled with anxiety. The world itself is in the throes of a universal "anxiety neurosis." Every civilized nation is desperately seeking peace; every family is frantically searching for security; every soul is seeking serenity—peace of mind, peace of soul.

This fact is attested to by the tremendous appeal of two recent books both of which skyrocketed to the ranks of the best sellers in the past few years: Joshua Liebman's "Peace of Mind" and Bishop Sheen's "Peace of Soul." And on all sides the clamor continues for the answer to the anxiety of the day.

The ultimate aim of the alcoholic also is serenity—peace of mind, peace of soul. Sobriety is merely the soil in which each one hopes to cultivate such. The A.A. program is the means and the instrument used in this cultivation. Without peace of mind and soul, sobriety to the alcoholic is an unbearable burden; and the bottle is not far behind. Still there are many members of A.A. who are dry, who do not have this serenity intended by the program. There are many such in every group. And from these confused souls come the most asked question in A.A.: "How can I get the serenity which so many talk about but which so few seem to have? Those who have it have something I seem to be missing? What is it? What makes the difference?"

We endeavored to answer this question in the preceding chapter: 'The Magic Action'[1] with a short synopsis.

Now, in seeking serenity, we must further analyze the above explanation. So, God willing and aiding, we give you the following with the fond hope and prayer that you too will join the ranks of those who have LET GO and LET GOD and thus have at last found peace and serenity.

We make no pretense to the erudition of Joshua Liebman; we shall never even faintly imitate the spiritual depth of Bishop Sheen; we are alcoholic and so must keep it simple—ever asking GOD to "grant us the SERENITY. . . ."

---

[1] Cf. p. 195.

THE SEARCH FOR SERENITY

"If only I could get again the PEACE. . . ."

Every alcoholic perhaps more so than the average individual has spent much time and energy in a futile attempt to find peace of mind; most alcoholics, at least on occasions, have desperately endeavored to find God; all members of Alcoholics Anonymous, prior to finding A.A., have failed to find either peace of mind or God. Another goodly number of alcoholics have failed to find peace of mind, or God, or A.A., and have stumbled off the cliff of despair as a tragic ending to their confused thinking and living. The papers left by one such unfortunate fellow give us a dramatic and realistic insight into the most misunderstood of minds, the alcoholic. On the verge of suicide, but still relentlessly searching for an exit from his mental prison, he wrote,[1] "all alcoholics who are struggling to throw off the shackles of their weakness are the subjects of my compassion. I feel that NO MATTER HOW DEGRADED AN ALCOHOLIC MAY BE, THERE ABIDES, SOMEWHERE DEEP WITHIN HIM, A DEATHLESS URGE TO REACH OUT BEYOND THE SORDIDNESS, DECEIT, FOLLY, IGNORANCE, AND SHAM OF THIS WORLD TO GRASP THAT ELUSIVE SOMETHING WHICH SPELLS KINSHIP WITH THE LOVELY IN LIFE. And I believe, once one even so much as brushes his fingertips against the greater understanding, he has attained that for which every literate soul seeks—maybe by varied and divergent channels, but nonetheless seeks.

"It is a strange and miserable world in which the alcoholic lives, made so much more strange and miserable by the fact that he lives in two hemispheres—normal and abnormal, and... THERE IS NO REAL UNDERSTANDING ON THE PART OF THE NORMAL FOR THE ABNORMAL.

"Of all humans afflicted, physically and mentally, the lot of the sensitive alcoholic is hardest. And just AS THE LOT OF

---

[1] **From THE THIRD STRIKE by Jerry Gray. Copyright 1949 by Pierce & Smith. By permission of Abington-Cokesbury Press, Nashville, Tenn.**

THE MAN STRUCK BLIND IS MORE AGONIZING BECAUSE HE COULD ONCE SEE, SO IS THE ALCOHOLIC'S LOT THE MORE DIFFICULT BECAUSE HE WAS ONCE FREE.

"Few sufferers can lean upon the straw of conviction that they are expiating wrongdoing through mental torture when they are unable to understand WHY they erred when THEIR ACTS WERE CONTRARY TO THEIR INNERMOST CONVICTIONS OF VIRTUE.

"And so I go on trying, trying to understand, to grasp Him Who could help me. It is a battle of a soul unsupported now.

"If only I could get again
The peace I had in the dark of God.
When the dream of Jesus opened like a rose on the night,
And He came all alone to my hushed, empty soul,
And all the paths of the night were still under His feet.

I had only to wait for Him then,
To cover myself with darkness and be still;
I had only to open my soul's door,
Only to stand on the threshhold and keep watch,
And I had him there in the stillness;
And when he had gone
All day long I went in peace, remembering Him.

And He will not come to me.
I go out into my beloved night
Where He hides in star and rain and rustle of leaf,
I climb all the heights of darkness—
Perhaps I shall find Him standing on the last height.

He is not there—
I go through the paths of the night;
Perhaps at the end He will be awaiting me;
There is no end to the darkness and He is not there.
I sink, I drown in the darkness and He will not hear me.

My heart knocks at my breast
And struggles like a live soul in a dead body.
My body is weighted with lead,
It drags me down through the darkness.
I cannot undo the clasp of the clinging flesh,
In the thick net of the senses I am bound,
If I die utterly and go to the place of the dead,
I shall not find Him;
Beyond death He will hide from me.

It is I who have driven Him from me.
How can He come to me?
How can I hold Him?
How can my dream of God break through the darkness,
When always this Thing, this vile Thing
Hangs as a satanic chalice above the threshold of night,
Lighting the secret ways
So that no god may pass?
When my body cries for scum
And my thoughts are poisons and arrows,
And futility, like black magic, wounds His blessed Image,
And my heart in the darkness
Is a three-tongued flame of despair, self-condemnation, and terror!"

Every alcoholic will quickly recognize the workings of his own mind as mirrored in the above quotation. We in A.A. shall pause a bit—and bow our head—and utter a reverent and sincere "Thanks be to God for A.A.!" And we'll probably muse to ourselves, echoing the words of the "Hound of Heaven,"

"I fled Him down the nights,
And down the days—
Down the labyrinthine ways of my own mind
I sped...."

UNTIL we, privileged in Providence, were caught up just short of despair and through A.A. were enabled to break through the clouds and "rise and clasp His hand and come."

Remember? The first time we got a chance to read the Alcoholics Anonymous book? We came to chapter five and there read those superbly written directions on "How It Works"—THE directions on how it works. Remember what it says? "Rarely have we ever seen a person fail who THOROUGHLY follows our path.... Some of us tried to hold on to our old ideas and THE RESULT WAS NIL until we LET GO absolutely...."

And then we read the twelve steps. We re-read them. Perhaps again and again we re-read them. Why? We wanted to hang on to—US, OUR OLD IDEALS. We did not want to LET GO. But we read on and we finally realized

"(a) That we were alcoholic and could not manage our own lives
(b) That probably NO HUMAN POWER could have relieved our alcoholism.
(c) That God could and would if sought."

So we decided to LET GO of our own ideas at last and to LET GOD take over. For again we read in the A.A. Book that "This spiritual life is not a theory. WE HAVE TO LIVE IT.... If we are painstaking about this phase of our development, we will be amazed before half through.... We will suddenly realize that God is doing for us what we could not do for ourselves." And it worked!

And then came along our first prospect. We didn't pull punches in those days about the "God angle" and about the "spiritual side." For we lived by the book then. We lived by the directions. We lived A.A. And hadn't we read in the A.A. Book about the prospective member, "Tell him exactly what happened to you. STRESS THE SPIRITUAL FREELY. If the man be agnostic or atheist, make it emphatic that he does not have to agree with your conception of God. THE MAIN THING IS THAT HE BE WILLING TO BELIEVE IN A POWER GREATER THAN HIMSELF AND THAT HE LIVE BY SPIRITUAL PRINCIPLES." Yessir, that's what the A.A. Book says right on page 105! And it goes a bit further to state:

"Abandon yourself to God as you understand God. Admit your faults to Him and your fellows. Clear away the wreckage of your past. Give freely to what you find, and join us. We shall be with you, in the Fellowship OF THE SPIRIT, and you will surely meet some of us as you trudge the Road of Happy Destiny." And the very last line in the A.A. Book reads "We find that no one need have difficulty with the spiritual side of the program. WILLINGNESS, HONESTY AND OPEN MINDEDNESS ARE ESSENTIALS OF RECOVERY. BUT THESE ARE INDISPENSABLE."

So we lived a spiritual life to the best of our ability. We were happy. We LET GO—and WE LET GOD manage our wills and our lives.

And then something happened. Either from one or from many; from the "1st Step Johns" or from the "dry-drunks"; from the "no-spiritual angle guys and gals," or from astute whisperings of a deceiving pride deep down within, we heard that good, solid and sober guys like us just don't need all that pietistic stuff. We were gradually deceived into the conviction that all that spiritual "stuff" was all right for the weak ones; that it was all right in the beginning; that it was right for the "Bible thumpers," but not for us. We had been sober a long time now and we just didn't need it. And after all, what had all that spiritual "hokum" to do with alcohol? Just stay around the group, we heard, that was all we would need.

Which we did!

And now we are unhappy. Sober, but very unhappy. We are easily irritated. We are hard to please. We are missing something—desperately.

Or maybe we are members who never have fully taken the 3rd step. Maybe we heard all the 'clap-trap' just mentioned above BEFORE we turned our lives and wills over to the care of God. So, having taken the 3rd step with reservations we too are missing something. We are not fully happy. We haven't GOT what so many we meet along the way of A.A. have. And we too are searching for that "something"—desperately.

Or maybe we are members who are only now toying with the "senselessness" of keeping up this spiritual "stuff." Maybe we are "about" to cut corners here or to omit things there. Maybe we are just "wondering" whether we really DO need all that spiritual business after all.

It matters little into which class we fall. For we either HAVE taken back our decision made in the 3rd step; or we are ABOUT to take back that decision; or we have never FULLY made the decision. And in all these classes is found unhappiness, discontentment—a lack of peace of mind, peace of soul—a lack of serenity.

LET GO – LET GOD

"At THY word. . . ."

A couple of incidents happened many centuries ago which might help us KEEP, or MAKE, or make AGAIN that decision in the third step.

Old, impetuous Peter had been all night in his boat with his companions on a fishing expedition. And as they sailed back toward the shore, they were grumbling to themselves about the bad "luck" they had had. All night—and no fishes! However, as they approached the shore Whom should they run into but the Lord. He asked them about their fishing. And Peter immediately told Him, "We have fished all night and have caught nothing." But the Lord did not sympathize with him, and quickly replied, "Launch out into the DEEP and let down your nets."

We can imagine what Peter's own thoughts were about this time. He had fished all night, hadn't he? Hadn't he tried all the places he knew? And he had caught nothing. Now the Lord comes along and tells him to launch OUT INTO THE DEEP—away from the places Peter had tried so unsuccessfully. To Peter it did not seem logical. It did not make sense. BUT Peter LET GO of HIS ideas and BECAUSE THE LORD SAID SO he "launched out into the deep." "AT THY WORD," he replied in COMPLETE SURRENDER, "I'll let down the net." We know what happened. Peter caught so many fishes that the "nets broke." And he no longer grumbled—he was happy. Not in what he had accomplished, but in what the Lord had accomplished through him. For he realized that he had nothing to do with the success. The Lord had done what he had tried all night to do. The Lord had done for him what he failed to do for himself.

The second incident occurred about thirty years previously. A young Jewish maiden was kneeling in prayer. Suddenly an Angel appeared to her and told her she was to become the Mother of the Savior. We know her thoughts at this time. "How can this be? I know not man." She even expressed those thoughts to the heavenly visitor. She was then told that GOD HIMSELF would bring this about. So MARY LET GO of her own doubts and LET GOD accomplish in her what no human power could have accomplished. Her "surrender" is so beautifully expressed in her answer: "Behold the Handmaid of the Lord. Be it done to me according to THY Word." And to that she adds, "My soul does magnify the Lord, and my Spirit hath rejoiced in God my Savior, BECAUSE HE THAT IS MIGHTY HATH DONE GREAT THINGS TO ME and Holy is His Name." So she too was happy, NOT AT HER ACCOMPLISHMENTS, but BECAUSE GOD'S WILL was being accomplished in her.

In the past decade and a half, thousands of other "incidents" have happened which strikingly bring home this truth. Thousands of A.A.'s have found in their unconditional surrender in taking the 3rd step "that GOD WAS DOING FOR THEM WHAT THEY COULD NOT DO FOR THEMSELVES." They have LET GO and LET GOD take over their wills and their lives; they have LAUNCHED OUT INTO THE DEEP: they have once and for all humbly breathed, "Be it done to me according to THY word." These are the A.A.'s who have both sobriety and serenity. These are the A.A.'s who will bluntly tell you, "I had nothing to do with it, GOD HAS DONE IT ALL." We all have heard this statement many times, but ONLY THEY WHO HAVE UNCONDITIONALLY SURRENDERED to the Will of God can fully know the true meaning of such depth of peace that follows this surrender.

Now let's see if we can find out a bit about the HOW of this surrender. Let us analyze what it really means to LET GO and LET GOD. Let us try to LAUNCH OUT INTO THE DEEP.

The A.A. program is not so much one of repeated efforts to build up or to re-build character; it is rather one of REPEATED ACTS OF SURRENDER in order to DESTROY CHARACTER—our own twisted one! The new one? God will take care of that in His own time and way—PROVIDED we LET GO and LET GOD take over. Thus we need little of the knowing HOW to rebuild our lives; but we need a LOT of WILLINGNESS for God to do so.

The program is not so much one calling for STRENGTH of will as it is one for the WEAKENING of a REBELLIOUS will. And this is accomplished only by repeated acts of SURRENDER, by LETTING GO and LETTING GOD give the end result. Ours is as always only the willingness and cooperation with HIM.

The program is not so much a way of learning new ideas and ways of achieving sobriety and happiness but a means of LOSING our PAST WRONG ideas of sobriety and happiness. It is a program for LETTING GO of all these erroneous and selfish ways to APPARENT happiness and one by which we LET GOD guide us to true sobriety and permanent peace of mind and soul and true happiness—in HIS Will.

So when we hear an A.A. make the statement that he had nothing to do with it, that God has done it all, it is not just a pious musing but the statement of one who has achieved one hundred percent submission to God's Will and by that unconditional surrender has permitted God to DO WHAT HE COULDN'T DO FOR HIMSELF. It is the same attitude expressed by Matt Talbot, the Dublin alcoholic who died in 1925 and whose process of canonization has now begun—a statement found among his papers: "I had nothing to do with it, God has done it all." It is also the same attitude expressed by Christopher Columbus in a letter to Ferdinand and Isabella shortly after he successfully reached the continent of America, quote: "But these great and marvellous results are not to be attributed to any merit of mine... but to the holy Faith... for that which the unaided intellect of man could not encompass, the SPIRIT OF GOD HAS GRANTED."

Too many think that they themselves have to do it all, that everything depends on them. The urge toward external activity, the craving to shape our lives by OUR OWN WILL AND WIT, our restlessness and our haste, are a weakness of the time in which we live. The very best of people are infected with this disease; the alcoholic is in its throes "nigh unto death." And when our progress is according to our wills we go off the deep end on the springboard of egotism; when our wills are crossed and frustration constantly meets our every push, we fall back into the mire of self-pity and resentment. What we need therefore, before all else, is to realize once and for all THAT REGARDLESS OF OUR WISHES, WE DEPEND IN ALL THINGS ON GOD WHETHER WE ADMIT IT OR NOT. And then we shall no longer need to chart our course. God, our Father, will be steering the ship of our lives so as to ACCOMPLISH THE GREATEST RESULT WITH THE LEAST EXPENDITURE OF ENERGY AND WITH THE UTMOST PEACE OF MIND and all that remains for us to do is to be READY. "Lord, what will Thou have me do?"

"Sculptor, God, strike! I am the stone!"

Must we not desire anything beyond this? Yes, and no. What God wills, I must fully desire and accept—but I must still do the footwork, using His headlights (Will) instead of my own (will). Shall we then no longer plan and care? Shall we rather be passive and inactive? Again, yes, and no. The inactivity of this constant preparedness for the Will of God IS ONLY APPARENT. IN REALITY IT IS BOUGHT WITH VIGILANT ACTION—i.e., ACTING AS IF EVERYTHING DEPENDED ON US, AND TRUSTING AS IF EVERYTHING DEPENDED ON GOD; ACTING AS IF THE OUTCOME WAS OF UTMOST IMPORTANCE, BUT CARING NOT AT ALL WHAT THE END RESULT MAY ACTUALLY TURN OUT TO BE; IT IS DOING WHATEVER WE POSSIBLY CAN OF OURSELVES, AND ACCEPTING ALL ELSE AS GOD'S WILL. Finally, it is USING OUR WILLS, but NOT CHOOSING OUR WILLS. And so in all of our actions it is indifferent to us what we do, where we are, whether we progress or not, or how quickly we do advance; such questions do not trouble us; we do not CONCERN ourselves with them. For again, GOD, our Father is directing our life—ALL of it.

We are idealists, but realists also. We live not in the dreamland of wishful possibilities, but in the world of solid reality. And wherever God has placed us we stand with both feet, doing the best we can without care and anxiety. We are not troubled with useless cares about the past and the future. We are AT-

TENTIVE only with the things of THE PRESENT TWENTY-FOUR HOURS and thereby wrest from the present moment the utmost, which includes peace and serenity. And we ACCEPT the reality of that present: by refusing none of the pleasures and joys God may grant us, nor any cross His hand may choose to lay upon our shoulders. WE REFUSE nothing; we SEEK nothing—we ACCEPT, we SURRENDER, we LET GO, we LET GOD.

So ALL THAT WE NEED IS WILLINGNESS. For neither effort, nor character, nor talents, nor money, nor anything else that is ours will give us peace of mind, peace of soul and serenity; NOTHING SAVE OUR WILLS TURNED BACK TO GOD will do this. And if we hold on to our own stubborn wills, even God cannot give us either sobriety or peace of mind and soul or happiness for our wills are free. This state of affairs is very well exemplified in the story of the fellow who was coming off a drunk and had the D-T's. He called for help. And when his sponsor came, he was told to quit his fretting and to trust that God would give him help. To this the drunk replied: "I just asked God for help. And you know what He told me? He told me, 'I'm doing all I can!' "

This surrender of our will and our life to God is the way of spiritual childhood and is the way that heeds the warning, "Unless you become as little children." It is the imitation of the little child who knows nothing of fear, nor of hunger, nor of any possible need—because its mother provides for them all. Left to itself, the child stumbles all over the place, but in its mother's arms it finds rest, and peace and contentment and protection from all harm.

Accompanying this state of spiritual childhood, this state of habitual surrender, is a rare quality of SIMPLICITY. And we know that the one thing that is necessary for the alcoholic is simplicity. Because for most alcoholics the complexities of life and their confused thinking present a most difficult problem. Their sincere desire to reconcile all the loose ends of their thinking, their problems, and their lives usually begets futility. And thus a state of equilibrium—so necessary for peace of mind and soul—is achieved only through the habit of surrender without analysis and by accepting all things as a small child, simply and humbly.

To do this is very simple. It consists in thinking and acting, under the influence of God's grace, and in the spiritual order, the same as a small child feels and acts in the natural order. It means acting toward God exactly like a very small child would act toward its mother and father, with absolute trust and with absolute surrender.

The child realizes its weaknesses and can give us a great lesson on this point, especially to us alcoholics who have admitted our powerlessness. For it calls attention to THE INDISPENSABLE CONDITIONS TO ALL PROGRESS IN THE SPIRITUAL LIFE, namely THE REALIZATION OF OUR OWN FRAILITY AND OUR OWN INCAPACITY FOR ANY SPIRITUAL GOOD IN OURSELVES and the necessity of looking to God FOR EVERYTHING.

This spiritual childhood excludes all feeling of pride, or the presumptuous thought of attaining ANY SPIRITUAL PROGRESS OF GROWTH by merely natural means, and the deceptive wish TO RELY ON ONESELF IN THE HOUR OF TEMPTATION AND DANGER. On the other hand, it presupposes a living Faith in the existence of God, a practical homage to His power and mercy and a CONFIDENT recourse to the Providence of Him Who alone can give us both the will and the strength to avoid evil and to do good.

Our greatest enemy is our "strength," which is pride. Only when we fully understand the words of God: "Without Me you can do NOTHING" do we fully realize our nothingness and the allness of God. The "little child" is aware of its weakness and thus is continually expecting and dependent.

So the two truths that suddenly will become clear from this childhood simplicity are: that GOD IS ALL and that we are NOTHING. 'Todo y nada' (all and nothing) was the way John of the Cross put it.

To summarize in simple language: To remain a little child is to recognize one's nothingness, to EXPECT EVERYTHING from the good God, as a little child expects everything from its father. It is to worry about nothing, and not to be concerned with amassing anything material. It is not to fret about one's weakness BUT EVEN TO REJOICE IN IT because it glorifies God. It is knowing IN ALL THINGS that GOD will PROVIDE. Let's remember it is only when a child grows up that it has to earn its own living!

So in our attempt at a total surrender of our will and our life to God, we must take ourselves AS WE ARE, and go straight to God as a little child runs to its mother, without making any unduly long effort, without any affectation and without any fear or reservation. We must LET GO completely and LET GOD be truly our Father, for it is only thus that He can and will provide EVERYTHING.

How many A.A.'s fail to find true peace of mind precisely because they complicate the program for themselves! By drawing up (mentally or otherwise) a long list of directives; by listing virtue after virtue to be practiced; by getting both their minds and their souls enmeshed in a maze of entangling "do's" and "don't's"—they completely lose sight of the simple core of the program and close the door on the very serenity for which they are seeking.

THE TWELVE STEPS AND SERENITY

"We made a DECISION. . . ."

Now let us DESCEND the Twelve Steps one by one as a little child. And as we take each step let us keep our gaze directed upon Him Who is to restore us to sanity—and SERENITY. And when we have achieved it, we shall realize that we had "nothing to do with the end-result," but THAT GOD DID IT ALL—that we merely "tagged along" WILLINGLY guided and supported and perfected by HIM.

Are you ready? Let's go—let us LET GO—so we can LET GOD.

1. *WE ADMITTED WE WERE POWERLESS OVER ALCOHOL, THAT OUR LIVES HAD BECOME UNMANAGEABLE.*

Has our admission been a full admission without reservations of any type? Did we really mean POWERLESS to a point where we really could mean "we are NOTHING?" Or were we holding on to a bit of a thought that maybe someday we could be "on our own again"? Better let go—of that reservation!

When we admitted that we were powerless "over alcohol," did we mean ALL ALCOHOL? Beer, wine, and what have you? Or was and is there another "maybe some day" present? Better let go. . . .

And when we said that our "lives were unmanageable," did we really mean ALL OF OUR LIVING? Or did we rather hold on to the idea that SOME of it was still o.k.? Don't you think we better let go?—if we have reservations IT WON'T WORK! Books don't tell us this but thousands of "slippees" did and do! We simply MUST let go of ALL of our reservations in the first step—else WE CANNOT LET GOD take over in subsequent steps.

2. WE CAME TO BELIEVE THAT A POWER GREATER *THAN OURSELVES COULD RESTORE US TO SANITY.*

Here we meet three general types of difficulties:

a) *The atheist or agnostic.* The alcoholic who has never or does not believe in a God has difficulty with the second step because HE WON'T LET GO OF HIS FALSE PREMISE that he won't believe except that which he can see or experience. And only when he does LET GO of this premise, and ACCEPT a higher POWER, does Faith begin to dawn—GIVEN TO HIM BY GOD. But only by letting GO of his own ideas, can he let GOD give Faith—which HE will. A classical example of this is the story of the agnostic who finally agreed to pray thus: "O God, if there be a God . . . !"

Here many "agnostics" get into further difficulty AFTER they have accepted a belief in God. In THEIR eagerness to clarify THEIR belief in God in THEIR way THEY search and frantically read books-on-end on religions, theism, and 'isms' of all types. As a result instead of getting a clearer picture of God in their mind's eye, they only become more confused. Why? They LET GO—but they DIDN'T LET GOD in HIS time and WAY, which is usually not at a fast pace. They "searched on their own" and He was not there, instead of abiding their time and simply and humbly praying, "God, that I may see." "Wait on the Lord, and HE will come." Again ours is merely the WILLINGNESS to accept when HE gives conviction.

b) *The confused believer.* In this class are the bulk of alcoholics. They believe in a God, but they have all mused within themselves thousands of times, "It doesn't make sense!" They too must LET GO—of the confusion which is their own making—and LET GOD disperse the clouds with HIS LIGHT and grace. So just put those confused thoughts aside for the moment—GOD WILL CLEAR THEM UP IN HIS OWN WAY AND TIME—for the present ACCEPT the PRESENT, and LET GOD take care of the rest.

c) *The frustrated church-member.* These individuals have time and time again—so they think—TRIED to achieve sobriety through their church, and failed. So they think the church has let them down. Many in this group nurse deep resentments as a result: resentments against God or Church, or pastor, or priest, or minister or ecclesiastical authorities. We must LET GO of these disappointments and resentments. That shouldn't be so difficult, for WE were wrong, not God or the Church. Remember what we just admitted above, "WE were UNMANAGEABLE"? Others, also, COULD have been wrong, but we are SURE WE WERE. So let's LET GO—of our ideas about what WAS wrong, and WHO was wrong, and let's LET GOD do it ALL this time, huh?

3. *WE MADE A DECISION (without reservations) TO TURN OUR WILL (all of it) AND OUR LIFE (all of it) OVER TO THE CARE OF GOD AS WE UNDERSTOOD HIM (always).*

What ARE we waiting for? All we need is ABSOLUTE confidence! Like the confidence of a small child, remember? No "if's," no "and's," no "but's," NOTHING! Let EVERYTHING go and LET GOD! Come on, chum, let's try it—

"My God, I believe so firmly that Thou watchest over all who hope in Thee, and that we can want for nothing when we fully rely on Thee in all things, that I am resolved no longer to have any anxieties, and to cast all my cares upon Thee. 'In peace and in the self-same I shall sleep and I shall rest; for Thou, O Lord, has singularly settled me in hope!'

"I may lose all my material things; sickness may take from me my strength to do your work; I may even lose Thy grace by sin; but my trust shall never leave me and I shall preserve it to the last moment of my life and no power shall wrest that from me. 'In peace and in the self-same I shall sleep and I shall rest!"

"Let others seek peace and happiness in their money and their talents; let them trust in the purity of their lives, the severity of their sacrifices, the number of their works, the many whom they have sponsored, the calls they have made, the talks they have given, the number whom they have helped, yes, the length of their sobriety, or the fervor and number of their prayers;

as for me, O my God, in my confidence itself lies all of my hopes and my trust. 'For Thou, O Lord, singularly hast settled me in hope.' And I know beyond any doubt that my confidence can never be in vain. 'No one has ever hoped in the Lord and been confounded.'

"I know, alas, I know but too well that I am weak and changeable and helpless, that my life, all of it, has been unmanageable. I know the power of temptation against the strongest virtue. I have seen the strong fall and the pillars totter; but these things alarm me not. For it is precisely because I am so absolutely powerless that I become so strong in You and this trust in You shall endure because Thou Thyself will sustain it in me.

"Finally, I know that my confidence in Thee cannot exceed Thy bounty; therefore I shall always expect from Thy goodness alone and because of no merit of mine, strength in every struggle; grace in every temptation; victory in spite of my weakness; and peace of soul in every disturbance.

"Dear God, our Father, my will and my life I consecrate entirely to Thee this day: my eyes, my ears, my mouth, my heart, my whole being without reserve—wherefore, dear Father, as I am Thine own keep me and guard me as Thy property and possession, always and in all things."

And now let us be on our way, and whatever we meet, day in and day out, within or without, from others or from ourselves, let us say: "GOD IS MY SUFFICIENCY." For NOW our GOOD, our PEACE, our SERENITY IS TO COUNT ON GOD FOR EVERYTHING.

"Let nothing disturb thee,
Nothing affright thee,
ALL THINGS ARE PASSING,
God never changeth;
Patient ACCEPTANCE
Attaineth to all things
Whom God possesseth
In NOTHING is wanting;
Alone GOD SUFFICETH."

Our job? The foot-work? It's easy now, chum—it is just ACCEPTANCE . . . and ACCEPTANCE plus FAITH is all that God has ever asked anyone for a cure. "Do you believe that I can do this unto you. . . ? If thou canst believe, ALL THINGS ARE POSSIBLE TO HIM THAT BELIEVETH" . . . so again, let go, let God. . . . "It will be done unto thee according to thy faith" in God as we understood Him. . . .

It works, chum, it really does. . . .

4. *WE MADE A SEARCHING AND FEARLESS MORAL INVENTORY OF OURSELVES.*

Now we turn on the "heat"—the heat and warmth of God's grace and light, and we SEARCH our innermost selves for all the defects, and faults, etc., that have been accumulating for years. We have looked at ourselves many times in the past. But every picture we got was a false one, discolored by pride and prejudiced; or darkened by the ramifications of our own rationalizations. We looked and thought we saw perfection—and we were puffed up with pride. We looked at other times and saw putrefaction—and we were cast down by self-pity. Now we LET GO of those false pictures. We look, we search, aided by the light of God's grace—We LET GOD give us a TRUE PICTURE. We see ourselves AS WE ARE—AS WE ARE SEEN BY GOD AND OTHERS. And we are neither puffed up nor are we cast down for we have the knowledge now that the perfections we see (and there may be one of the other such) have been placed there BY GOD; and we also know that the putrefactions we see will be REPLACED BY GOD, i.e., if we LET GO of the past and LET GOD do so.

And now no longer shall we be afraid to look at ourselves. Our inventory is FEARLESS—the FEAR of a lifetime has been replaced by FAITH in GOD. "Be not afraid" . . . "Fear not, it is I" . . . "If God be with us, who can be against us?" . . . "Even if I walk through the valley of death, I shall NOT FEAR." . . . "Even though He slay me, I shall trust Him" . . . so away with fear . . . LET IT GO the way of all phobias . . . and LET GOD direct our inventory . . . and as we begin and many,

many times in making it—(take it EASY, time means nothing and EASY STILL DOES IT)—let us breathe a fervent and sincere "O God, that I may see!"

5. *WE ADMITTED TO GOD, TO OURSELVES AND TO ANOTHER HUMAN BEING THE EXACT NATURE OF OUR WRONG.*

Three possible obstacles confront us in this step. We hesitate to admit our true selves to God because we are AFRAID OF WHAT HE WILL THINK AND DO. Actually we should realize that GOD CAN only think the TRUTH. And after all are we not seekers after truth? So let's LET GO of our double standards—one for us to look at and another for God and others to look at. And let us LET GOD think and do WHAT HE THINKS BEST knowing that it will BE BEST for us. It may HURT, but so does an operation.

Again, we may hesitate to admit our true selves TO OURSELVES because we are afraid of THE CHANGES we may have to make in our living. Whom are we kidding? Remember not too far back when ANY CHANGE WOULD HAVE BEEN SWELL AND WELCOMED AS AN IMPROVEMENT? Now, let us go ALL the way. Let go and LET GOD "give us the courage to CHANGE THE THINGS WE CAN AND THE SERENITY TO ACCEPT THE THINGS WE CANNOT CHANGE AND THE WISDOM TO KNOW THE DIFFERENCE."

Finally, it is almost certain that MOST of us are going to be afraid of what that other human being is going to think or say. But, you know what? It won't make a bit of difference what anyone might think or say IF WE LET GO OF OUR PRIDE and LET GOD substitute a little humility. And you know something else? It is amazing how much serenity and peace of mind is always mixed in with every bit of humility!

6. *WE WERE ENTIRELY READY TO HAVE GOD REMOVE THESE DEFECTS OF CHARACTER.*

Are you ready?

Then let us LET GO of ALL of them: resentments, fears,

self-pity, dishonesties, sinful relationships, double-dealings, and all of the rest. For, it is only when WE LET GO OF ALL OF THEM that GOD can remove them. We simply must let GO, if we hope to be ready to LET GOD. "O God, make me ENTIRELY willing, to LET GO all the way."

7. *HUMBLY ASKED HIM TO REMOVE OUR SHORTCOMINGS.*

LET GO! RELAX in the Presence of God. Go to Him with Faith and trust. Go to Him as a small child with a bruised thumb goes to its father. Go to Him with COMPLETE confidence as one goes to the surgeon KNOWING THAT HE IS COMPETENT, INFINITELY COMPETENT TO REMOVE ALL OF THEM WITH LEAST PAIN—for He usually won't hurt. It is WE who usually cause the hurt BY BALKING, BY KICKING AGAINST THE INCISIONS AND THE BANDAGES, BY KICKING AGAINST HIS WILL. The child gets hurt the most by trying to ESCAPE from the arms of its mother; the child who ACCEPTS its mother's arms goes peacefully to sleep there, completely oblivious of the bruised thumb.

So, let us LET GOD take over the job of rebuilding our lives in HIS WAY. "Unless the Lord build the house, he labors in vain who builds it." We have built for years, in OUR way —and failed miserably. So, now we let go of all of our old blueprints of what should be and LET GOD do it in His way.

As the sculptor sees the finished work in the rugged stone, so God sees the finished product in us no matter how "jagged" we may be. And thus, to Him we go and humbly ask that HE remove the jagged bits and bring out in us His Image. . . .

"Thus I have formed Thee with my shaking hand:
Lest I should be the greater sculptor,
Form me—e'en though filled with faults—
According to Thy Image, make me truly free!
The first of men Thou madest of clay;
Of hardened clay, alas, am I;
Thou wilt have to use a hammer.
Strike, O Sculptor God, I am the stone!"

What does not belong here must be hewn away. "Remove my shortcomings." We cannot contribute much to His work in removing these shortcomings except by patient and humble acceptance of all that happens, each day, as God in His Providence working on our character. The less we disturb Him in His work, the more patient we are, the greater will be the work of God and the deeper will be our peace and serenity. "Let naught disturb thee." All will be well IF WE ONLY LET GO—AND LET GOD have a complete free hand. So let us fully realize this and "humbly ask Him to remove our shortcomings." He will—really He will!

8. *MADE A LIST OF ALL THE PERSONS WE HAD HARMED AND BECAME WILLING TO MAKE AMENDS TO THEM ALL.*

For years we carried around in our confused minds a very long list—OF THE PERSONS WHO (so we thought) WERE HARMING US. Remember? And now we are to replace that phoney list with a TRUE LIST of the PERSONS WE HAD HARMED. So, therefore, we must first LET GO of all those former false notions of the many harms that were done to US. We must LET GO of our habit—and probably it is a very deeply ingrained one—of BLAMING OTHERS AND CIRCUMSTANCES FOR OUR DIFFICULTIES. Then, and then only shall we HONESTLY ADMIT THAT WE WERE RESPONSIBLE and be able to LET GOD direct us in listing HONESTLY all those whom we had harmed.

Before we attempt this list we should ASK GOD TO DIRECT US and to give us the grace to see ourselves AS HE SEES US—and we might throw in a prayer that HE MAKE US WILLING to make these amends. It is so much simpler, easier, and surer when HE does it. But in order to have Him take over we must LET GO of OUR IDEAS in the matter so we then can LET GOD clear them up.

9. *MADE DIRECT AMENDS TO SUCH PEOPLE WHER-*

EVER POSSIBLE, EXCEPT WHEN TO DO SO WOULD INJURE THEM OR OTHERS.

First and foremost in this step we must LET GO of our PRIDE and VANITY. Then we are able to LET GOD give us doses of HUMILITY and that is our paramount need.

We must also LET GO of our vain FEARS of approaching these persons whom we had harmed and thus LET GOD instill into our hearts and minds more and more FAITH and COURAGE with each successive apology, or restitution, or what have you.

And let us LET GO of our habit of dishonesty in dealing with others. Remember all the "if's," and "and's," and "but's" that we used to drag out to EXCUSE us in this, that or the other obligation? LET THEM GO and LET US GO DIRECTLY to ALL of the persons—with only ONE exception: when to do so would injure them or others. Then we shall be LETTING GOD bathe our souls in TRUTH and honesty, and He will again give us that CLEAN feeling and clear thinking which we haven't had perhaps since childhood.

And right here some will object. "But, what will these people say? Or what will so-and-so DO to me if I let him know I did this or that or the other thing?"

You really want to know? It is very simple: LET those uncertainities GO and LET GOD HANDLE THE RESULTS. Now if you go and get your big Alcoholics Anonymous book and look on page 92 you will find a factual example HOW GOD does it—i.e., if we LET GO and LET GOD. (If you haven't a big A.A. book it is about time you're buying one!)

"EXCEPT WHEN TO DO SO WOULD INJURE THEM OF OTHERS." Here above all we must LET GO of our wishes in the matter and LET GOD handle the entire situation. Oh, we know, we WISH WE COULD make this, that or the other thing up. But we CAN'T without injuring them. So we LET GO of our PRIDE—for that is what is making us wish that WE could make it up. So LET IT GO and LET GOD make it up. He'll do a much better job anyway.

10. *CONTINUED TO TAKE PERSONAL INVENTORY AND WHEN WE WERE WRONG, PROMPTLY ADMITTED IT.*

Here we must LET GO of our former EXCUSES that we always had ready, even if we had to manufacture them, to justify almost any and all of our aberrations, faults and failings. So let them GO—we're finished using them. LET GOD throw His searchlight of grace upon our soul in our inventory so that we may KNOW AND ACCEPT our faults AS OUR OWN. "O God, grant us the grace to see ourselves as YOU SEE US; so that knowing ourselves and Thy Will we may be enabled to carry it out in our daily lives."

We also LET GO of our old time habit of always looking for SUCCESS or FAILURE and making something of it. That's over with too. Now we are going to LET GOD GIVE SUCCESS OR PERMIT FAILURE. Thus we shall be neither puffed up by the former, nor cast down by the latter. IT IS NOW ALL HIS WORK—ours is ONLY the footwork. So we no longer go to God to give Him instructions as to what we want and expect, we simply report for duty! We therefore merely DO WHAT we can, we LET GOD DO THE REST.

THE TOTAL VIEW AND AIM OF OUR INVENTORY IS THE ACCEPTANCE OF THE WILL OF GOD. By this fulfillment of our entire self will be transformed and rebuilt along HIS LINES. Thus we prevent selfishness and pride from insinuating themselves into the practice of virtue which would happen if we practiced freely chosen virtues. A LITTLE SELF-WILL, a bit of vanity and pride, however small and hidden, is in EVERY SELF-INITIATED VIRTUE. This is readily seen should we criticize such virtue in another. That is why Augustine tells us "Vice begets vice—vainglory alone is begotten of virtue." Especially is this danger present in the personality of the alcoholic. So, in our inventory, we DO NOT AIM AT THIS OR THAT VIRTUE, or aim at eliminating THIS OR THAT VICE—we AIM AT TOTAL CONFORMITY TO GOD'S WILL—ACCEPTING everything that happens each day as His

Will and thus we shall find that ALL the virtues necessary to our circumstances in life will unfold in the sunlight of the Divine Will. We take our inventory so we can the more conform to that Will—our inventory is our textbook of ACCEPTANCE, of SURRENDER—more and more learning and practicing LETTING GO, so we can LET GOD.

"PROMPTLY ADMITTED IT." This is to LET GO of our upsets, etc., mental, moral, and emotional. We LET them GO—out of us by admitting them to another PROMPTLY. Thus we LET GOD support us, we having continued to remove all the emotional obstacles as they arise.

11. *SOUGHT THROUGH PRAYER AND MEDITATION TO IMPROVE OUR CONSCIOUS CONTACT WITH GOD AS WE UNDERSTOOD HIM, PRAYING ONLY FOR KNOWLEDGE OF HIS WILL FOR US AND THE POWER TO CARRY THAT OUT.*

Humble prayer and meditation! We LET GO completely of all of our cares, problems, work—of EVERYTHING and LET GOD take over entirely for a little while. WE RELAX WITH GOD! WE LET GOD speak to us—we LET GO of all else and listen. We LET GO also of ALL of our problems—one by one—and LET GOD solve them, for which solution, again, we simply listen. "Speak, Lord, thy servant heareth." We also LET GO of the management and LET GOD'S WILL manage us and GOD'S POWER sustain us—always. We no longer TELL Him what we need, we ASK Him what He wants of us.

12. *HAVING HAD A SPIRITUAL AWAKENING AS THE RESULT OF THESE STEPS, WE TRIED TO CARRY THIS MESSAGE TO ALCOHOLICS AND TO PRACTICE THESE PRINCIPLES IN ALL OF OUR AFFAIRS.*

A spiritual awakening—i.e., complete new attitudes toward God, toward our fellow man and toward ourselves. So we must LET GO of all of our FORMER ATTITUDES. May they rest in peace! We have had a spiritual awakening. We have had a CHANGE of ATTITUDES. We now shall see all things THROUGH GOD'S EYES—as HE sees things. So, let us LET all of our past attitudes GO—once and for all. Then we can LET GOD DIRECT our gaze and our actions ALWAYS.

"WE TRIED TO CARRY THIS MESSAGE TO ALCOHOLICS." We ONLY TRY. We LET GO of our former DETERMINATION TO ALWAYS SUCCEED. Thus we worry not as to whether we shall succeed or not with the new prospect. We LET GOD decide that. WE ACCEPT. Remember?... "We are going to LET GOD GIVE US SUCCESS OR PERMIT FAILURE. Thus we shall not be puffed up by the former, nor cast down by the latter. IT IS NOW ALL HIS WORK—ours is only the foot-work... we simply report for duty."?...

We don't even worry as to what we are going to say to the new prospect. We LET GO of our former habit of "figuring out what we're going to say." And we LET GOD direct our words and conversation.

One very successful sponsor was asked by another member of his group what he thought about on his way to call on a new prospect. He replied, "I don't think anything, I PRAY!" Let go, chum—LET GOD accompany you on your twelfth step calls, it won't be nearly so lonesome!

"PRACTICE THESE PRINCIPLES IN ALL OF OUR AFFAIRS." "These principles"—let's keep it simple. All of these principles can now be boiled down to one! "Let GO—LET GOD" which interpreted means in ALL things GOD'S WILL be done—IN ALL of our affairs.

So our whole day each day we place under the will of God. We use ALL occasions and in ALL of our affairs we simply practice ACCEPTANCE, ACCEPTANCE, *ACCEPTANCE!*

So the day begins. Our plan for the day is upset. WE ACCEPT it as God's Will, and in humble submission we go on with the temple of our mind and soul unruffled. A certain obligation demands great sacrifice; GOD asks it; it is His Will; we do it gladly. An unpleasant call demands our attention; we are inclined to avoid it; many excuses suggest themselves;

but we do it—God's Will instead of ours. An inconsiderate person offends us; our ire is aroused; but we think quickly, God permitted this, it is His Will; we ACCEPT. We feel depressed; cares force themselves into our heart and soul; but we immediately remind ourselves that God is guiding us and protecting us; and that He permits the darkness as well as the light; so again we say an humble "Yes, Father," and the depression passes; or if its tentacles but grow the more, we ACCEPT until God wills to release us, all the time doing what we can. We pray; distractions come; we ACCEPT them by ignoring them as we do all the varied distractions that come to us when we are holding converse with a dear friend. We are suddenly pleased or buoyed up by a good fortune; we thank Him, ACCEPT it, and offer it to Him and enjoy it as His gift and His Will. We are busily occupied; someone asks a favor; we say "yes" and thus in our neighbor too we have done His Will. And on through each TWENTY-FOUR HOURS we go . . . simply doing the foot-work of the daily rounds of our work and our play . . . always ACCEPTING; always giving a cheery "Yes, Father" to ALL and to EVERYTHING because it is GOD'S Will.

We may have a struggle for a time to become adept and ready with a wholehearted and ready "Yes, Father" in all circumstances. But if we make a new effort every day, we shall be amazed at the progress and facility we shall soon accomplish; and at the ease we shall acquire before long to reply quickly, deep down inside, consistently and readily in ALL things, "Yes, Father." And at the end of each day when we again take our inventory, we shall indeed find many marks and bruises and stains, but THE CITADEL OF OUR SOUL WILL HAVE REMAINED SERENE and we shall know true PEACE—NOT in ESCAPE, but IN ACCEPTANCE!

And thus we go on . . .

Taking our inventory . . . (10)

Praying and meditating . . . (11)

Doing our twelfth step work (12), with a song in our heart and a prayer constantly on our lips:

"God grant us the SERENITY to ACCEPT."

About this time some "wiseacre" is going to come along and whisper "Look at so-and-so, he is becoming a regular 'pious-puss.' " And then we are going to be tempted to draw back from our path to serenity and happiness BECAUSE OF WHAT OTHERS MAY THINK OF US. And here we seal our serenity once and for all by inscribing deep in our heart and mind and soul: "To practice these principles in ALL OF OUR AFFAIRS" means that in ALL of our actions there is ONLY ONE THING NECESSARY—WHAT DOES GOD THINK OF US?

By the way—honestly—what DOES God think of you, chum?

PROBLEMS AND SERENITY

"In all of our affairs." ALL of them, without exception. And, because we are alcoholic, we shall find this practice of surrender and acceptance particularly effective in the handling of those problems more or less accentuated in our personalities. Let us apply it to a few:

1. *Resentments*—Here we face the number one enemy of all alcoholics. But if we handle our resentments by LETTING GO and LETTING GOD—by ACCEPTANCE, we shall find that our enemy is merely another Goliath.

First, we must LET GO OF OUR "I'S," and the reason we have so much "I" trouble is because WE HAVE OUR "EYES" FOCUSED TOO MUCH ON OURSELVES. And if we let our "I'S" GO we shall not have nearly so many resentments; we shall find it so much easier than to LET GOD (in our fellow-man) have more room in the picture of our lives. So, let us practice letting GO of OUR interests for awhile and letting GOD'S (and our neighbor's) guide us more. We then shall be much more concerned as to what GOD is saying about us instead of what the other fellow is saying. And, all of the gossip, slander, hurts, circumstances that irritate us and tend to make us resentful, we simply let them GO—we simply ACCEPT—we simply—if repayment be just—LET GOD REPAY them. "I am the Lord and I shall repay." Again, LET GO—of God's lines just quoted. Quit using and acting on them. See the "I" in them? That means GOD—so LET GO chum and LET GOD.

2. *Self-pity*—The number two enemy. But here our "I" is not gleaming, but is bruised. Ain't it a pity. Poor ME! For other people the birds SING! And on and on. Let us quit DEPENDING ON SELF—let us let GO OF "I," and let GOD give the strength, the will, and the success. After all, whatever is, IS GOD'S WILL—and that "ain't a pity" that is wonderful, for it is exactly what we have been praying for—or is it? ? ? Or were we still "gimmeing"? Let GO, let GOD GIVE.

3. *Temptations*—So many A.A.'s complain of severe temptations—"the bottle, the flesh and the alcoholic." But temptations aren't nearly so severe or so frequent, either of the flesh or of the bottle IF WE LET GO OF THE OCCASIONS of temptation; If we LET GOD'S plan occupy our minds; or if they still persist, if we simply LET THEM GO, don't bother them, turn our thoughts to God and LET GOD take over.

4. *Nervousness*—Much nervousness and restlessness is caused by TOO MUCH CONCERN ABOUT OUR AFFAIRS; by wanting TO MANAGE TOO MANY OF OUR AFFAIRS. Let GO of the MANAGEMENT; let GOD manage—ALL OF OUR AFFAIRS. This will positively eliminate all WORRY (an ingredient of most nervousness) for WORRY IS THE PROPERTY OF THE MANAGEMENT. OURS is only THE FOOT-WORK. And if our nervousness is physical in origin, then LET IT GO—ACCEPT, let GOD alleviate it or permit it to remain.

5. *Neurosis—depression*—Something most alcoholics are heir to—either slight or severe. But, you know what is the cause of most neuroses? (Except those that are caused by a physical condition which we must ACCEPT if we can't remedy). Most neuroses are a result of one's NEVER HAVING FULLY MADE UP ONE'S MIND WHO IS TO BE BOSS—the body or soul; we or God. So LET GO—LET GOD PROVIDE EVERYTHING, which He will IF WE let HIM MANAGE.

6. *Suffering*—when suffering comes to our lives as it must for all, there is nothing that will make it more desirable but ACCEPTANCE—by LETTING GO OF OUR DESIRES IN THE MATTER AND LETTING GOD'S WILL BE DONE IN US.

Philosophers tell us that "suffering is the human lot and we must grin and bear it." But that does not make it more desirable. WE can bear it—but ONLY GOD can give us the grace to grin!

Others will tells us that in suffering we should bear in mind that "there are others who have it worse." But what about the fellow who has it worst?

To many, suffering in human life just doesn't make sense. But neither does the music of the opera and the symphony make sense to many. To the musically uneducated the music of the masters is but a conglomeration of disagreeable sounds. But to the composer, it is perfect harmony. So in life—to the prayerless, the atheistic, etc., suffering and the like are evidences of lamentable disorder, BUT TO THE ONE WHO SEES IN ALL THINGS THE WILL OF GOD—OF THE DIVINE MASTER, everything is perfect harmony, because everything is GOD'S WILL and that is perfection. So, let GO of our fear of suffering; LET GOD send WHAT He will, WHEN He chooses, for AS LONG AS He chooses. He then will also send the strength to bear and with serenity.

7. *Fear*—The alcoholic's plague. Here we must simply LET GO of ALL of our FORMER PROPS, and LET GOD be OUR SECURITY in ALL the circumstances of our daily lives. "GOD WILL PROVIDE"—really He will! Remember a material "prop" is good until it wears out; a Divine "prop" is eternal. "God alone sufficeth."

8. *Past wrongs*—Often a "disturber of the peace." What is the cause of this unrest? This worry over past sins and wrongs? Too many think that THEY must save themselves and that THEY must make up for wrong, instead of LETTING THE PAST GO, and LETTING GOD make up for it. God alone can satisfy for sin. We can do no more than say humbly: "Father, I have sinned" like the prodigal son. THE REST WE MUST LEAVE TO GOD.

Without fully realizing it such people doubt God's mercy and power. Why don't we have confidence? God's grace is always greater and more powerful than sin. That is why we were told a long time ago, "Where sin abounded, grace did more abound." Or in other words, THE MORE PAST SINS YOU HAVE THE MORE GRACE YOU CAN EXPECT. Let us remember that God is not a tyrant who constantly rehearses past faults and sins or who can never close an issue. When it comes to past repented sins "God has an awfully bad memory and eyesight." Child like trust in God HONORS HIM A THOUSAND TIMES MORE THAN REPEATED ACTS OF SORROW FOR PAST SINS LONG FORGIVEN. So forget them—God has—let them GO—and LET GOD take care of them.

9. *Avarice*—Now comes the "enigma of A.A." Thousands of alcoholics, HAVING SOBERED UP, NOW BECOME "TIGHTER" THAN THEY EVER WERE DRUNK—with money! And the poor abused and over-used EXCUSE "no fees, no dues, no nothing"—salves their consciences and sets them in their "tightness."

Gosh, fellows, LET GO OF SOME OF THOSE "BUCKS"! And if it is hard to do so—LET GOD MOTIVATE YOUR GIVING! Where do you think you got those extra coins? You say you worked for them? Who gave you the ability to work for them? And the health, and the talent, and the job? GOD DID! If you think differently someone is kidding no one but himself! Better give some back. How? Through your fellowman, your group, the Central Office, your Church—there's plenty of objects if we'll just LET GO of a few of the coins.

Someone will say, "I'd be glad to give, IF I KNEW SO-AND-SO WAS WORTHY or that SUCH-AND-SUCH A CAUSE WAS A GOOD ONE. A nice excuse if we could use it, but only an EXCUSE. For WHY ARE WE GIVING? Worthiness means nothing except that in such a case we OWE it out of JUSTICE; if it is not worthy or needy then we GIVE it out of CHARITY because of GOD. So let's LET GO; let's GIVE; because of GOD. We shall then sober up also financially—and incidentally thereby purchase a lot of serenity!

10. *Humility*—Humility—for the alcoholic a "consummation devoutly to be wished" and the CORNERSTONE AND FOUNDATION AND THE ENTIRE STRUCTURE of SERENITY.

Fundamentally humility is truth. So in its acquirement, we should aim primarily at acquiring absolute truth—and that is: WE ARE NOTHING—GOD IS EVERYTHING. We thereby LET GO of all of SELF and LET GOD be our everything.

Let go—of our former ideas of ourselves—the big-shot ideas—the big-shot aims and ambitions—the scrambling for high places. Thus we can LET GOD put us in the place HE has selected for us.

Let go—of our "I-sight"—and put on the "spiritual awakening," the new vision through "God's-sight." "God grant us the grace to see ourselves as You see us, so that knowing ourselves and Thy Will, we may be enable to carry It out in our daily lives."

Let go—of the credit-taking; let go of the bragging; let go of the boasting. LET GOD take the credit. "He did it all; we had nothing to do with it."

Let go—of our uncharitableness, the gossiping, the dishonesties, the scandal-mongering. Let GOD USE US always as His instrument to HELP our neighbor, FOR "THERE BUT FOR THE GRACE OF GOD GO I."

Let go—of the reins of government in running our lives; let go of the determination to have OUR way; let go of the desire to always win. LET GOD run the show—all of it.

Let go—of the intolerance and the bigotry; let go of the criticisms and the sniping; let go of the "better than thou" attitude. LET GOD be our FATHER and ALL of our fellowmen our BROTHERS under that GOD—be they white or black, rich or poor, Catholic, Protestant or Jew, drunk or sober, drinking or staying on the program.

Let go—of our desire to correct evils; of our incessant endeavor to CHANGE things; of our tendency to a pietistic apostolic zeal. LET GOD eliminate evil in HIS time. Evil has its day; GOD will in His way and time have His. So let others, and what they do or how they do it, GO!

LET GO—in short—LET GO OF THAT ONLY OBSTACLE TO THE GRACE OF GOD AND THE MAIN OBSTACLE TO PEACE AND SERENITY: PRIDE. Let God replace self with HimSELF.

One time a certain member had a slip in A.A. He called his sponsor and, crying on his shoulder and full of self-pity, he moaned: "And to think, I have lost all of my pride!"

"Swell," his sponsor bluntly remarked, "Now we can BEGIN."

11. *Anger—irritability*—Another tendency that is always found accentuated in the alcoholic. And why do we get "mad" so easily? Someone has punched us in the "I" again! We are still hanging on to self. We won't LET GO of self. We won't turn ALL of our will over to God. If we did, we couldn't get "mad" any more unless it be at God—could we?

12. *Decisions*—One of the most difficult jobs in life for the alcoholic has been to make decisions. It was precisely our abhorrence of making decisions that made us procrastinators and dreamers. And most of this running away from decisions stemmed from our perfectionist creed. WE WANTED TO BE SURE OF SUCCESS, WE DREADED FAILURE and this very dread drove us on to the latter—through constant INDECISION.

Now we LET GO of this false idea THAT WE ARE RESPONSIBLE FOR THE RESULTS OF OUR ACTIONS and we ACCEPT the fact that WE ARE ONLY RESPONSIBLE FOR THE ACTIONS. The results ARE GOD'S BUSINESS. Again, we are only responsible for the foot-work—for a sincere effort. And thus it becomes easy to make decisions, for in every dilemma God has either clearly indicated His Will or He hasn't indicated His Will. In the former there is to the sincere person only ONE DECISION—to do God's Will. In the latter the principle that applies is that where God has not indicated His Will specifically, HE EXPECTS US MERELY TO USE OUR JUDGMENT, DO THE FOOT-WORK and then TO LEAVE THE RESULTS UP TO HIM. We ask for guidance, we made a decision, we leave the outcome TO HIM.

Our worry and indecision generally arises from the fact that we attribute far too great importance to our own share of the work in our partnership with God. Remember—"Our SUFFICIENCY IS FROM GOD," so let's LET GOD give it.

Let us take for example the father of a family. He must provide for the education of his children. This involves innumerable decisions—figuring out the means and ways, supervising their upbringing, arranging for finance, etc., etc. God does not want the father to wait for HIS DIRECTIONS in all of these decisions. He wants the father TO MAKE THE DECISIONS THE BEST HE CAN but to LEAVE THE RESULTS TO GOD. God does NOT COMMAND SUCCESS. Such a father's attempt to educate his children may be partially frustrated by the non-cooperation of the children, by mistakes on the part of the teachers, by illnesses, or by any of a hundred happenings. But still ALL THAT GOD ASKS is the sincere ATTEMPT—the REST IS GOD'S GUSINESS. So let us make our decisions AND LET GOD take care of the rest.

13. *The "unsolvable problem"*—Many members have some type or other of the so-called "unsolvable" problems. In other words they have a problem about which NOTHING CAN BE DONE towards a factual solution. This may be in respect to money, job, family, marriage, or what-have-you. Time and time again they have sought a solution—always unsuccessfully. And now there seems to be no solution. What to do? ACCEPT it as a problem, then let it GO and LET GOD solve it WHEN, HOW and WITH THE MEANS HE wills.

It may be well to analyze one such problem that is quite common: how to get the wife back, (or the husband back), or the family back, or the job, or the good name, or whatever has been lost through our drinking days. Many expend much energy and time "trying" themselves to reclaim such lost circumstances, whereas the simplest, the surest, and the quickest way is TO LET THEM GO and LET GOD bring them back. It really works—and often amazingly! ALL WE HAVE TO DO IS TO BRING OURSELVES AND OUR OWN LIVES BACK TOGETHER—TO SANITY; God will bring the others back to us AND USUALLY WHEN HE SEES THAT WE ARE CAPABLE OF HANDLING THE RETURN. So—LET THEM GO; ACCEPT the situation AS IS; adjust and CHANGE YOURSELF; and let GOD DO THE REST. He will!

A PRAYER AND SERENITY

"God grant us the SERENITY to ACCEPT the things we cannot change; COURAGE to CHANGE the things we can; and the WISDOM to KNOW the difference."

The most important part of this prayer is the last line PLUS willingness and effort. If we have the "wisdom to know" WHAT to ACCEPT and WHAT to CHANGE and are willing and make an honest effort to do so our lives will be happy and serene. And here many will ask "How can one be sure he 'knows the difference'?"

This question was answered in part when we spoke of "decisions." There we saw that ordinarily we ask for guidance, we make the decision, do the foot-work and LET GOD do the rest. However it will be a great help to us in knowing what we have to change and what we have to accept if we set for ourselves a general rule. And from the experience of the human race we evolve the following pattern: MOST THINGS WE CANNOT CHANGE AND MUST ACCEPT ARE THOSE OUTSIDE OURSELVES AND INVOLVE OTHERS—MOST THINGS WE CAN CHANGE ARE INSIDE OURSELVES AND INVOLVE US. A good fifteen-minute "think" over that statement will generate a lot of "wisdom" . . . right? And isn't it true that MOST OF OUR UNHAPPINESS CAME FROM TRYING TO CHANGE OTHERS TO OUR WAY OF THINKING? It goes without saying we have always ACCEPTED OURSELVES! And now for peace of mind and serenity we finally realize that we usually can't change others but we can change ourselves.

And so the answer to our A.A. prayer is SURRENDER to this realization. And the more we go on day by day, the more we will find that IN MOST THINGS IT IS ACCEPTANCE. Always doing the foot-work BUT ALWAYS ACCEPTING THE RESULTS AS GOD'S WORK. And thus in time we shall achieve true PEACE OF MIND, TRUE PEACE OF SOUL, TRUE SERENITY even amidst the strongest efforts and the worst storms. For IN ALL THINGS the citadel of the soul shall remain SERENE. Like the little duck, even in the most turbulent water—calm and unruffled on the surface, but underneath paddling for all he's worth; A perfect example of the coordination of SERENITY in ACTION. Only in eternity will the feet too be still.

Yes— only in eternity will ABSOLUTE and complete unruffled peace be ours. In the meantime let us "rejoice (let go) in the Lord (let God) always; again, I say, REJOICE . . . BE NOTHING SOLICITOUS, but in EVERYTHING by PRAYER and supplication with thanksgiving let your petitions be made known TO GOD. And the PEACE of GOD which surpasseth all understanding, keep your hearts and minds . . . and the GOD OF PEACE shall be with you."

And when the reality comes, which it will for all of us sooner or later and soon at the latest, and we are bidding our last farewell to this world, then that prayer that has fallen from our lips thousands of times in life shall surely be heard in that dread hour : GOD will "GRANT US THE SERENITY to ACCEPT the final thing we cannot change"—DEATH; and HE will give us the "COURAGE to CHANGE the final thing we can"—our temporal abode for one eternal; and He too will give us "the WISDOM to realize" that we are merely taking the THIRTEENTH STEP into eternity. And then all will be over—the loneliness and the heartaches; the disappointments and the deceptions; the pain and the sorrow; the anguish and the conflicts; the sin and the shame—and all the "interruptions" to our happiness shall be a thing of the past. And throughout eternity we shall thank God that he has given us twelve little steps on which we have DESCENDED to peace of mind and peace with our neighbor here—in order that we might thereby ASCEND ultimately to ETERNAL SERENITY with HIM.

And then and then only shall we FULLY understand the "enigma of God"—His greatest paradox: that WE MUST DIE TO LIVE; that WE KEEP ONLY WHAT WE GIVE AWAY; that WE ACHIEVE VICTORY ONLY THROUGH SURRENDER.

THE DAWN OF TRUTH

"WITH DESOLATION is the land made desolate . . ."

Somewhere along the path of life of every human being there comes a dread moment when he suddenly sees himself for what he is. Minus all the sham, the surface and the show, he then stands face to face with truth. Minus the deception of his own self-seeking and selfishness, he sees himself clearly outlined in the aura of God's grace as it tears away all the foolish self-deceptions and shows a man for what he really is—selfish, deceitful, full of excuses, dishonest even to himself and full of faults and failings.

To some few it may come in the green and virile freshness of youth when failures still are only theory and cocksureness still the order of the day. Blessed are they if they can then and there see the truth for what it is and follow it faithfully on down through all the subsequent years of struggle and still retain it as their guiding star even to the eventide of declining years.

To another some the moment is delayed until remaining years are few and fast fading and the will is battered and torn by life's long struggles and hardships. But to them truth remains obscure, enmeshed over the long years in the deceptions and the excuses of "the world, the flesh and the devil." A miracle of providence and God's grace alone can pierce the hardened shell.

To most of us this moment comes at a time when many of life's battles and years have passed, but at a time when there still remains sufficient years, vigor and initiative to "seek truth and pursue it," in order to make it the motive of our living, the motive of our struggles and the security of our declining years.

This moment may be brought about by the death of a loved one, the loss of worldly goods, or it may be directly occasioned within by the grace of God speaking to the depth of our soul. To most alcoholics it comes at that instant when they face the inevitable choice: death, insanity or absolute sobriety. It often comes with a blinding flash that seems to tear away the very foundations of life, and whether alcoholic or non-alcoholic, layman or professional, young or old, their arises from the very innermost sanctuary of the soul and heart the cry "My God, what a mess I have made of things! How pitiful is the good done, how sparing my help to others, how innumerable my mistakes, the wrongs—how all-pervading my self-seeking, how dishonest my every motive! How seamy the finished, but now battered product!"

This "moment" may last for an hour, a day, a month, a year or for years. But whenever, however it comes—it is a dread and fearful moment, because UPON THAT MOMENT AND THE DECISIONS OF THAT MOMENT MAY DEPEND OUR VERY LIFE AND OUR ETERNITY. And from that time on one can never be the same again.

For it is then that he sees fully and clearly without rhyme or excuse what he has so far made of himself and how he has done it. He sees the great and the small failures—the great and the small successes. He for once now knows things for what they really are in themselves and not in their labels. He sees the total effect of what seemed to be little compromises—the little treasons, the little dishonesties, the little failures to live up to God's plan. He sees himself and his life for what it is—an intricate tissue of choices in which the smallest choice has given direction to other choices—like the tiny strokes of the artist's brush, in themselves meaningless—but in their union with others bringing forth the full portrait. And so he suddenly realizes that he has been down through the years like the artist who ever lifted the brush to canvas but never produced a picture; like the musician who ever touched the bow to strings but never emitted a harmony; like the sculptor who ever placed the chisel against the stone but never brought forth a statue.

It is then that life's greatest decision must be made and then it is that it seems that an angel has him by the hands and a devil by the foot. And having caught, perhaps only for a fleeting instant, a vision of himself naked in the white light of truth and the piercing rays of grace—having seen the abyss that separates him from what he should be, from what he has believed or tried to believe himself to be—and having at the same time recognized his own complete helplessness, he can do one of three things:

First—he may rush in confusion back to the old surface view of self and try by a thousand and one-half remedies to dress up the haunting vision, to explain away the stubborn reality, TO EXCUSE, and to attempt forgetfulness by courting the sham fancies of the night and by rushing headlong through the chores of the day. THIS IS THE CHOICE OF THE VAIN MAN.

Second—the shock may be so great, the failure so undeniably real, the disillusionment so crushing that he despairs and in one way or another he seeks to destroy himself—either factually or by the bottle. THIS IS THE PROUD MAN.

Third—this is the way of the Prodigal Son, who dropped on his knees in the swine pen and cried: "Father, I have sinned" or with its echo "I am powerless . . . my life is unmanageable"—and perhaps for the first time in his life that man REALLY prays and begins to MEDITATE. THIS IS THE HUMBLE MAN. And day by day he prays and he MEDITATES on TRUTH lest again he fall back into his former dishonesties, into his former self-deception, into his former life-long HABIT OF EXCUSES. For the LIFE OF ALL IS LOADED WITH EXCUSES—AND SYSTEMATIC, PERSISTENT AND CONSISTENT MEDITATION ALONE WILL DISSIPATE THEM. "With desolation is the land made desolate because there are none who thinketh in their hearts."

THE HABIT OF EXCUSE

"I pray thee, hold me excused . . ."

The habit of excuse is as old as the human race. It had its beginnings with the beginning of the human race. It began with the first man and the first woman—with Adam and Eve. And ever since that time history is filled with people who in order to justify themselves, in order to escape from responsibility, in order to minimize their guilt and/or in order to salve their conscience, EXCUSED themselves.

Let us take a look at the sequence of the events that brought about the first excuse ever used.

According to the scriptures, Adam and Eve were created by Almighty God and placed in the garden of Eden. They were given everything therein for their pleasure and happiness with but one exception. They were told not to eat the fruit of the tree of the knowledge of good and evil which grew in the center of their paradise. And they were also told that if they did eat it they would die.

Then along came the serpent. He asked Eve how it was that she did not eat of the fruit of the tree. And Eve told him that the reason was that God had forbidden them to do so and if they did eat of it they would die.

But the crafty serpent countered with: "You will not die. God knows that in what day soever you shall eat thereof, your eyes shall be opened; and you shall be as gods knowing good and evil."

Then Eve doubted God, believed the serpent, and ate the fruit.

And immediately realizing the evil she had done, she in turn offered the fruit to Adam and he (like so many husbands down through the ages!) in order to please his wife, also ate of the fruit.

And then both Adam and Eve began to be afraid. And when God asked them why they had eaten the fruit, SEEKING

TO ESCAPE FULL RESPONSIBILITY FOR THEIR ACTIONS, they began to make excuses.

Adam excused himself and endeavored to put the blame and responsibility upon Eve, "The woman you gave me as my companion gave it to me."

But Eve too tried to escape responsibility and she in turn put the blame upon the serpent, "The serpent deceived me, and I did eat."

And thus began the use of excuses TO JUSTIFY ONESELF, TO ESCAPE FROM RESPONSIBILITY, TO MINIMIZE ONE'S GUILT, AND/OR TO SALVE ONE'S CONSCIENCE.

A little later in history we have another excellent example of using excuses. It happened in Adam's immediate family.

Cain and Abel were sons of Adam. They both, the scriptures tells us, offered sacrifices to Almighty God. And we are told that God accepted Abel's sacrifice, but did not accept Cain's. So Cain in his resentment and anger, killed Abel.

Then the Lord called to Cain and said, "Where is thy brother Abel?" And Cain replied with that classical oft-repeated endeavor at excuse, "Am I my brother's keeper?" in order to quiet the fear within and to minimize his own guilt.

Centuries later, the Lord Himself gave three more vivid examples of excuses in His parable about the man who gave a great supper and who invited many of his friends to partake of it. Here's the story:

"A certain man gave a great supper, and he invited many. And he sent his servants at supper time to tell those invited to come, for everything is now ready. AND THEY ALL WITH ONE ACCORD BEGAN TO MAKE EXCUSE.

"The first said to him, 'I have bought a farm, and I must go out and see it; I pray thee hold me excused.' And another said, 'I have bought five yoke of oxen, and I am on my way to try them; I pray thee hold me excused.' And another said, 'I have married a wife, and therefore I cannot come.' "

And in all of these instances, they EXCUSED themselves seeking to JUSTIFY THEMSELVES, TO ESCAPE RESPON-

SIBILITY, TO MINIMIZE THEIR GUILT AND/OR TO 'SALVE' THEIR CONSCIENCES.

The alternative in all of the above instances? There is only one alternative to all excuses and that is the TRUTH or as a very common current expression tells us 'LET'S FACE IT.'

And what would Adam and Eve have said in place of excusing themselves? Just the simple TRUTH which would have been: "I did wrong, Lord, I disobeyed your law, I am sorry." And you know something? I don't think the good God would have punished Adam and Eve nearly so severely had they done just that: given an HONEST reply, the TRUTH instead of attempting to excuse themselves.

And Cain? It would have been just as simple, "In a fit of anger, I killed him, Lord, please forgive me." And I don't think Cain's punishment would have been as great either.

And the three who were invited to the supper? That would have been simple too, "We don't want to come to your supper."

If this had been done in all the above instances, from Adam on down, they would not have endeavored to justify THEMSELVES but would have let the truth seek the justification of God which always is MERCY. Whereas an excuse is but a lie cleverly cloaked in a semblance of truth endeavoring to deceive another but usually only ending in self-deception. Its root is in FEAR, usually fear of reprisal or punishment. Its primal stirrings are echoed in the words of the small child, "Mommy, I COULDN'T HELP IT!" instead of "I'm sorry, mommy, the next time I shall be more careful."

And thus in the alcoholic we find this age old habit of excuse very accentuated to the extent that every alcoholic is a past master at giving and manufacturing excuses from the initial, "I fell asleep" to the ultimate "I ain't been in the gutter yet." Remember?

And in the alcoholic personalities we find two causes of this over-accentuated characteristic; fear and sincerity.

Most alcoholics are very sincere by nature and in a frantic endeavor to avoid insincerity in facing their human failings, they, more than the average individual, rely on an excuse TO

JUSTIFY THEIR ACTIONS, TO ESCAPE FROM RESPONSIBILITY, TO MINIMIZE THEIR OWN GUILT, TO 'SALVE' THEIR CONSCIENCES.

Coupled with this circumstance within, every alcoholic is goaded on in many of his actions by an ABNORMAL FEAR ELEMENT operative in either his consciousness or subconsciousness.

Thus fear leads one to attempt to escape and over-sincerity leads one to self-justification. He (so he thinks) HAS to escape; and also he (so he thinks) *has* to have justification for his actions. And thus, (so he thinks) he retains his SECURITY and his CHARACTER but in doing so he REALLY only retains the shell of both which ultimately completely deteriorate in his alcoholic excesses. And the more he lies, the more he has to lie to justify his lies—and so the cycle goes on and on until at his 'level' he fails to find another excuse and he comes face to face with reality and truth in the ultimate dilemma of every alcoholic: INSANITY or DEATH or TOTAL SOBRIETY.

The habit of using excuses comes from a habit of rationalization, and an excuse may be defined as "an attempt to find a reason, where there is none," in order to avoid FACING THE WHOLE TRUTH.

This fact is excellently brought out in the story about the Pharisee who asked Christ, "Who is my neighbor?" He wasn't really looking for a true definition of his neighbor, but he was endeavoring to find some definition which WOULD ENABLE HIM WITH SMUG CONSCIENCE TO OMIT SOME OF HIS OBLIGATIONS TO HIS NEIGHBOR. That is the reason the scriptures preface his question with "Seeking TO JUSTIFY HIMSELF."

The same rationalizing takes place wherever you find a gathering of A.A.'s discussing 'ad nauseam,' "What is an alcoholic?" In such a gathering you can usually be certain that one or more of the gathering is LOOKING FOR AN OUT: "Seeking to JUSTIFY himself"; seeking to justify ANOTHER DRINK. He is looking for a reason which would permit him without qualms to disassociate from A.A. and to drink again.

But there ISN'T ANY SUCH REASON, so he queries on and on "What is an alcoholic?" hoping sometime to find an ingredient given by someone WHICH DOESN'T APPLY TO HIM, and which he can use then as an EXCUSE for drinking again. And thus he JUSTIFIES HIMSELF, HE MINIMIZES HIS GUILT, HE ESCAPES RESPONSIBILITY FOR DOING IT (until the 'Brooklyn boys' appear on the scene!) and HE 'SALVES' HIS CONSCIENCE. The little child again, "Mommy, I couldn't help it."

Now, since the habit of excuses is a basic human fault, let us analyze a few of the more commonly used ones and endeavor to find out this fallacy.

1. *"Everybody else does it"*—One of the most common excuses used to justify almost any behavior no matter how wrong in itself. The more people we can adduce who do something which we are trying to justify in ourselves, the more is our own guilt minimized—so we think. And in the thinking we DO 'salve' our own conscience, don't we? But DO we change the basic law we are breaking? Now really DO WE? Or rather doesn't it remain the same even if EVERYBODY acts contrary to it?

2. *"They all say . . ."*—Here we have coming to the rescue of the excuser that old familiar "they"—did you ever meet "they"? Quite a fiction, not? But when an excuse is needed "they" are so easily quoted; and exactly as WE wish them to be, in order to justify ourselves, and it DOES 'salve' our conscience, doesn't it? The only difficulty is "they" did not MAKE the law we are breaking, did "they"?

3. *"Men of importance (or position, or distinction) do thus and thus."* A very common excuse of the modern era. "Men of distinction" do it so we simply MUST too, and since "men of distinction" do it, it simply MUST be RIGHT. Or must it? To commercialize on this common excuse of human nature, a certain liquor firm used to portray "men of distinction" who used their brand. At one time they used for a long time the same man as model in their advertising. Then he appeared no more. But the writer met the gentleman a short time later—

in a sanitarium on the west coast—coming off a binge, in a ward of drunks!—where there no longer seemed to be much "distinction."

What "men of distinction" do or say does not point to what is right, or good, or best—but gosh, it does 'salve' our own conscience somewhat, doesn't it?

4. *"My mother told me so"*—Poor mom! She's gone now, and what a lovely one to blame for our shortcomings! She can no longer dispute it. And it is a wonderful 'trump' excuse excellent for use on the spur of the moment when we can't seem to find another. And it will shift the blame; it will enable us (so we think) to escape responsibility: and it certainly will 'salve' the ole conscience quite a bit.

5. *"Every bucket must stand on its own bottom"*—A trite little phrase. And one that is commonly and widely used to excuse from innumerable obligations of charity. When we are too stingy, or too lazy, or too bitter to extend a helping hand to our neighbor, this excuse is a wonderful one to dish out. Or when a twelfth-step call is to be avoided for the same reasons of stinginess, or laziness, or bitterness, just come up with "every bucket must stand on its own bottom" and after all, let the guy or the gal have a little 'cold' treatment and furthermore one doesn't want to 'pamper' one, does one? And ecce, our conscience is quiet! Shades of Cain! "Am I my brother's keeper?" But you know, bub, it's a funny thing about this law of charity and brotherly love, YOU ARE.

6. *"Well, after all, one doesn't HAVE to do this or that—to stay sober, or to accomplish this or that or the other thing."* A long one, but an old stand-by so often used by our 'first-step Johns and Jills' and our 'twelfth-step busy-guys and gals' and the 'meeting every-now-and-then gents.' Since everything in A.A., including the twelve steps, is only suggested, this excuse is a fine one to permit one to omit almost anything not strictly of obligation with a clear conscience. How often do we not hear this excuse in the spiritual life: one doesn't HAVE to pray every day; one doesn't HAVE to go to the Sacraments frequent-

ly; one doesn't HAVE to meditate regularly—and on and on. No, one doesn't, but one does gotta die, doesn't one? And then? You take it from there.

7. *"I don't (didn't) have the time"*—This is perhaps the most widely used excuse there is and also probably the biggest lie frequently told. Listen to the guy or gal just back from their vacation: "I would have loved to write you, but I just didn't have time!" Listen to the fellow or girl reneging from helping with a church, or A.A. or social affair: "I would love to help, but I just don't have the time!" And listen to the A.A. slipping out of a twelfth step call: "I would love to make it, but I can't find the time right now!" Such really mean they don't WANT to TAKE the time, but using the verb HAVE in place of TAKE does justify them, nor does it disquiet their conscience either.

8. *"I don't FEEL well"*—The obligations that are side-stepped by this, one of the most common of excuses! Duty beckons, but gosh I just don't feel well, SO I can thus omit the duty, justify myself, and 'salve' the conscience!

There is a story told about a certain young man who went to his boss and asked if he might go home for the rest of the day, because as he expressed it, "I just don't feel well." To which his boss very aptly and with much wisdom replied: "My boy, there is one thing you can never learn too soon nor remember too well, and that is this: MOST OF THE WORK IN THIS OLD WORLD OF OURS IS DONE EACH DAY BY PEOPLE WHO JUST DON'T FEEL WELL."

They also tell the story about a certain member of A.A. who had promised to lead a meeting at a neighboring group. However, on the day he was to do so, he called the secretary of the group and begged to be excused because he had laryngitis and the doctor told him he should not speak over a few minutes at a time. It was forty minutes later when he hung up the phone after talking that length of time to the secretary!

9. *"At least I'm not a hypocrite"*—A wonderful conscience-salver used profusely by alcoholics and even on occasion by many others. "I don't go to church, but 'at least I'm not a hypo-

crite about it'—I admit it!" "Sure I drink—even too much on occasion, but 'at least I'm not a hypocrite about it' and I could stop any time I choose!" "Yes, I know I should do something about my faults, but 'at least I'm not a hypocrite about it'—I admit I have them!" So not being a hypocrite excuses from anything that I have a sneaking suspicion I CAN'T or DON'T WANT TO do anything about. And lo and behold there is peace within my conscience. Is there really, chum?

10. *"I'm not a saint"*—A very potent excuse for any fault, wrong-doing or sin that I may not want to or be able to correct. And the funny thing about this excuse, it has more of truth than the usual mine-run ones. There can be no doubt about it—I'm NOT a saint. But you know something? Do you know what the Lord is going to say when we used that one with Him? He is going to simply query back, "WHY?" "With all of My helps, and opportunities given you of grace and strength and direction, why?" Then, what will the answer be? Huh?... but for the nonce it is a lovely excuse, isn't it?

11. *"You gotta let go once in a while"*—And to this rationalization is often appended as verification, "and my doctor, or the psychiatrist said so." So thus I can indulge in anything good, bad or indifferent and conscience is at rest, for after all, "You gotta let go." And strange as it seems, one hears the same advice when one comes to A.A. but it is a bit different in its content. It contains the whole truth—"LET GO"—but "LET GOD" direct the extent of it. Remember? Let go—LET GOD? And then, strange as it may seem to some, we no longer NEED excuses if we LET GO—and LET GOD! FOR GOD IS TRUTH!

12. *"I know a fellow (gal) and he (she) is a WONDERFUL CHARACTER who does this, or that or the other thing..."*—It is amazing how many very ordinary people become WONDERFUL CHARACTERS, WONDERFUL A.A.'s or WONDERFUL CHURCH MEMBERS when we want to use them as an excuse! D'jever hear it? "I know a fellow, and he is a wonderful A.A. and he doesn't go to meetings very often, or he

doesn't do much twelfth step work, or he doesn't go for this prayer and meditation stuff, etc. etc. etc." . . . ad infinitum. And having identified ourselves with this imaginative 'WONDERFUL fellow' our conscience is easily lulled and we stand justified —so we think!

13. *"If I don't, he will"*—The favorite excuse for the one in business. The fact that one's competitor does this, that or the other shady business certainly does not change the basic moral law for us, but it certainly does provide a wonderful excuse for our breaking it because after all, "If I don't, he will," and so we are justified . . . are we, really?

14. *"It's a woman's privilege*—The ladies would like it much better if we left this one out, but then this is no time to be using an excuse, is it? And the one thing we could never find out about this almost universally used excuse about a woman's privilege, is who gave them the privilege? But gosh, it surely does excuse almost every eccentricity of womanhood, and justifies their every aberration, and gives them a blissful conscience, doesn't it?

15. *"I'm a little 'wacky' "*—Why some people would rather be considered a "little wacky" than a sinner is incomprehensible, but the fact is that many would. But do you know the real reason behind such 'screwy thinking'? Being a 'little wacky' excuses one from doing anything very seriously about all the faults and failings and sins. And it does soothe the conscience and blind one from the real truth. The real truth? If one is a sinner, he has an obligation of changing, hasn't he?

16. *"But, you see, I'm different"*—Different from what? But that matters very little, just so we are different from others —and who isn't, pray tell? "But to my mind if I am different (no matter how little or hazy that difference may be) I must then have *different* obligations, and since everybody else accepts most basic human obligations I must, since I am 'different,' be freed therefrom—especially those obligations I do not want to live up to." And so our conscience is 'salved' and we are justified in our misdeeds—well, at least in our own mind. Peace —it's wonderful!

17. *"I have changed"*—and of course since "I have 'changed' one would hardly hold me to anything I may have promised, or planned, or agreed to before 'I changed,' now would they? And, by 'changing' I have set aside rather easily, if not so truthfully, quite a number of old responsibilities. And then too, one would hardly be expected to have to live up to a promise made so long ago. And now I can go merrily along without the slightest pang or twinge of conscience and I do feel so justified."

18. *"Times change"*—This old stand-by takes several forms and is first cousin to the one above. "You gotta be modern" or "you gotta keep up with the times" express the same theme and are but two of its many dresses. And since the modern crowd does this or that, one simply must "keep up with the times." But we wonder what would happen to this excuse when placed side by side with the time-proven truth: "Times indeed do change a lot; but souls change very little; and God not at all." Gotcha thinking, hasn't it?

19. *"Well, I am always very frank and outspoken"*—And with that trump up my sleeve we may say what we please no matter whom it hurts or how much it may sting to the very depths the heart and soul of one to whom or about whom we are 'so frankly' speaking. Gosh, what an out: No effort needed now to "hold back" this or that unkind remark—just be frank! And so we are justified in omitting all that tedious discipline necessary so often to keep back the uncharitable dagger—which the Scriptures themselves tell us is the most difficult of disciplines. But you know something? The Scriptures also state that "he who thinks himself to be religious not bridling his tongue, that man's religion is "vain." And "vain," brother means 'worthless' in the English language.

20. *"You see, I'm the nervous type"*—And thus tantrum after tantrum; explosion after explosion: and fault after fault will go uncensored—for after all since "I'm the nervous type—it's nerves." Faults? Of course not, it's nerves! And that label so nicely fits any and all aberrations I don't want to overcome—listen: "I wasn't angry, I was only nervous!"; "I didn't 'blow-up' at him, it was my nerves!"; "I'm not lazy, just resting my

nerves!"; "I'm not jealous, she just simply makes me nervous!"; and on and on and on—by the way, who's kidding whom?

21. *"A.A. comes first"*—And thus, my friend, we are exempted from many, many obligations—to wife, home, work, and what have you. The excuse that has produced so many 'A.A. widows' throughout the ranks of A.A. And believe me, it is amazing how many otherwise honest fellows and gals blissfully side-step obligations of every sort with a smug: "A.A. comes first." It's the number three on the hit parade!

We could devote much space to a discussion of this, one of the most common excuses in A.A., but suffice it to repeat what we have written in our chapter on Attitudes, namely: A.A. does come first, BUT that means, chum, the twelve steps in one's daily living, not necessarily the TWELFTH STEP with all of its activities.

22. *"No dues, no fees, no money needed in A.A. so why should I give to this or to that . . ."*—And here comes the one in the number two spot on the hit parade of A.A. excuses. But a wonderful one to use for soothing the ole conscience when one wants to avoid giving to any A.A. project—from the weekly 'kitty' to the special 'kitty,' the Club, the banquet, and every request for financial donations. And to the above rationalization some subtly add: "And furthermore you can't buy and sell sobriety."

Since this excuse is one of the very "fine-line" ones, perhaps a little story might throw the light of exposure on it.

One time a preacher was urging all of his listeners to 'be saved.' And in flights of oratory he told them again and again: "And the salvation of the Lord costs us nothing; it is absolutely free."

After he had finished speaking, one of the audience approached him and queried: "Say preacher, you talk and talk and you say that salvation is free, that it costs us nothing. And then how is it that every time you preach you pass the collection basket?"

To this the preacher replied with an answer that is a classic: "Yassuh, I did and I do say that salvation is free, that it costs you nothing; just like the water that the good Lord has given us—it costs absolutely nothing, BUT when it comes to the 'piping,' we gotta pay for it!"

23. *"I'm an alcoholic"*—Lo, the number one excuse in A.A. And with this trump card up one's sleeve almost any aberration can be easily excused, and our conscience will feel peaceful, and our responsibility practically nullified. For what can one expect? "I'm AN ALCOHOLIC!"

We get angry—but what can you expect? We're alcoholics!

We are lazy—but what can you expect? We're alcoholics!

We are dishonest—we lie—but what can you expect? We're alcoholics!

We chisel and cheat, we nurse every fault we ever had—but what can you expect? We're alcoholics!

And on and on—but you know what? It won't be long until such will have to add an adjective to that excuse; or perhaps just another line: "We're alcoholics, and we're drinking again!"

But after all what DID YOU EXPECT?

Really, let's face it, aside from the compulsion to drink, there isn't any difference between the alcoholic and the rest of men. Remember the saying: "If you can't smell 'em, you can't tell 'em"?

THE TWELVE STEPS AND EXCUSES

But the lives of all are LOADED WITH EXCUSES which is but another way of saying that poor human nature is frantically endeavoring to justify itself and its actions, is trying to escape from responsibility, is trying again and again to minimize its guilt and is attempting at every turn to 'salve' its conscience so that it may somehow or other live IN PEACE WITH ITSELF.

Books and books could be written and much space given to little else but a listing of the thousands upon thousands of excuses that human beings have and do use. However such is not the scope of this book, and the above is merely a cross-sampling of the excuses that you and I, that all of us are familiar with. And as alcoholics we were past masters at the art of excuse making.

When we came to A.A. and were confronted with the twelve steps, again we were faced with a 'big' order to handle. And again we, with hangover of habit or designedly, used excuses in taking these steps; so that many members along the twelve steps' path have so rationalized and excused that they have never FULLY and HONESTLY taken the twelve steps LITERALLY. Why? It is the old story: we want to escape responsibility, we want to minimize our guilt, we want to justify ourselves in our omissions, and we want to thus 'salve' our consciences. Because we as alcoholics must have serenity even though it be 'FRANTIC' serenity.

1. *WE ADMITTED WE WERE POWERLESS OVER ALCOHOL AND THAT OUR LIVES HAD BECOME UNMANAGEABLE.*

Because of the necessity of admitting, perhaps for the first time in our lives, an absolute truth: THAT WE ARE POWERLESS; and because of the humility necessary to make such an admission, the alcoholic is adept at finding hundreds of excuses that will enable him 'in good conscience' and with 'self-justification' to avoid taking this step in a one hundred percent fashion. And among all of these rationalizations, perhaps the most common is that one that has been used for years and years. "But I'm not THAT bad." "Yes, I get drunk, I get into trouble, etc., etc., but POWERLESS? Oh no, I'M NOT THAT BAD!"

Some months ago the writer had a long-distance call from a party who was interested in helping a certain individual who had had difficulty with his drinking. His problem had become such that for many months he had not been able to work. And somewhere along the way someone had given him the writer's name whom he had been told might be able to get him work.

When the one with the problem himself came to the phone, he was asked whether he had had any contact with Alcoholics Anonymous. But to this 'insult' he quickly replied in typical excusing fashion: "O, but I'm not THAT BAD!"

To which came back just as quickly: "Then why in the world aren't you working?"

He now is a very active and sober member of A.A. and has an excellent position in which he is making a fine record.

However, there are many alcoholics who are not so easily exposed in their excuse-making and who thus come forward with many an added one to 'justify themselves'—in their drinking.

2. *WE CAME TO BELIEVE THAT A POWER GREATER THAN OURSELVES COULD RESTORE US TO SANITY.*

It is amazing and amusing to hear the many excuses that the fellows and gals produce in 'wholesale' fashion to get around this step—this 'God-business.' Let us examine the one most frequently expressed. It is an excellent fit for the present materialistic era. Listen:

"Yeah, I could possibly go for this God stuff, but after all You GOTTA BE PRACTICAL." So, in case you do not realize it, that excuses from all spiritual obligations, and in the excusing one is justified, escapes any responsiblity for so doing and lullabies to sleep that wee voice which most mortals call conscience.

It may not be out of place to mention at this juncture an observation on this second step which we feel is often overlooked, but which also often evokes excuses, and sometimes very amusing ones.

We say in the latter part of the second step that we could be "restored to sanity." Now it is the writer's opinion that we cannot be *restored* to anything unless we have been away from it. Therefore in this part of step II we are admitting that we HAVE BEEN INSANE. Else how could we be "*restored* to SANITY?"

And, of course, if we have been 'insane' or are 'neurotic' there are many other obligations that come along which will necessitate the sincere person's working at changing these 'personality patterns' which so often—WHETHER WE ADMIT IT OR NOT—got and still get us into trouble.

And here again—to justify our eccentricities and neurotic tangents of character—we are very expert at producing an excuse. Here's a rather amusing one heard at an A.A. meeting some years back:

The discussion had drifted into the question that is often 'kicked around' at A.A. gatherings, namely, "Are all alcoholics neurotic?" Pros and cons were given by the members—'pros' by the honest ones; 'cons' by the rationalizers. Then from the back of the meeting room came the pay-off. Suddenly in the middle of a lull in the discussion came this apt observation—a very patent excuse: "I object," this member answered to the remark that all alcoholics ARE neurotic, "Neurotics is nuts, and I ain't nuts!"

"I beg you hold me excused!"

3. *WE MADE A DECISION TO TURN OUR WILL AND OUR LIVES OVER TO THE CARE OF GOD AS WE UNDERSTOOD HIM.*

Much has already been written on this step and the difficulties in taking it in our chapter on Happiness. But there is one excuse used in side-stepping it that is a most common one, and which is very frequently used by human nature in escaping responsibility of all sorts and in justifying all of our procrastinations. And that excuse is just one little word: "Mañana" —which translated means "tomorrow" and which Augustine so aptly calls the "corvina" or "raven" of work, duty, and virtue. "Tomorrow"—"yessir, I'm going to take the third step—TOMORROW." But, you know—there happens only and always to be just TODAY. For we can never do anything tomorrow—not until tomorrow becomes TODAY—and if we are always going to take the step TOMORROW—that means in plain language—NEVER! But it does make us seem to have GOOD WILL, and GOOD INTENTIONS, (but incidentally not many GOOD ACTIONS) and that justifies us, and 'salves' our conscience and permits us to escape without too much disturbance many, many responsibilities.

And thus always and everywhere: "I beg you hold me excused TODAY—because I'm going to do it TOMORROW!"

Whom ARE you kidding?—besides YOURSELF!

4. *WE MADE A SEARCHING AND FEARLESS MORAL INVENTORY OF OURSELVES.*

A job and a big one. And a rather 'nasty' one, too—very unpleasant. So we need a good excuse here—and a very common one is taken from the Scriptures—that gives it authority. "A searching and fearless moral inventory? Why, I just don't believe in such things for the Scriptures say: 'Let the dead bury the dead,' and again, 'Let sleeping dogs lie,' and furthermore it 'disturbs my peace of mind'!"

And having what we think is scriptural backing, our conscience is in fine mettle, we are justified, and escape much guilt and responsibility of restitution.

By the way, where is it also written: "Woe be to them who cry, 'Peace, peace where there is no peace,"?

'FRANTIC' serenity!

5. *WE ADMITTED TO GOD, TO OURSELVES AND TO ANOTHER HUMAN BEING THE EXACT NATURE OF OUR WRONGS.*

In this step we very often find used another excuse that justifies procrastination in order ultimately to side-step or omit all or part of the humbling experience intended by the fifth step. And again, under the mantle of truth, an axiom of A.A. is adduced in the role of an excuse. "Easy does it"—so why make oneself go to another human being? "Easy does it"—so why take a chance in revealing my misdeeds to another one? "Easy does it"—there's plenty of time to take this step. And lo and behold "Easy does it" gets an entirely new meaning, which translated means: "Keep putting it off, chum—that's the EASIEST way out of it!"

6. *WE WERE ENTIRELY READY TO HAVE GOD REMOVE THESE DEFECTS OF CHARACTER.*

"Who, me? Why, I'm too bad for that. You just don't know what I have done. I've done too many wrongs for God to forgive and to change me." An excuse stemming from 'big-shot-itis' in reverse. It is positive that we're not the best guys now, so why not be the worst? And then, too, that excuses us from doing anything about all of our past. And it justifies us in retaining all of our defects of character, and soothes our conscience, and we are freed from all responsibility.

It seems like one of God's greatest attributes has disappeared—His mercy. What is that He tells us: "the greater the sin, the greater the mercy"?

7. *HUMBLY ASKED HIM TO REMOVE OUR SHORTCOMINGS.*

"Humbly"—which means that it demands humility. And wherever there is a question of practicing humility, the pathologically proud alcoholic immediately seeks escape and becomes the master again in excuse-making. And in the seventh step one of the most common goes something like this: "God knows me, so why should I bother to ask Him to remove my shortcomings?" or "Who am I to tell God what to do." Very subtle, very suave and very effective—in justifying one's faults, and in minimizing their guilt.

They tell the story of the old fellow who was asked by his minister why he did not say his prayers. To the query of the minister the old fellow always replied: "Me pray? Why who am I to tell the good Lord how to run his business?"

"I beg you hold me excused!"

8. *WE MADE A LIST OF ALL THE PEOPLE WE HAD HARMED AND BECAME WILLING TO MAKE AMENDS TO THEM ALL.*

In this step the most often used excuse consists of only one little word: "BUT." "Yes, I did a lot of wrong, BUT—it wasn't ALL my fault—BUT—HE also harmed ME—BUT—it just couldn't have been helped."

And thus, in blaming others our responsibility is minimized, we 'salve' our consciences and we are justified in omitting many 'harms' from our list.

By the way, who is going to even THOSE up?

9. *WE MADE DIRECT AMENDS WHEREVER POSSIBLE EXCEPT WHEN TO DO SO WOULD INJURE THEM OR OTHERS.*

In this step many fail to derive any benefit and excuse themselves from the many valuable acts of humility intended by it by glibly coming forth with, "My priest, (minister, adviser, etc.), said it wasn't necessary." Having gone to such a one who although perhaps thoroughly grounded in theology was not familiar with the basic needs of the alcoholic, these individuals indeed were told that it would be sufficient to make INDIRECT amends, and that such would suffice to satisfy justice and rights and restitution. However any solid A.A. could have told them in the twelve steps 'something has been added' in this matter of restitution, that DIRECT amends are advised because thus and thus alone does the alcoholic acquire true PRACTICE of humility, which humility the alcoholic needs perhaps more than anything else. But by INDIRECT amends we keep our anonymity, don't we? Yea, chum, we keep our PRIDE too... ! And incidentally, we are laying aside a 'leetle' drink for a rainy, blue day! ? Indirectly!

10. *WE CONTINUED TO TAKE PERSONAL INVENTORY AND WHEN WRONG PROMPTLY ADMITTED IT.*

Stepping all around this step but never taking it are all of the many "extroverts" in A.A. And with the mental 'ambidexterity' of such they proffer a time-worn excuse: "It disturbs my peace of mind." But of course such do not hear the echo that always accompanies such an excuse, and which has been and is sounded down through the ages: "Peace, peace, and there is no PEACE"—except on the surface. So these deluded souls go blissfully on in their frenzied activity with their 'frantic serenity,' and their consciences are 'salved' but never HEALED until the day sooner or later when their 'problems' will 'come busting out all over'—with the help of the bottle. Better continue the process begun in the FOURTH step, fella, it is much easier to daily 'dislodge' than to ultimately 'dynamite'—remember? ? ?

11. *WE SOUGHT THROUGH PRAYER AND MEDITATION TO IMPROVE OUR CONSCIOUS CONTACT WITH GOD AS WE UNDERSTOOD HIM, PRAYING ONLY FOR KNOWLEDGE OF HIS WILL FOR US AND THE POWER TO CARRY IT OUT.*

In approaching this step, which, incidentally, could contribute so much to peace of mind, sobriety and serenity, one very frequently sees it side-stepped by the much over-worked excuse: "I ain't no 'Bible-thumper,' I ain't no 'pious-puss,' I don't go for that constant prayer business." And to this is usually added an echo of the excuse used in the seventh step, "and furthermore, God knows what I need, He knows what to do."

How very true, chum, BUT do YOU? !

12. *HAVING HAD A SPIRITUAL AWAKENING AS A RESULT OF THESE STEPS, WE TRIED TO CARRY THIS MESSAGE TO ALCOHOLICS AND TO PRACTICE THESE PRINCIPLES IN ALL OF OUR AFFAIRS.*

Since this step comprises much on the activity side of the program with its speaking, twelfth-step calls, meetings, etc., etc., we find hundreds of excuses offered. But again, let's look at only one—a very frequent one: "I wouldn't mind speaking, (or I wouldn't mind making twelfth-step calls, etc.), but I have so many other things to do!" And so, with smug conscience, we enjoy all the blessings of sobriety without having to make an effort to give in return. Shades of the parables! "I bought a farm and must go see it; I have bought five yoke of oxen and must go try them; I married a wife . . . I beg you hold me excused." But you know what? It won't be very long until those old excuses are again slightly changed—"I bought a 'fifth' and must go sample it." Which you WILL.

LET'S FACE IT

"And the TRUTH shall make you free . . ."

As we have tried again and again to point out in previous chapters, the tenth, eleventh and twelfth steps are the DAILY living of the A.A. program. And if we look a bit closer in our analysis, we shall find that all three have ONE AIM—namely, TO LEARN TRUTH IN ORDER TO ELIMINATE THE HABIT OF EXCUSE, so that gradually and little by little we can motivate our daily living WITH TRUTH instead of the habit of excuses.

In the TENTH STEP we take our REGULAR inventory so that we may be able to see ourselves AS WE ARE—faults, talents and all; IN ORDER TO LEARN THE TRUTH ABOUT OURSELVES and thus eliminate EXCUSES about ourselves.

In the ELEVENTH STEP we seek through daily prayer and meditation to LEARN THE TRUTH ABOUT GOD AND OURSELVES, and thus knowing the TRUTH about our relationship with God, we are able to eliminate the habit of excusing ourselves in our obligations to GOD.

In the TWELFTH STEP we work with others, with our neighbor, IN ORDER TO LEARN THE TRUTH ABOUT OUR NEIGHBOR AND OURSELVES so that thus knowing the true RELATIONSHIP between OUR NEIGHBOR AND OURSELVES we are able to eliminate the habit of excuse which so often wrongly freed us from so many of our OBLIGATIONS TO OUR NEIGHBOR.

In these three steps we also find on further analysis that there CORE is MEDITATION which is nothing more nor less than A SEARCHING WITH GOD FOR TRUTH IN ORDER THAT WE MAY ULTIMATELY MOTIVATE OUR LIVING WITH TRUTH INSTEAD OF THE HABIT OF EXCUSES. And so we do not hesitate to offer as our opinion that WITHOUT MEDITATION CONTENTED SOBRIETY IS IMPOSSIBLE; and WITHOUT CONTENTMENT, SOBRIETY WILL NOT BE PERMANENT. "We SOUGHT through . . . MEDITATION."

This is probably the most talkative age of history—not only because of the abundance of mechanical devices to diffuse our talking, but also because we have little inside our minds which did not come there from the world outside our minds, so that human communication seems to us a great necessity. There are few listeners, although St. Paul tells us that "faith comes from hearing." IF THE BODIES OF MOST OF US WERE FED AS LITTLE AS THE MIND, THEY WOULD SOON STARVE TO DEATH. Many otherwise good and pious individuals wonder why they make little or no progress in their spiritual life in spite of daily and frequent vocal prayer. The real reason is that THEY ARE SPIRITUALLY MENTALLY STARVED. They say hundreds of verbal prayers—but they never regularly meditate and as a result they are attempting to live in a SPIRITUAL VACUUM—a methaphysical impossibility. And so there is of necessity hyperactivity, restlessness, talkativeness—and a tremendous over-emphasis on activity and movement. One's soul and body in this contradictory state of affairs is constantly attempting to REST IN MOTION. Whence such excuses as "I went out to a party to RELAX!"; or for a drive, or dancing, or on a trip! Someone has said that the rocking chair is symbolically of this vacuum-starved mentality of the era —it enables one to sit in one place and still be on the go.

ANYONE WHO BECOMES ILL AT EASE OR DISQUIETED WHEN THE ACTIVITIES OF THE DAY OR EVENING CEASE AND ONE IS ALONE PROVES THAT HE OR SHE IS LIVING IN FLIGHT FROM HIS OR HER TRUE SELF. Gregariousness, the passionate need for a crowd, or the "gang"; or the incessant urge to identify oneself with the tempo of the time; or the continual "pushing the day into the night" is proof positive that one is seeking distraction from innerself, because innerself is a void, is a vacuum, is SPIRITUALLY MENTALLY STARVED. As we mentioned above in the beginning: "they attempt forgetfulness by courting the sham fancies of the night and by rushing headlong through the chores of the day"—EVEN THE SPIRITUAL CHORES.

In their spiritual life, not even having stopped long enough to KNOW GOD in meditation, they again resort to constant activity—prayers, services, novenas—by the dozen. Thus they cover up their true spiritual status which is built upon activity and not on God's will. They merely WORK for God; they do not LOVE Him. They do not want to be on the "outs" with God, as a clerk does not want to be on the "outs" with his boss. And so, with so little love operative in their arid and empty spiritual life, God's law and prayer are regarded as mere correctives, as something negative and restraining to their wishes. They ask of prayer that they keep from serious sin—that they will be enabled to restrained themselves MODERATELY in their avarice, in their selfishness, in their intemperances, in their sins of the flesh. Their excuses in pursuing this half-track to God which always ends in wreckage here or hereafter are ridiculous. Listen to a few: "just a 'white' lie; just a 'little' drink; just a 'little' petting or 'pitching'; God can have this and that BUT THIS AND THAT I SHALL KEEP FOR MYSELF, and after all I do say a lot of prayers." Like the wife who sets out just what her husband may and may not do and then adds: "And after all I do 'yackity-yack' at you so much!"

Such souls have no REAL desire to know what God WANTS —they only wish to TELL Him what THEY want Him to do— SO MUCH, NO MORE. One finds out what God really wants ONLY IN MEDITATION.

MEDITATION feeds the mind with TRUTH about God, themselves and their neighbor—it breaks down and through the self-deceit and the excuses which so foster the aimless and ceaseless activity of which we have spoken. It puts back again into one's life the only safe guide-post: HIS Laws as He meant them to be, to offset the excusing habit of His laws as WE want them to be FOR US.

But here after human ingenuity and diabolical rationalization side-steps what seems to be such an evident truth and necessity for both peace of soul and salvation—with an excuse. ANY excuse—just so it will justify more activity, just so it will EXCUSE one from FACING THE TRUTH in meditation. A common one: "I'm too busy"—and of course, with the overactivated-mind-starved-triphammer-gregarious-soul there is little doubt but that they are VERY BUSY—in fact they ARE too busy—PERIOD. For, if one is TOO BUSY to meditate regularly, that person is TOO BUSY.

Little do they realize that logic (of which they have seemingly such paltry knowledge) would point out to them that it is IMPOSSIBLE not to have enough time to meditate. Rather, it is just the opposite: the MORE ONE MEDITATES THE MORE TIME ONE WILL HAVE. We don't have enough time for God because we don't think enough of Him in meditation. The time one has for anything or anyone depends on how much one values such. THINKING DETERMINES THE USE OF TIME; TIME DOES NOT RULE OUR THINKING. So the problems of spirituality, of spiritual reading, of prayer and meditation IS NEVER A MATTER OF TIME; it is A PROBLEM OF THOUGHT. Silence and thought have made many a saint; WORDS AND TALK NEVER HAVE—it is POSSIBLE to pray VOCALLY until life's last hour and still lose one's soul; it is IMPOSSIBLE to MEDITATE regularly and lose one's soul—for, it does not require much TIME or ACTIVITY to make a saint—it requires only MUCH LOVE—and who can LOVE a person without FREQUENTLY thinking about them???

So let's take a closer look at this meditation business, which seems to prove such a stumbling block to so many. Why, we know not, for in reality MEDITATION IS SO SIMPLE. Again, it is merely A THINKING ABOUT TRUTH IN THE PRESENCE OF GOD IN ORDER TO MOTIVATE OUR LIVES WITH TRUTH INSTEAD OF THE HABIT OF EXCUSES.

It need not be formal. We personally feel that the less formality the better. We need only to see that there are THREE ingredients:

1) *The presence of God.*
2) *Thinking.*
3) *A decision to apply the truth to our lives.*

It is immaterial WHERE we meditate, or WHEN we meditate, or WHAT POSITION WE TAKE when we meditate. We can meditate ANYWHERE, because God is EVERYWHERE especially inside us, so that no matter WHERE we may be GOD IS PRESENT.

We may take any POSITION when we meditate. We may sit down, or stand up, or lie down, or walk up and down—or, should it more facilitate the matter for some alcoholics—we may even "stand on our heads" to generate the thinking process! Many may prefer to kneel, but we should bear in mind that all of this makes little difference to God who is not looking at our position but at OUR HEARTS. Just so we "set and think" instead of only "settin'!"

Likewise, one may meditate morning, noon or night. For this too makes no difference to God, we feel sure. However, it will facilitate the forming of a HABIT of meditation if we set aside a REGULAR time each day. It gives our wills something to hang on to. It is good psychology.

What should one meditate about? We should meditate about TRUTH—ANY TRUTH. They may be truths about God, about our neighbor, about ourselves, about objective things—about ANYTHING. A few examples: death, God, marriage, alcoholism, drunkenness, Christ, the Bible, the universe, the laws of nature, the virtues, the vices and on and on—ANY of the thousands of truths. ALL we need to do is to EXAMINE IT IN THE PRESENCE OF GOD; APPLY IT TO OURSELVES AND OUR LIVES; MAKE A DECISION TO MOTIVATE OUR LIVING BY IT.

A good spiritual book will be a great help to many in guiding their thinking—especially in the beginning. SPIRITUAL READING provides the FUEL FOR MEDITATION, it gives us FOOD FOR THOUGHT. And we should never forget that the MORE SPIRITUAL our reading is, the MORE PRACTICAL IT WILL BECOME!

Is there a METHOD for our meditations? There are hundreds in the many volumes written about meditation. But here again, let's keep it simple. We are alcoholics, remember? And of all the methods, we feel that there is one that is very simple, very effective, and very easy to use. That we like to call the "Who, which, what" method. And in using it, all we do is to present the truth to be meditated about to our minds and ask the SEVEN BASIC QUESTIONS OF ANALYSIS:

Who?
What?
Why?
Where?
By what means?
How?
When?

The answers to these seven questions will give ample analysis of any truth and will provide an excellent and effective meditation. A detailed example will be given later on in the meditation on death, appended to this little booklet.

The secret of every meditation is the DECISION, for action is still the magic word. In other words, when we meditate we should always conclude by thinking to ourselves: IF THIS OR THAT OR THE OTHER THING BE TRUE—THEREFORE WE SHALL DO THIS OR THAT OR THE OTHER THING—TODAY.

Let us never forget that the more we meditate the less we shall excuse ourselves; the less we excuse ourselves, the more we shall accept; the more we accept, the less conflict shall we have; and the less conflict we have the more peace of mind; the more serenity we shall acquire. An it is our opinion that UNLESS A HUMAN BEING MEDITATES OF HIS OWN FREE WILL, THE DAY WILL COME AND HAS COME FOR ALL OF US WHEN GOD WILL FORCE US TO MEDITATE—and THAT meditation will not be so pleasant. Remember coming off the last binge?

THEREFORE if we regularly meditate, we shall never HAVE to meditate! So—

LET'S FACE IT!

A MEDITATION

"It is appointed unto man ONCE to die . . ."

There is one truth about which there is no controversy—and that truth is death. We do not believe that any of our readers would deny that some day sooner or later and soon at the latest, we are all going to die. It is the most universal of all facts—the most undeniable of all truths—the one immutable law that admits of no exception. SO let's meditate . . . and place before our mind the truth—WE . . . MUST . . . DIE. And let us place ourselves in the presence of God . . . each in his own way . . . ever mindful of His Presence and ever asking His guidance. . . .

Down through the ages from the very beginning of the human race, every one who has ever lived has finally died. First let us look at the Scriptures and see how they in their story of the early years of time tell us that we must die.

In the Scriptures we read that Adam lived nine hundred and thirty years, and then . . .HE DIED. And on through its pages the Scriptures always appends those two little words to close the chapter of every mortal.

There we read that Seth lived nine hundred and twelve years, and . . .HE DIED. Enos live nine hundred and five years . . . and . . .He DIED. Methuselah, supposedly the longest-lived of any man, lived all of nine hundred and sixty-nine years, but in the end is appended those two little words: "HE DIED."

And on through its pages, again and again . . . to close every life . . . is DEATH . . . as expressed in those two simple words . . . "HE DIED" . . . David and Solomon . . . and Abraham. . . and Isaac . . . and Jacob . . . and Daniel . . . and Joseph . . . and the Apostles . . . and Paul . . . and Mary . . . and even Christ on Calvary . . . each telling us over and over again . . . "It is appointed unto man ONCE to die." So that should we ask the Scriptures they will tell us on almost every page . . . WE . . . MUST . . . DIE.

And likewise, all of nature tells us the same truth.

If we would ask the sun which rises in the dawn and slowly ascends to its zenith at mid-day and then sinks almost imperceptibly in the west at even-tide and disappears, the sun would tell us that such is our life. We enter life at birth and through the years grow into manhood and womanhood only to finally sink into the grave and disappear from this world . . . forever.

If we would ask the seasons which so orderly follow one another, the seasons would tell us that just as summer follows spring; and spring, winter; and winter, fall; and fall, summer again; so too, in life we follow our forefathers, and others will follow us, and others them again, each closing his or her chapter of life . . . in death.

If we would ask the streams that flow through the fields, the streams would tell us that life is like a stream. The first years of the stream are spent in obscurity—then it hastens on over rugged rocks, through gloomy forests, and dashes over yawning precipices, and passes through blooming landscapes . . . and on and on until . . . at last . . . it sinks into the silent ocean never to return. Thus too is our life—a life of joy and sorrow —a life of pleasure and pain—a life of innocence and sin. We hurry on and on until at last we sink into the silent ocean of eternity—NEVER MORE TO RETURN.

If we would ask history, all history would tell us that we must die.

Where are the nations of old? Those nations that once gloried in their splendor and achievements? The power of Rome? The splendor of Egypt? The talent of Greece? And their leaders? The Napoleons? The Ceasars? The Washingtons? The Mussolinis? The Hitlers? . . . they . . . are . . . dead! And their glory and their splendor and their power is buried with them.

Where are many of the companions we ourselves knew in our youth? The companions of the dance? Of the games? Of the theatre? Of the school? Our drinking companions . . . many are dead . . . and perhaps . . . God forbid . . . some may have died drunk? ? ? And in them all is mirrored the inevitable truth of death.

Every moment, the statisticians tell us, someone, somewhere, is dying. Right NOW . . . SOMEONE . . . SOMEWHERE . . . IS PASSING ON INTO ETERNITY. Some day . . . we . . . shall travel the same path . . . this fact we cannot possibly doubt.

YET we don't like to think about death! Even though every moment since birth has been a struggle to keep alive, we still try to shun the thought of death. We try to smooth it over . . . we try to minimize its impact . . . we *try* to *excuse* its reality. Listen. . . .

"He passed away. . . . "He left us. . . ." "He slept away. . . ." EVERYTHING BUT HE DIED! We attend a funeral, and what do we hear? "He is as he is asleep"—(as if we know how he looked when asleep!)

And why? Why are we afraid of the very thought of death? (We really shouldn't be afraid to die, for after all it is merely knocking off work for all eternity!) We are afraid of death, because we have a stinking suspicion THAT WE ARE NOT READY TO DIE TODAY. And that is the reason that we were told long, long ago: "In all thy works, O man, remember thy last end and thou shalt never sin." For death is the most powerful motive we have to live well and rightly. And IN DEATH we learn the TRUTH of LIFE. We learn ourselves TRUTHFULLY in relation to LIFE. In death we achieve our TRUE stature, and bring everything of life into TRUE perspective.

"I'll sing you a song of the world and its ways;
And the many strange people we meet;
From the rich man who rolls in his millions of wealth
To the struggling poor wretch on the street.
But a man though he's poor and in tatter's and rags,
We should never affect to despise;
But think of that adage: "remember my friends,
That six feet of earth make us all of one size!"

So, now let us 'who, which and what' awhile, huh?

And let us ask ourselves, "WHAT is death?" Well, ... death is the end of life. It is the end of all we know and have here in this world. The finale to our association with our family, our friends, or enemies, our hobbies, our home, our business our job, our pleasures, our pains, our joys, our sorrows—the end of all things material. And then? ... You take it from there a few minutes, for what happens after that last heart beat is a matter of divergent belief and of doctrine and a little bit outside the scope of A.A. to discuss. ...

And now "WHO is going to die?" We. I. YOU. That big ego whom we think so much of right now, some day sooner or later and soon at the latest is going ... to ... die. And then it is going to shrink ... and shrink ... and shrink ... into dust and ashes where finally as the poet told us above, we all achieve our true size. Yes, chum, YOU ... gotta ... DIE!

WHERE are we going to die? Away from home, friends, loved ones? Alone? Among strangers? or, God grant, at home surrounded by all those who were nearest and dearest in life. Where? We just don't know.

BY WHAT MEANS are we going to die? In an accident? After a long illness? By a painful illness? Suicide—actual or by the bottle? It COULD happen—it HAS HAPPENED!

And WHY must we die? But here again we are liable to step on someone's "doctrinal toes" so we shall let each one answer that in his own way. But for all Christians the answer is given in the Scriptures, "Death entered into this world by SIN" ... and so. ....

WHEN are we going to die? ... nobody knows the time nor the hour. It may be ten years, it may be ten months, it may be ten days or ... it may be ten minutes! That COULD happen. That HAS happened. The writer was speaking to an A.A. group in the middle west some years back and made just that remark. Just as the meeting ended, one of the members dropped dead! (And you can be sure that the rest of them got on the program that night!) But the fact remains, we simply do NOT know WHEN we are going to die, and it could happen at ANY moment.

A few interesting examples from A.A.:

Bill B. made our first A.A. Retreat back in 1946. The next day Bill dropped dead.

During one year in one of the groups, three members died. One dropped dead suddenly; one died after a prolonged illness; one was killed. We know not the time nor the hour!

A member of A.A. down in the southland had been sober for five years. But in all of these years he seemed never to be able to find contentment and happiness. He attended one of our southern Retreats. There he seemed to get all the answers to his problems and seemed very happy. Three weeks passed and suddenly after a meeting one evening, he got drunk! Within forty-eight hours he was in the hospital coming off it. Two days later, perfectly sober, he called the nurse and said: "Nurse, I'm going to die—but I'm ready."—And he dropped dead!

Another member had made a reservation for our midwestern Retreat. On the day he was to leave home to attend the Retreat, several other members came by his house to pick him up. He came out to the car, started to get in—and he dropped dead! He had already made his *last Retreat*—the year before.

Way down in Texas where A.A. is vibrant and full, one of the members was chairman of the meeting. He introduced the speaker—then he dropped dead!

Now what would all of these fellows have to say to us now about this question of WHEN. We wonder if they wouldn't tell us: "Since no one knows WHEN, it behooves all to find out HOW," and so. . . .

HOW are we going to die? And that is the sixty-four dollar question. For on that answer, bub, is going to depend an 'awful lot of eternity.' HOW are we going to die? A friend of God? Or His enemy? Prepared? Or unprepared? Sober? Or, God forbid, DRUNK? People HAVE died drunk, haven't they? Did you ever see somebody die drunk? And what is that we say in

A.A. so often and have on the placards of most of our meeting places: "There, BUT FOR THE GRACE OF GOD, go I." And that means that there is ONLY ONE THING THAT IS GOING TO GIVE ME A SOBER AND HAPPY DEATH—THE GRACE OF GOD. For neither money nor talents, friends nor relations, nor any material thing in all the world can assure us of a sober and happy death; ONLY the GRACE OF GOD obtained through humble and sincere, persistent and consistent "prayer and meditation."

In 1923, eight of the most successful business men in the United States held a meeting in a hotel in a midwestern city. They were:

1) The President of the largest independent steel company—a millionaire;

2) The President of the largest public utilities company—a millionaire;

3) The President of the largest gas company—a millionaire;

4) The greatest wheat speculator—a millionaire;

5) The President of the New York Stock Exchange—a millionaire;

6) A member of the President's Cabinet—a millionaire;

7) The greatest "bear" on Wall Street—a millionaire;

8) The President of the Bank of International Settlements —a millionaire—V.I.P.—very important people!

Eight men with perhaps the world's greatest accumulation of financial security! BUT

In 1952—just twenty-nine years later, these eight world's great and successful financiers gave the following amazing picture:

1) The President of the largest independent Steel Company—Charles Schwab—died bankrupt and had to live on borrowed money for five years before his death!

2) The President of the largest public utilities company—Samuel Insull—died penniless in a foreign land!

3) The President of the largest gas company—Howard Hopson—went insane before his death!

4) The greatest wheat speculator—Arthur Cutten—died abroad insolvent!

5) The President of the New York Stock Exchange—Richard Whitney—was prior to his death sentenced to Sing Sing prison!

6) The member of the President's Cabinet—Albert Fall—was pardoned from prison so he could die at home!

7) The greatest "bear" on Wall Street—Jesse Livermore—died a suicide!

8) The President of the Bank of International Settlements—Leon Fraser—died a suicide! R.I.P. God grant... !

"Sic transit... !"

Well? . . .

"Speak history! Who are life's victors?
Unroll thy long annals and say . . .
Are these whom the world calls victors?
Who won the success of a day?
The martyrs or Nero? The Spartans
Who fell Thermopylae's tryst?
Or the Persians or Xerxes? His judges
or Socrates?
Was it Pilate ? ? ? Or
Was it Christ?"

So come let us visit a deathbed NOW so we can know a bit about this dying business. Let us visit the deathbed of someone very near and dear to us—OUR OWN. And first let us see what our deathbed scene might be like.

And it COULD and MIGHT be a mess! For it COULD happen that we are DRUNK and DYING. Let's take a look.

That isn't really a bed we are stretched out upon—just a metal straw-covered cot. We are in a small, dingy, dark, damp room. It's just a small back room down skid-row way. AND we are alone—and awfully drunk.

The beads of perspiration are thick and heavy on our face and brow. There is a glassy, vacant, frightened stare in our eyes. ALONE and DRUNK and DYING!

Our friends? We have left them long ago. And with pride in our heart and a bottle to our lips we have progressively and persistently gone down and down. Each drunk became just a little bit worse. Each binge took us a little bit further away from our friends, our family, our loved ones.

A.A.? Huh, that wasn't for us! WE weren't that bad. Yeah, just a bunch of hypocrites. Well, maybe so, but they were HAPPY hypocrites weren't they? And especially they were SOBER hypocrites. Too bad we didn't get in with them—feel sure there would have been room for one more hypocrite!

Then there is a vision—or perhaps we better call it a nightmare—the D.T.'s, the old "Brooklyn Boys!" Back in all their demoniacal cussedness in death as they had visited us several times in life. The D.T.'s—and we are dying!

We turn from the horror of it all. We turn our alcohol-soaked body and our terror-filled mind away—away to a dingy, dirty cracked wall—and then the curtain of life slowly falls and we—drunk—meet our God—in Eternity! We die!

Possible? That COULD happen, IF we persistently refuse to DO anything about all those things in our life that MIGHT cause a slip. IF we persistently neglect this "prayer-business" and this "God-stuff." IF WE ARE DEPENDENT FOR OUR SOBRIETY ON ANYTHING LESS THAN THE GRACE OF GOD.

But now let us hasten to visit another deathbed scene. Let us visit the deathbed scene of OUR OWN DEATH as WE WOULD LIKE IT TO BE.

Finally the day has arrived—the hour has come. But we are not afraid. And why are we not afraid? Because we have frequently visited this scene during life in meditation and thus have lived each twenty-four hours as we would have wished to live on the day we are to die. So, we are ready. God is no stranger to us. Day in and day out we have "sought Him in prayer and meditation." In fact we have become very close friends with Him. And now in place of fear there is sort of a 'longing' to be with Him always—to know Him still better—to meet Him 'face to face.'

We are at home. We look around and see there gathered around us our family and our loved ones. Their lips are moving—in unison and in prayer. Nor do we see fear on their faces, but the semblance of peace of mind arising from a knowledge and conviction that we are ready for death and that they in turn before very long will follow but to be with us again—for always. And then in the midst of the darkness of death, there comes to our grace-enlightened souls the vision of all those we have known in life:—those we had merely met in passing along life's highway; those we had come to know well and to love; those we had met in A.A.—a hundred and fifty thousand friends! ; those we had sponsored and had helped and had confronted; those we had prayed for in life, now praying for us in death; and with that vision the curtain slowly falls upon our worldly abode and opens into eternity! What a beautiful scene!

Possible? Yes . . . even probable. In fact, it can BE CERTAIN . . . IF

We LIVE EACH DAY AS WE WOULD WANT TO HAVE LIVED ON THE DAY WE DIE . . . for as WE LIVE WE DIE . . . and, THEREFORE, if we LIVE EACH DAY WELL, NO MATTER WHAT DAY WE MAY DIE, WE CAN BE CERTAIN THAT WE SHALL DIE WELL . . . and THAT is all that matters!

Now—since we are facing this truth of death HONESTLY, let's see about a few things in our lives that maybe we should do something about if we REALLY hope to die well.

1) *Those decisions* we have been GOING to make for so long a time?

2) Those *resentments* that we are hanging on to; which we are doing NOTHING about?

3) That *pride* that we are letting push us all over the place—always in front; always first; always better than the next fellow; and on and on?

4) That insatiable determination to pile up *material* security? Remember the eight men?

5) That *illicit relationship,* which if we are honest, we KNOW is not right?

6) That habit of *gossip?* Of slander? Of unjust criticism?

7) That *intolerance?* Bigotry?

8) Those *dishonesties?* Debt? Injustice in business?

9) That neglect of PRAYER? OF GOD?

And all those things which are a stone wall separating us from the fullness of God's grace, and which COULD bring about the FIRST deathbed scene! Remember? There BUT FOR THE GRACE OF GOD . . . GO I!

AND NOW what ARE you going to do about it
TODAY?

THAT, my friend, is YOUR job!....

GRATITUDE

"Were not ten made clean? ... Where are the other nine... ?"

Most people prefer dogs to cats. It is therefore about a ten to one chance that you like dogs and do not like cats. You may like cats, but if you do you are the exception. And what is more you also will like dogs. In fact you will in all likelihood have a liking for most inhabitants of the animal kingdom, just as some people here and there have no use for any animals.

The reason that most people like dogs is a very real one. Primarily it is because dogs are such *grateful* animals. You rub them behind the ears, and they grovel with gratitude at your feet. You bring them their food, and they run to you, barking their appreciation and frisking about you with a friendliness that warms even the most forlorn heart. However hungry the dog may be, he takes time out to first look up at you with a misty thank you in his eyes which is unmistakable even before he begins to gulp his food down. When, on a cold winter day, you let him come into the house, he repays you his thanks by his tail wagging which seems endless. And when you are gone for awhile, and return home even after a brief absence, he welcomes you with an enthusiasm that makes your return seem to have been a very special favor to him.

But cats—on the average they are very selfish creatures. Even when they appear to rub themselves affectionately and gratefully against your leg, you seem to sense that they are doing it for purely sensory satisfaction. They purr and they press against you, not because you happen to be you and they are grateful, but they are delighting in their fur being rubbed back into place and in the pleasure they are receiving from it. Feed them, and they take their food with a sniffy-like condescension. Allow them to place near the hearth and they bask in its warmth, close their eyes, and proceed to drift into self-satisfied slumber without so much as a glance, grateful or contemptuous, in your direction.

Dogs are extroverts, pouring themselves out upon you. They are continually conscious of what is and what moves about them.

Cats are introverts, living in a smug little world of their own and always seeking therein their own comfort and convenience. It is only some happening about them which might provoke a fear of being disturbed that will awaken them to the surrounding events.

Dogs are loyal and show loyal gratitude to a master irrespective of the type of master he or she may be. It is because of this that a dog will follow his master, even though such master might be indifferent or even cruel, and he will follow that master into poverty, walk at his heels over the most uncomfortable roads, leave a cozy home for a miserable cabin, and then act all the while as if he were privileged to be accompanying his master.

Many a cat on the other hand will watch the best of masters go away and calmly and unperturbedly remain behind in the comfortable house which it much prefers to any human companionship. Even after a stray cat has been warmed and fed and housed for the night, try to coax it outside with you the next day if the weather be foul, you will find that the recipient of all of your favors will choose not to show its gratitude by following you, but selfishly remain inside the shelter of your abode. Indeed if you want a cat to go with you, the only way usually is to force it along in your hand basket. From the viewpoint of the average cat you personally happen to be just a convenience to which it has grown accustomed and which if necessary it can easily do without.

To a dog you are his world—you are his everything. And his tail is continually wagging in sonnets of gratitude. His bark, and even his playful growl—yes, even his snapping is usually a song of thanksgiving. And when he cavorts before you he flings himself about with gestures of worship which no pagan ever accorded to his idol. He loves you for the scraps from the table no matter how meager, and he is likewise appreciative for even an idle stroking of his head which you at times may do in absent-mindedness. And above all—he never fails to let you know it!

And that is probably why we like dogs. We all love gratitude and always react with a warm glow to the act of appreciation, to the cards of thanks, to the letter of gratitude. And maybe that is the real reason most people don't like cats—we all despise ingratitude and even the most hardened of men dislike the ingrate. And yet—there are very, very many humans in this old world who are ungrateful or at least who never take the time to show their gratitude. We hesitate to label such as ingrates—perhaps a better term would be 'thoughtless' in place of 'thankless.' But the fact remains, most people are not grateful in *action* no matter how deep the feeling of appreciation may penetrate on the occasion of a favor or kindness or gift. And it is without doubt because of this that the act of kindness whatsoever it may have been dies within the heart to which it was given—for it was not returned to its donor nor was it in appreciation passed on to another. "What we keep to ourselves we lose; for in the keeping we cannot reproduce" ... for self-containment is but synonymous with sterility.

For the past six years the writer has been enabled to publish the Golden Book Series—one each successive year. The thoughts of these booklets are first gathered together a year before publication. They are then used as the theme of our A.A. Retreats for that year. The following spring the thoughts are put into writing and another one of the Golden Books becomes a reality. On publication, we have always sent to our very personal friends a copy of the new booklet with our compliments. On the average about a hundred are thus mailed out. But you know something? Of this hundred only about eight or ten are acknowledged, and those only over a period of the ensuing year.

Came 1952. The Golden Book had been published and copies had been dispatched to friends here and there. The Retreat time was fast approaching. Our mental faculties seemed to become more and more sterile as the time approached. A new theme for the coming year seemed not to be found. Then we received a letter. It reads as follows:

"Dear _______ _______,

"I hope this reaches you. For want of a return address I am sending this to the publishing company. I do want you to know how much I've appreciated every one of your books. They never fail to galvanize and inspire me, and I keep going back to them again and again.

"If your books can mean this much to someone without an alcoholic problem, I can imagine what a lifeline they are to alcoholics. God love them all!

"Please remember me in your prayers. And thank you again for sharing your inspiration and wonderful work with me.

"Sincerely,

_______ _______"

We immediately thought of something that had happened many, many years ago and which had to do with ten men who had leprosy. The story goes like this:

"And as He entered a certain village, there met Him ten men who were lepers. They stood afar off and lifted up their voices and said, 'Jesus, Master, have mercy on us.'

"And when He saw them he said to them, 'Go show yourselves to the priests' And it came to pass that as they went they were cleansed.

"And one of them, when he saw that he was healed, turned back and with a loud voice glorified God.

"And fell down on his face at His feet, *giving Him thanks:* and he was a Samaritan.

"And Jesus answering said, 'Were not ten made clean? Where are the other nine?

" 'There are none found to return and give glory to God, save this *stranger.*' "

And then another thought came to mind. We thought of the question that is being asked all over the country in A.A., "Where are the old timers in A.A.? So many no longer take an interest in the group. So few will sponsor new members. Many no longer attend meetings. Where are they?"

And then we mused to ourselves: "Were not all of them made sober ? Where are the other nine?"

We forgot to tell you that the letter quoted above was from a non-alcoholic. But its contents should have told you that. And what was it Christ said: "... none ... to return ... save this *stranger*... ... and he was a Samaritan..."?

And the letter ... the writer was a *non-alcoholic.*

"The other nine ..."; human ingratitude; human thoughtlessness; failure to recognize a gift; A.A. leakage; the Twelfth Step: "Having had a spiritual awakening ... we tried to carry ..."; we received; we give; ... at last we had our theme: *Gratitude,* the Twelfth Step in *action* ... for

> *"What we give away—we keep; for it is in*
> *the giving that we receive:*
> *"What we keep to ourselves we lose; for in the*
> *keeping we cannot reproduce:*
> *"And when we die, we take with us only that which*
> *we have given away."*

GRATITUDE AND A.A.

"So that you being strengthened, you may in turn strengthen your fellowman . . ."

No one ever really got "on the program" of A.A. until he had taken the *first* step. Likewise, no one every stayed on the program unless he *continued* the *twelfth step.* For in the twelfth step is all the activity that insures, enlarges upon and matures our sobriety and our serenity. "Having *had* a spiritual awakening, we (in turn) tried to carry the message *to alcoholics."* In this we have expressed again in a little different way the so-called paradox of living: "We keep only what we give away; for it is in the giving that we receive." . . . In the twelfth step also we have indicated to us the value of *gratitude in action.* In it we have enunciated to us the principle that "all gifts are given to us by Almighty God *in order that we may give them in turn to our fellowman"* . . . and that is true gratitude.

This whole idea was explained to Peter when he was made head of the apostles. He was told at that time "I have prayed for you, Peter, that your faith fail you not . . . so that *you being strengthened, you may in turn strengthen your fellowman."* Which is merely another way of telling him, and us, that all of God's gifts are *loaned to us* . . . and that we keep them only as we in our gratitude in turn share them with our fellowman. And so too our sobriety in A.A. is loaned to us: so that we in turn *may give it to other alcoholics.* And the funny thing is, bub, that is *the only way* we can keep it! And the heart-breaking experiences of many, many 'slippees' bear tragic testimony to this truth.

But someone about this time is going to object. And they are going to say: "If it is gratitude that makes the twelfth step work, then how about the fact that we are always being told this is a 'selfish' program?" And such a one will insist: "Gratitude comes from love, and what has love to do with selfishness?"

We shall endeavor to answer. And first of all may we point out what many seem to overlook, namely that the 'selfish' part we so often are told about means we must take care of self *first.* For we are reminded again and again in A.A. that if we don't stay sober ourselves we won't be of any use to anyone or anybody. And so A.A. is definitely a 'selfish' program, for it teaches *prudent self-love.* But *so does the law of love!* What is it that we are taught: "Thou shalt love the Lord thy God with thy whole heart . . . and thy neighbor *as thyself"?* Which means we *must love our self first—prudent 'selfishness'!*

Thus in the twelfth step we learn that we shall *keep our sobriety* only if we in turn give it to someone else. And therefore . . . in order to *keep it* . . . in order to preserve *ourselves* . . . we carry the message to other alcoholics . . . which means *we practice and continue to practice the twelfth step in order to keep sober ourselves.* And that gives us the *motive* for doing it . . . a motive that cannot puff us up . . . a motive that will keep us humble . . . a motive that will not make us become patronizing . . . a motive that will continue to remind us of our need . . . a motive, finally, *that will enable the pathologically proud alcoholic to practice love of his fellowman and to show gratitude to his fellowman . . . and still avoid getting on the pedestal of the philanthropist.*

The founder of our A.A. group in Indianapolis had a pet phrase. It is a phrase that he used over and over again. Seldom did he give a talk in A.A. without repeating it again and again. It was a simple phrase. And in a very few words it expressed the whole gist of success in A.A., particularly in practicing the twelfth step. The phrase he so often used is: *"This is a GIVE program."*

Again we hear the echo: "It is in giving that we receive . . ." . . . "We keep only what we give away" . . . "So that you being strengthened, you may in turn strengthen your fellowman. . . ."

Yes, chum, this is a *selfish* program; but it is *not* a *take* program; it is a *give program.*

THE TWELFTH STEP

"Having had a spiritual awakening as the result of these steps, we tried to carry this message to alcoholics and to practice these principles in all of our affairs."

In the twelfth step we have three definite actions. One passive; one active; and both active and passive.

1) "Having *had* a spiritual awakening"; herein we are passive; we receive; the "compulsion to drink is expelled by Almighty God." As it is phrased in many A.A. circles: "The expulsion of a compulsion by a Higher Power." God has *given* us sobriety along with an entire new spiritual attitude.

2) "We tried to *carry this message* to alcoholics"; and herein we begin to *give;* we become *active;* we share with others what has been given to us.

3) "And *practice* these principles in all of *our affairs";* and herein we *continue* to be *active* on *ourselves*—"in all of *our affairs";* we *act* on *ourselves* and then are *passive* in *accepting* its discipline. As the big A.A. book tells us: "disciplining ourselves into habits of unselfishness and love."

One of the first mistakes made by many in A.A. relative to the twelfth step is a misunderstanding of what the term "spiritual awakening" means.

There are two things that it is definitely *not:* it is not a *sudden* happening (except in very rare cases); and it is not *emotional.*

Perhaps if we analyzed the word "awakening" we may more easily understand it. All of us "awaken" every day from sleep. And what happens when we awaken? When we awaken, we usually *gradually* change from a state of sleep to a state of wakefulness. Seldom is it sudden. That is why we so often say we were only "half awake." For some it may take hours to have full use of one's faculties clearly after being in a deep sleep.

A similar circumstance takes place in A.A. We *gradually* awaken to a *new life; a new attitude* towards spiritual values; a *new* ability to think clearly. That is the spiritual awakening. So now we see things *clearly*. For the light of God's grace has entered our minds and our souls and has awakened our spirit to a new consciousness of Him. It is like all the things that we can see now, and hear now, and recognize now in the light of the new day, but which in the night and in slumber were totally invisible.

Whence does this "spiritual awakening" come? The step is very explicit: "as a *result of these steps," i.e.*, as a result of steps 1, 2, 3, 4, 5, 6, 7, 8, 9, 10, and 11! So therefore the twelfth step *presumes* that the other eleven *have been taken.*

If one is not conscious of having had a spiritual awakening, perhaps such a one might check: where are the other eleven? !

Having received this gift from God, we then begin to *give.* "We tried to *carry this message* to other alcoholics." And right here our little theory about motivation mentioned above will play a very, very important role.

If we carry the message, if we do twelfth step work, if we sponsor a new member *in order to sober him or her up* we are likely to get into serious difficulty. For the fellow or the gal we are sponsoring *may* stay drunk. In fact the first ten we sponsor *may* stay drunk. And then what's going to happen with our motive? We are going to get an awfully bad case of self-pity. Poor guy! We tried and tried so hard—with *ten* of them—and they *all* stayed drunk. We simply must not be much good ourselves. And then—maybe a little drink might soothe our aching heart? !

Or it is possible that the first fellow or gal we work on will stay sober and really "get" the program. It might even happen that the first *ten* we sponsor *might* stay sober and "get" the program. And then what is likely to happen? "Gosh, I must be some sponsor! Look, ten guys, and they are all on the program!" And then we go home and in our pride-fed elation we just might possibly look into the mirror. And we just might possibly admire that "big-shop" sponsor we see in the mirror. And then

—we just might possibly invite that big shot we are looking at out for a drink. It has happened!

On the other hand *if we sponsor a new member*, if we *carry the message in order to give away what we have SO THAT WE MAY IN TURN KEEP IT*, then it *will not make any difference to us whether the new fellow or gal stays sober or not*—because we have *successfully accomplished what we set out to do—WE have stayed sober; we have kept what we had because we gave it away irrespective of what the other fellow did with it.*

What did we give away? What was the "message"? It is very simple. It is explained very tersely and very clearly in the big A.A. book: "Tell him what happened to you." In fact, that *is all you have to give away—what happened to you—period.*

"And practice these principles in all of our affairs." Which simply means putting into practice in "all of our affairs," i.e., in *all we do—socially, spiritually, in business, at home*—in everything—all the things we learned and were given in the spiritual awakening. And "putting into practice" means repeating over and over—day in and day out; hour in and hour out; yes, if necessary minute in and minute out.

"So that you being strengthened, you may in turn strengthen your fellow man."

"Where are the other nine?" They stopped —*giving.*

CARRYING THE MESSAGE

"We tried to carry the message . . . for it is in giving that we receive"

When we "carry the message to other alcoholics," this giving of what was given to us is not confined to twelfth step calls and sponsoring new members in A.A. Carrying the message includes *all* of what we refer to as "twelfth-step activity" including the *living* of the A.A. program.

So now let us take one by one all of those things which a sincere A.A. will take part in as part and parcel of his or her twelfth-step living and all of which, too, he will realize must be continued if he or she wishes to retain sobriety, serenity and happiness. We might say that the twelfth step is the "pay-off" step. For in pursuing it day in and day out, we keep on receiving a hundredfold in return in sobriety, in contentment, in peace of mind, in true friendship, in mutual esteem and through it all and in it all we gradually more and more *grow* and *mature* in body, mind and soul.

1) We *give* by *attending* meetings. Many times we refer to A.A. meetings as a means of "insurance against a slip." The reason for this is that in *giving* by attending meetings, we *receive* and *keep* what was given to us—*our sobriety,* and an increase in serenity. But here again old man "motivation" comes in. Why do we go to meetings? Do we go to *give* or *get?* We will always *get,* and *much,* from meetings *provided our purpose in going is to give,* if only by our presence encouragement to the newcomers and others present. But if we primarily go to *get,* many, many times we shall leave the meeting empty-handed. For perhaps we went to hear a *good* talk and the speaker was "lousy." So all we take away is disappointment. Or perhaps we want to learn, and hearing nothing we did not already know, we again went away short of our expectations.

On the other hand, if we always go to the meetings to *give,* then no matter what might happen at the meetings, we shall always accomplish our purpose in going—an opportunity to *give* of ourselves. And then the One Who gave us our initial sobriety, again gives the increase and the peace and the serenity. "For it is in the giving that we receive."

Furthermore, if we attend meetings for what we receive from the talk, or associations, etc., the time comes when these things are no longer attractive enough to motivate our attending and so often then begins excuses for staying away, for missing the meetings, because of the terrible speakers, or because they bore us to death, or because of this or that personality, etc., etc. *But* when we continue to attend meetings for the *purpose of giving in order to get and keep what we have,* we shall never be open to the deception of excuses for staying away. For no matter how bad the speaker may be, no matter how boring the meeting may be, no matter who is present or what takes place *we still can and do accomplish our purpose*—we still shall *always* have *opportunity to give even though as mentioned above it only be giving by our presence encouragement to the newcomers and others.* Remember your first meeting? Wouldn't you have had an awful shock if there had been *no one* else there? And it *could* happen *if all went to meetings for only what the meeting had to offer.* But on the other hand there would *always be a huge crowd if all went for what* they could GIVE—for there then could *never* be a reason or even an excuse for staying away.

"Were not *all* made sober? Where then are the other nine?"

"And you being sobered, so that in turn you may sober your fellowman. . . ."

"For it is in *giving* that we receive. . . ."

That's right—this is a *give* program. Remember?

What else besides our presence at the meetings can we *give?* Let's analyze a few more ways to *give.*

2) We can *give* of our knowledge and experience to the discussion during the meeting. We can give constructive criticism and bury all destructive habits of criticizing the talk, or the speaker, or the other members, or what goes on in the group.

We can *give* encouragement to the speaker, ever mindful of how we expect a handshake, a thank you or a pat on the back after we have spoken or led a meeting. "For it is in *giving* that we receive. . . ."

Once there was a very famous public speaker whom all seemed to applaud and compliment after every speech. One day a little old lady said to the speaker after one of his fine talks, "You must, sir, get a lot of satisfaction out of all the compliments that are paid you after every talk you give."

"Not at all," he replied. "You see, madam, all of that just runs off like water off a duck's back."

"That I know, sir," she insisted, with a twinkle in her eye, "but shure and the duck like it"!

3) We can *give* our *attention* to the talk. And this is really the only way we can ever hope to receive much from even the best of talks. They who jabber on and on with their neighbor while the speaker holds forth; they who take a little nap during the talk; they who are thinking about the thousand and one things of the day instead of listening *attentively* to what is being said—all of these can *take* little home with them for they *fail* to give the first requisite: *attention*. "Where are the other nine?" Some, I believe, are sleeping!

4. We can bring to the meeting and the talk and the discussion, and we can *give* an *open mind*. The big A.A. books tells us: "Willingness, honesty and *open-mindedness* are essentials of recovery. But they are *indispensable*." It is the closed mind that begets criticisms, and doubts, and monotonies, and boredom, and dislikes and all the other things that eventually make for *missing* meetings. We *must* give to *every* talk or discussion an *open mind*. It is essential. "So that we being strengthened in our sobriety, we may in turn strengthen our fellowman."

5) We can *give ourself* to the talk or discussion—*not* the other fellow. How often do we not hear the remark, "Boy, I hope Jim was listening tonight. He really *needed* that talk." We shall never get much from the talk to improve our sobriety

and our living unless we *give* of *ourselves* so that we can *apply* what is said *to ourselves not* to the fellow or gal sitting in the next row. And it is *only* when we apply what is said *to our lives* that we can take it home with us. "If the shoe fits, *wear it.*" Then it will still be there when you get home. But it won't be there if you put it on someone else's foot!

6) We can *give action* on what we hear. To merely listen and then proceed to forget what was said will never bear fruit in our lives. It is only action on what we hear that will do that.

The story is told of a certain fellow who was consistently late for services on Sunday at his church. In those days the sermon was always given *after* the services. So this Sunday morning, he was hurrying to church and as he approached the steps he noticed the people beginning to leave. He accosted a woman who came down the steps and queried why so many were leaving church. And he asked, "Is the sermon over?"

"No, it is not," was her short reply.

"Then why are so many leaving church, madam, if the sermon isn't over?"

"Because the priest has stopped speaking," she again answered tersely.

"Come now. You say that the sermon is not over. And now you say the priest has stopped speaking. What do you mean?"

"Indeed, sir, the priest *has* stopped speaking. But the sermon now only *begins.* For we take it home to continue it and use it in our daily lives!"

We learn in order to *use*—so that we "may in turn strengthen ourselves and our fellowman." *Action is the magic word!*

7) We can *give encouragement* to the newcomers and to those having difficulties with their living or the program. In short we can *give a good shoulder* to them to cry on. Remember when you needed just such a shoulder? Be a good listener. *Give* an ear. Don't join the "other nine" who always side-step the newcomers and the problem guys and gals. Want to keep your courage? Then *give* a little!

8) We can *give* a *talk* once in awhile when asked. And no matter how poorly trained you may be in speaking you *can give* a talk and a *good* one. Remember you are only there as the instrument anyway. What are you going to say? Well, that's in the book, too. In the big A.A. book it again says: "Tell them what happened to *you*." That is really *all* that you have to *give*. And that is what everyone wants to hear: what has happened to you in A.A., how the program is working in your daily living. You say it isn't? Well, then tell them just that—for that is what happened to you. And always bear in mind, *someone somewhere is waiting for that very particular thing in your talk which is in no one else's and which is the very thing that is going to give them or strengthen their sobriety.* "That you being strengthened, you may in turn strengthen your fellowman." Give of *yourself* therefore in your talk in all honesty and simplicity. Such talks don't have to be practiced—they are always *inside*.

9) We can *give* to our time and of our talent to be chairman of the meeting, the picnic, the annual banquet; yes, even to the job of secretary. This is all practicing the twelfth step. This is all *giving*. But here in particular there is much "avoiding." Perhaps it is because in these jobs and similar ones in the group activities, one has to *give* a lot—of time, of thought, of talent, and particularly of *patience* in weathering the barbs of the "aginers," and the 'slingshot artists." But let us never forget, the *more* we *give* the *more* we receive—from *God*—not from the others in the group. With this in mind one will do a good job in the group and not tend to be discouraged and disappointed when "the wolves" come a-running. For whatever happens, we *always* then *accomplish* what we set out to do—to *give*. "This is a *give* program."

10) We can *give* the *big book* to those we sponsor or to those who haven't the financial means to buy one. And the neglect of doing this is in the writer's opinion one of the biggest "canker sores" of A.A. today. It is amazing how many, many so-called members of A.A. have not the big A.A. book nor have ever even read the big A.A. book. One in ten have one! "Where

are the other nine?" Why is this? In most cases because their sponsor was too "tight" in his sobriety to buy them the book. Five-fifty for a fifth and nary a four-fifty for a book! It's all in the book. That's the therapy of A.A. from the ones who started this thing. It tells "how it works" as it was meant to work—effectively and proven from experience, without all the novelties and the new fandangles one sees so often here and there today, but which are not too sure to give sobriety.

To give some idea of how widespread this lack of the big A.A. book is, an amazing thing happened last summer. A member of A.A. from the west coast of southern California, where there is never a meeting without the reading *from the book* the first part of the fifth chapter of "How It Works" down to and including the twelve steps, was on a trip in a certain part of the country and dropped in an A.A. meeting in a strange town. Learning that he was from a distant group, the chairman asked him to speak. He said, "Sure, get me the big book."

"Big book?" queried the chairman in confusion, "What is the big book?"

Their group—the whole group—had never heard of the big A.A. book! We would have loved to hear the gentleman-from-California's talk that evening.

Distributing, and *giving* the big A.A. book—and other A.A. literature to "other alcoholics" is "carrying the message" and all part of the twelfth step work. Whereas "knocking" or "libeling" or "minimizing" the big A.A. book and other A.A. literature is *not carrying the message* but *stymieing that message* whether the literature we are "damning" be published by the A.A. Publishing Co. or not. There is much good A.A. literature published by other sources than the A.A. Publishing Co. To deny this would not be honesty—and this is a *program of honesty.* To deny it would also be no longer *giving,* but *detracting from*—and this is a *give* program. Remember? "That you being strengthened in sobriety and in knowledge of A.A. from the big A.A. book, you in turn *may enlighten your fellowman."* It's in the book!

11) We can *give* of our *money* to help the group help our fellowman. And here is the enigma of A.A.: How "tight" an alcoholic becomes after he is sober in A.A.! Over a hundred thousand members of A.A. having difficulty supporting one Central Headquarters. Is it ingratitude? Is it thoughtlessness? I don't know. But I *do* know it is fact. And I also know that too many A.A.'s just don't *give.*

Every group is plagued by this "enigma." One of the prime sources of troubles in A.A. is financial. And let the secretary, or the chairman or let anyone ask for a bit of "extra" money for this or that or the other thing and the howl of protests sometimes reaches to the highest heavens. And although tattered and torn, that now aged excuse struts through each echo: "No dues, no fees—A.A. don't cost nuthin'." "You can't *buy sobriety"*—and "We have nothing to sell."

Very true. We have nothing to sell. We cannot buy sobriety. There are no dues nor fees in A.A. *But*—we have an awful lot to *give away.* And not the least of the things we have is some of that green stuff that wasn't there when we were drinking. That too was *given* to us *to share* it in turn with our fellowman.

You say you *worked* for what you have? Maybe you did, bub, but *who gave* you the ability, the talent, and the health, and the job that brought what you have? *Better* give some back else that same Person Who gave it to you may some day take it *all* away again. It *has* happened on one grand and glorious binge! What is that we have been repeating about everything else: "We keep *only what we give away;* for it is in *giving* that we receive." Now how about that *extra* buck or so for the "kitty" or for the General Headquarters or for—well, just for the sake of *giving!* This is a *"give"* program. Let it not be said in your group when the "kitty" is counted, "What? Only *one* buck? Where are the other nine?"

12) Finally, we can *give* of the special talents with which *God* may have endowed us and by the use of those talents "strengthen our fellowman."

To many individuals God has *given* special talents. They are given so that those individuals in turn may use them to also "carry the message" to alcoholics. And we know that among all the media of "carrying a message" the pen is foremost. So those who have the ability, time and talent can *give* by writing about A.A. and all of its facets in perhaps a little different way even though basically nothing new is ever added. So all the fine pamphlets and booklets and books that have been written by the many talented members of A.A. here and there in the country are one of the most effective means of "carrying the message"; and it is one of the finest ways to *give*—all opinions to the contrary notwithstanding. It would be a strange honesty abroad in A.A. if all without exception could "carry the message" *verbally,* but only the "powers that be" could do so in writing! Who's kidding whom? If you have talent to write, get out the old pen and write—*give,* and don't pay any attention to the growls of the jealous "johns" and "jills" and you can be sure that the same God Who endowed you with that talent and Who enables you to write will also see to it that your written message is carried throughout the length and breadth of the land, if it be His Will. And if it is His Will, you can also be sure that no human will stop it. "It is the pen that paints the truest pictures, and one that carries on when the spoken word is but an echo."

To another some are given other talents. Those too we can give; talents of entertaining, of speaking, of teaching, etc., etc. When we use these talents of A.A. to help our fellow members, no matter what type of help that might be, we are *giving* of ourselves. And so in that giving we shall again receive—more help, more sobriety, more serenity, more of everything that is good and desirable. For all talents are *given;* they are *gifts* of God; and we *give* them back when we *use* them for our fellowmen.

Undoubtedly many of our readers have heard the famed story of the juggler. It is told on radio and television and by word of mouth each Christmas time. But it is so striking and has some bearing on this use of talent that we give it now for thoughtful analysis.

There once lived a juggler. He was very expert at juggling, but he was also very poor. One Christmas Eve, he visited the monastery church to pray. And as he knelt there in the shadows, he saw the monks entering the chancel and in single file wend their way to the statue of the Virgin. As each one reached the statue, he paused and in humble reverence placed something at her feet. Curious, the juggler inched toward one of the monks who had been to the statue and then returned to one of the pews to kneel in prayer. He nudged the monk.

"Father," he whispered, "what is it that all of you were doing tonight going to the statue of the Virgin?"

"We were all placing at her feet our Christmas gift—something each had made himself during the year. It is our token of gratitude to our Lady on Christmas."

The juggler returned to his place in the shadows with a heavy heart. He had *nothing* to give the Lady for Christmas. And he was so poor he could buy nothing. And he knew no art nor trade, so he could make nothing for her. Then suddenly a thought came to his wondering mind. "The *only* thing I have is my juggling. I shall juggle for the statue. That, small as it is, will be my Christmas present."

He approached the statue, and in full view of the monks, he juggled. They were horrified at this apparent sacrilege. They rushed to the altar and were about to stop him when suddenly they all saw a strange, yes, a miraculous sight. The Lady was waving them back—and in her eyes there shone a light of heavenly joy, and across her lips there played a beautiful smile, a smile of approval to the poor juggler.

He *gave*—what he had. And thus he received—the approval of heaven.

"For it is in giving that we receive" . . . and A.A. is a "*give* program."

What to *give?* That is simple. We only have to paraphrase the big A.A. book when it tells you to tell them "what happened to you" . . . *"Give* whatever was *given to you!"*

One of the most heart-warming experiences the writer has had recently was to see the many members of the profession in Hollywood groups so frequently *giving* of their talents to entertain, to encourage, to help along someone or something in A.A.; time and time again actors and actresses and radio guys and gals *giving what was given to them.* No wonder A.A. enjoys such phenomenal growth in those parts: what is that we hear so often, "it is *God* who *giveth* the increase."

GRATITUDE AND SPONSORSHIP

"What we give away—we keep . . ."

Our biggest opportunity to *give* in A.A. is in calling upon and sponsoring some alcoholic who still has not known of the blessing of sobriety through Alcoholics Anonymous. In doing so we fill *two* people's needs—theirs and *ours.* And it is only when we get that conviction once and for all that we shall sincerely accept sponsorship in A.A. And it is only in *keeping* that conviction that we shall *continue* to sponsor others and to mature in sobriety and serenity. Because "It is *only* in giving that we receive; and what we give away—*we keep.*"

The drinking alcoholic, the alcoholic who, still in his confusion and sickness, is looking for the door that will lead him out of his darkness and despair to the light of true sobriety, *needs you. But* never forget, mister, *you need him just as desperately* if you want to *permanently* and *contentedly* keep that sobriety that you now enjoy and which some other alcoholic *gave to you.* Again we repeat as we stressed in the early pages, *that is the only way you will keep your sobriety.* And if you have a doubt, just ask the next 'slippee" you meet, especially if he happens to be one of the ones who were sober for a "long while in A.A." before he slipped.

Let's write it in our minds and hearts with never-to-be-erased letters: GIVING IN A.A. IS SELF-PRESERVATION! This is a *selfish* program; and so it *must be a give* program. "What we give away—*we keep.*"

And the most essential *giving* in A.A. is in *making twelfth-step calls* and *sponsorship.* In no other activity of the Twelfth Step do we *give* so much of *ourselves* as we do in sponsoring the new member; in making a twelfth step call. Time, talent, money, sobriety, encouragement, guidance—we *give our all.* And yet, isn't it true that in most groups *only a minority are willing to make twelfth step calls; only a few are willing to sponsor other alcoholics?* "Were not *all* made sober? Where then are the other nine?" You know where they are? They are basking at present in the sunshine of their own sobriety. *And* it won't be too long—maybe a year, or two or three—or even eight or ten, but sooner or later, and soon at the latest, that sobriety which they are now so closely keeping to themselves, is going to become awfully boring, and heavy, and a terrible burden. And to such a "stinking," stingy, self-centered mentality—there will be only one *apparent* easement—the bottle. Again, we suggest: ask the next 'slippee' you meet. He found out—the hard way.

Ingratitude? Thoughtlessness? Laziness? We know not, but we do know it is true. So how about *you* and *me?* Let's keep what we have. Let's improve our sobriety, our serenity, our whole theme of living. Let's *give in sponsorship.* For even though we don't *want* to; or even if we don't *like* to; or even if we feel it's a *burden;* the truth from experience tells us over and over again: *We got to!* "Selfish gratitude"—the A.A. paradox!

PRACTICAL SPONSORSHIP

"This is a GIVE *program"*

A sincere A.A. may make many mistakes in his twelfth step calls and in sponsoring new members, but on the average he *won't be hurt thereby* nor will he seriously hurt his protege. For the sincere person is more than any other an instrument in the hands of the Almighty and *He* will give or permit whatever results. And after all, as we pointed out previously, the sincere person making a twelfth step call or sponsoring a new member has accomplished *his* purpose no matter how blundering or erroneous may have been his 'technique'—for he *has given*—and in the giving has kept and improved his own sobriety.

But twenty years of A.A. experience has picked up a lot of suggestions as to what works best and what is best to be done and what is best to be left undone. There are no 'dues nor fees' in A.A. And likewise no matter what experience might point out, there are also no "do's nor don'ts." Each member's autonomy is the basic solidarity of the entire A.A. membership. So, in A.A. each group, each member *does* his or her or their A.A. in the way *they choose to do it.* Nor is there ever to be anyone to bid him or her or them 'nay.' However, common sense demands that we *for our own* sakes ordinarily follow the paths which experience demonstrates to be the better. So the following 'guides' (we hesitate to label them 'rules') are merely given as a result of our own experience and the experiences of thousands in A.A. which we have picked up here and there. So far literary succinctness and using our literary license, we shall here and there use 'do' and 'don't'—or maybe even a 'be sure to'—*but* when we do, just remember your *don't* gotta! First, a few questions:

I) *How many should one person sponsor at one time?* The answer to this question must always be relative. Such a number will always vary greatly between the fellow who works twelve hours a day and the gal who has no job or family obligation. But there are ways and means of judging how many one can prudently sponsor at one time. We can *sponsor only that number to whom we can GIVE THE FULL benefit of our sponsorship.* Many get into difficulty here and neglect is the result because in their eagerness they make many calls, but have not the time to give these same new 'babies' all that true sponsorship demands. It is certainly much better to sponsor *one* and *give* him or her the *full* benefit of our time, than it is to sponsor *many* and then neglect the follow-up in the 'other nine.' We feel that an average sincere A.A. will be always sponsoring *one* new member, although at times because of lack of prospects or of time difficulties, such will go for a time without a prospect 'under his wing.' Whether you can sponsor *more* than one at the same time, *that will depend entirely on how much time you have to give.* May we suggest: *give what you have, to whomsoever asks, whenever time permits.*

II) *How soon should a new member sponsor somebody else?* In handling this problem, we find all sorts of "rules,' 'regulations,' and 'traditions' in various groups and areas. And as with so many things in A.A. there exists a wide difference of opinion, varying from the "not for at least a year" to "the sooner the better." In between we find the 'six-month rule,' the 'ninety-day rule,' the 'six-month continued-sobriety rule' and what have you. Let us analyze the reasons they adduce and then let's try to evaluate the one which seems to be the one that 'follows the program.'

Those groups and individuals who maintain that a member must be 'dry' for six months or a year before such a one should sponsor a new member or make a twelfth step call give the following reason: "You do not level off in A.A. for six months or a year; you can't learn A.A. in a few days or weeks; so you can't tell the new fellow or gal much about A.A. until you have been a member for a sufficient length of time."

In our opinion, this reasoning places too much emphasis on "learning" and "teaching," whereas we feel that such really are unimportant in A.A. After all the A.A. book tells us: "Tell them what happened to you." And certainly everyone is quite conscious of what happened from the first day of sobriety—in fact *more* conscious of it than six months or a year later.

So we think that the best procedure is to sponsor someone —the sooner the better. (Of course we are presuming that the one who starts sponsoring is *completely* sober and not still reeking of liquor or paraldahyde!)

A.A. is *not a learn* program; it is *not a teach* program; *it is a GIVE program.* Remember?

And what has a fellow or gal who has been sober only a week to give? A week of sobriety! Which is a week more than the one on whom he is calling has. And such a one, with only a week of sobriety, certainly has the qualifications asked for in the A.A. Book—which interpreted means: "GIVE!" Surely length of sobriety does not determine one's ability to do that.

III) *How MUCH should one give in sponsoring?* Perhaps the biggest "DO" we should quote here is *"Do avoid using excuses."* And we might add that it is difficult to *give* too much. However, there is often present the danger of "spoiling" or "over-pampering" the new prospect. And surely this is one circumstance that has already contributed to his or her drinking in the past—over-indulgence of a mother, wife, husband, friend, etc. And in our experience we feel there are more "slips" occasioned (we hesitate to use the word "caused") by too much pampering than by too much neglect. The sincere sponsor will endeavor to avoid both extremes. But it is impossible to determine what is too much and what is too little in general. Every alcoholic, although having the same basic problem, and pattern, has a *different need.* How can we determine that? There is only one "sure" method: *Stop—ASK for the right answer in humble prayer—and then act. The results then are truly in the hands of God—where they should be.*

IV) *How often should one call again on a "slippee"?* We shall answer this by giving the reply given by a member of one of the midwestern groups during an A.A. Forum:

In a certain group was a fellow who again and again slipped. Seventeen times he slipped; and seventeen times one of the members of the group answered his call for help. And then the group all decided to call a halt and agreed that the next time no one would go to see him if he slipped.

A few weeks passed and once again the unfortunate fellow slipped. Frantically again he called the group for help. All refused—*save one.* One member decided to make the call. The "slippee" was sobered up again—and to this day never has had another drink and is a solid member of the group!

Their curiosity having been aroused after this one member had made the call, the rest of the group asked him why he had made it particularly after all had agreed not to. His answer is a classic:

"When he called for help, I got to figuring, and decided that if I *didn't* go, I was *sure* to lose all the effort expended on the other seventeen calls. So I went."

How often? Your guess is as good as mine. We just can't presuppose on the Lord. We can only *give.*

And now a few "guides" for what they may be worth. We did not pick them out of books. They are only our conclusions as a result of experience. They are not rules, not even suggestions, but only what in our humble opinion have worked in many, many instances.

1) *Always follow up every call.* Don't be a "one-call-that's-all" fellow or gal. If we make a twelfth-step call, let's follow through on it. Let's see that the one we have called on gets to a meeting, etc., etc. And even if it is one of those "not-yet-ready" individuals, it is a good idea to "look-in" every once in a while. We can never know just when he might be ready.

2) *Do not be alarmed at initial zeal.* So many new members go all out in the beginning and try to sober up every person they can find—in the jails, hospitals, skid-row, etc. Let them go! They aren't doing any harm. They may not have much success, as we all know, but it is all a part of such a personality's maturing. Let us not criticize, nor forbid them, nor become alarmed. Let them make all the calls, cold or otherwise, they want to.

3) *Don't EXPECT success.* And don't *fear* failure. Let us remember what we said earlier about "motive." We make twelfth-step calls in order to give what we have so that in giving what we have we shall be enable to *keep* what we have. We are not making the calls to *sober up the other fellow, nor to keep the other fellow sober by sponsoring him.* We make the call; we sponsor a new prospect *only* to *keep* what *we have.* Selfish-gratiude! Such a motive will keep down pride; it will prevent many heartaches and disappointments.

4) *Don't brag.* We ought not to brag to the new fellow about *our own sobriety;* nor should we brag about the *wonderful* fellows and gals in the group. Nor should we indicate that there are many "big shots" socially, or otherwise in the group, even if we do not use their names. *We do not have anything to SELL.* All we have is *ourselves* to GIVE away—*by "telling them what happened to you!"*

5) *Exclude no one.* If one is *honest* and *humble* and *sincere,* he will make a twelfth-step call and sponsor *all who ask*—whether they be black or white; rich or poor; Catholic, Protestant or Jew; coming off a drunk or completely sober.

We also feel that it is foolish concern, irrelevant and ineffective to endeavor to have someone of "equal" social statue, or profession, etc., to make the call. The effectiveness of the A.A. approach lies in one ALCOHOLIC talking to another ALCOHOLIC; not in a lawyer talking to a lawyer, nor a doctor talking to a doctor, nor a clergyman talking to a clergyman, nor a laborer talking to a laborer. Let's don't lay the foundation for a "silk-stocking group" in the twelfth-step calls.

6) *Dispense no medicine.* And we cannot stress this too much. For in many instances much harm and even death has been caused by the "self-appointed-M.D.'s" in A.A. And giving the drinking alcoholic *any kind of a pill COULD CAUSE DEATH.* And *no* layman is able to tell whether *any* medication is needed or even safe. *Only the doctor can do that.* The only thing we know anything about at all is alcoholism and alcohol. So if you feel the prospect needs something *give him a shot or*

two of liquor. It may make him a little drunker, but it won't kill him!

7) *Ascertain the prospect's NEED from someone who is capable of judging.* On the average, whenever a prospect seems to us to be very sick or very drunk, we still are not capable of judging whether he or she should or should not be hospitalized. When there is doubt, *let a doctor make that decision.* That is HIS profession, not ours. And by incompetently deciding *not* to hospitalize a sick alcoholic, we *may* do a lot of harm or even occasion death.

8) *ALWAYS SEE TO IT THAT THE PROSPECT GETS THE BIG A.A. BOOK.* In our opinion this *"do"* is the most important of them all and could profitably be placed in large lettering in all A.A. club rooms and meeting halls. *Always give the prospect a big A.A. Book!* If he or she should happen to "hock" it for another drink, so what? *We have given*—and *this is a GIVE program.* And, then, too, who knows, the fellow running the "hock shop" might join!

9) *Don't PRACTICE what you are going to say to the prospect.* "Practicing" what we are going to tell the new guy is what leads to "making-up" what we are going to say, and to "selling" the program. And we don't have anything to sell through a sales talk. "Tell them what happened to you." We all know that *very well.* And we do not need *practice to relate it.* But you know something? We might need a little *humility!*

The founder of A.A. in Indianapolis was asked in a meeting one time what he thought about on the way to call on a new fellow. He answered in his own simple yet sincere way: "I don't think about anything; I *pray.*"

We think he has something there!

10) *Don't give PROFESSIONAL advice.* Many times harm is done and the new member is left more confused than ever simply because his sponsor assumed the professional role of doctor, or psychiatrist or clergyman. *Medical advice* should be given *only by doctors; psychiatric advice* should be given *only*

by competent psychiatrists; and advice about religion or the worship of God, should be given *only by clergymen.* Whenever our "sponsee" asks for such advice *guide him to one who is competent by profession to give it,* and *don't in egotistical vanity give it yourself.* Remember, chum, it is the fellow's body, mind or soul you're dealing with and *that "ain't" unimportant.*

The same thing holds true relative to family problems, i.e., serious ones. *On the average we are not competent nor should we ever presume to advise in such problems.* Guide the new member to one who is competent to do so. Rash advice given here and there by A.A.'s on family problems and relationships has often times done untold harm and damage. And on occasion presumptuous dribble has broken up a family where it was not necessary.

The only thing we can give advice about is *liquor* and *drinking*—and there is an awful lot about that which we still don't know.

11) *If possible, TAKE SOMEONE along on calls.* There are several very sound reasons for this. In the first place, it is *prudent security.* For we can never know what circumstances we are going to run into on a call. And many, many times having someone along is self-protection morally, physically, and legally.

It will also often times prevent "jealousies" at home. And it will often prove more effective in making "contact." One can "irritate" the new prospect; the other then all the more gets his confidence! There are some groups who use this latter procedure and approach with great success.

12) *Don't give MONEY on calls.* Giving money to the individual on whom we are calling is always bad practice. Our own charity shall dictate whom to help and whom not to help financially, *but it should never be given to the individual who is still drinking or just coming off a binge.* If there is definite need, and we feel inclined to fill that need, then give it to a third party to use for the new fellow.

A.A. does not deal with financial problems; nor is there anything in the A.A. program about giving, loaning, or paying anyone else in A.A. *What one does in this matter is up to each one to decide for himself.* As in politics and religion, so also in money affairs *each member does what he chooses to do and in the way he chooses.* Although we may remark that in most instances *financial transactions between A.A.'s or in A.A. end up in much difficulty and misunderstanding.* That is why we are advised in the big A.A. book to keep *politics, religion and finance out of A.A.* So whatever one does in these matters ought to be transacted outside and away from meetings, club rooms, etc., etc.

13) *Man shouldn't sponsor woman and woman shouldn't sponsor man.* We are fully cognizant of many instances of successful sponsorship of a woman by a man or vice versa. *But we are also horribly cognizant of the untold number of instances where very serious harm, moral and otherwise, has come from such procedure.* And we know too that in many groups it is not tolerated, because of such grave danger.

Man sponsors woman. Man falls in love with woman. Woman falls in love with man. Both stay sober, marry and live happily ever after. That's a fine story for the films, *but it is not solid A.A.* For the usual way it works is: *Man sponsors woman. Man falls for woman. Woman falls for man. BOTH FALL—period.*

There is one excellent reason why this No. 13 "shouldn't" is solid advice. It is the reason given by a clergyman asking for a marriage dispensation for a couple he was about to marry: "He's a man; she's a woman."

14) *Don't PREACH or MORALIZE to the prospect.* We are not calling on the alcoholic for the purpose of saving his or her soul (although that might come about too). We are making the call to *give* what we *have* so we shall be enabled to *keep* what we *have.* And that is *sobriety.* He will get a lot more—*later—and in his own way.* Give him God, but don't try to impose *your* beliefs upon him. Let's keep in mind: most alcoholics *have been subjected to preachments and moralizing thou-*

sands of times, and by experts—but *it did not take.* So *let's get him sober FIRST*—physically and mentally. Then let us *let God* do the moralizing and preaching *through his ministers,* if the new member should so choose to approach them later.

15) *Don't AVOID nor APOLOGIZE for God.* The other extreme to the above is the fellow who for fear of "scaring" the new guy won't even bring up the subject of God. Prudent "giving" of God never "scared" anyone. *But not even mentioning God has often left the new fellow without any prop and he has as a result slipped.* Go read your A.A. Book. It has an excellent treatise on how to broach God to the fellow or gal on a call. *It's all in the book!*

16. *Don't LOOK DOWN on the new fellow.* We should never be patronizing in our approach. We are *not helping a poor drunk—we are making the call to HELP US.* What did we say about motives? We certainly can and should feel genuine sorrow for the plight of the individual in the throes of coming off of a glorious binge. We can pity such. We can sympathize with them. *But our purpose of being there should never be patronizing*—with the idea of helping the "poor devil" out. Let us not forget that we need him as much, if not quite so urgently, as he needs us. *We are giving in order to keep what has been given to us.* Selfish-gratitude—the A.A. paradox!

17) *Don't FORCE sobriety.* It just cannot be done—permanently. We may force one to stop drinking as of here and now, by forcefully taking him away from all liquor. But unless *he wants to stop now* it is foolish and a waste of time and never effective to *make him stop now.*

On many occasions, in order to save his job, or for some such reason, an individual has been forced to sober up. *But that binge will out sooner or later.* And for the good of all concerned it is much better to let him finish it here and now, than to have it continue from where you interrupted it later on and with only added heartaches and problems.

If the one upon whom we call is not ready to quit, *let him continue*—and remind him: "call us when you are ready."

18) *Don't GOSSIP about or reveal what happens on a call.* In making twelfth-step calls it often happens that we are let in on many family and personal problems and secrets. *Let them die within yourself.* It really is a damnable thing to hear someone bragging and gossiping about what he found, or saw, or heard on a twelfth-step call. Gossip itself is a detestable habit, but when it has to do with what we learn in confidence, it becomes truly diabolical. "Tell him what happened to you," but do not "tell others what happened on a twelfth-step call."

19) *Don't make PROMISES.* It is both presumptuous and a false premise to *promise* to the new prospect what the future will bring if he joins A.A. So many do this only to pave the way for later disappointments, self-pity and the eventual "slip." We cannot guarantee that the new member by joining A.A. will get his job back, or his family back, or make a lot of money or anything else *materially.* The *only* thing we know is that *IF he follows the program sincerely he will stay sober and CAN be happy.* What else may happen is entirely in the hands of the Almighty. And hard facts point to the truth that *most* A.A.'s have as many or more problems, hardships, and difficulties *after* they are on the program. *But if they are ON the program they retain both sobriety and serenity in spite of problems and hardships and difficulties.* A.A. will give peace of mind, serenity, happiness and sobriety, *but not necessarily a better job, more money, more pleasure or even better health.* (In case you do not realize it , there is a big difference between "happiness" and "pleasure." In fact people who have most pleasures are usually the least happy.)

Such false promises are often made from the speakers podium in A.A. meetings as well as on twelfth-step calls. We have many times listened in silent musing and amusement while the erstwhile speaker of the evening was in glowing terms painting the beautiful, though false, picture of the endless material benefits which would inevitably accrue to every member of A.A.—a bigger and better job; more income; a better home; better health; and endless pleasures. He left out the bottle pleasures—but he'll come to that—in a month or two or more!

20) *Be sure the prospect and his family know how to get in touch with you.* If you hesitate to do this for fear of being unduly disturbed, then it is better not to make the call. It is, in the writer's opinion, ridiculous to only tell the fellow that you are "Bill from A.A." In this way, to him you will still be a nonentity. And how in the world a member of A.A. can tell the new fellow much about himself, and not reveal his full name is difficult to understand. The tradition of anonymity respects the "public level of the press, radio and movies." And yet there are a few groups here and there who advise members not to tell one's last name—ever—not even to the other members of the group. No wonder they enjoy snail-like growth. "Tell him what happened to you," but *tell him who you are.*

21) *"Do" or "Don't" make COLD CALLS as you choose.* There always has been and still is much discussion on whether to call on a person with the idea of giving him sobriety even though such a one has not asked anyone to call. These are the so-called "cold" calls. And we feel it is entirely up to an individual whether he wants to make such. And certainly neither the one who makes such calls nor the one who refuses to make them are to be condemned. In fact no one in A.A. no matter how he or she works the program is to be condemned. That too is God's business.

22) *Don't PROGNOSTICATE.* It is the height of folly to prophesy who will and who will not "make the program." The longer we are in A.A. the more we realize how impossible it is to pin the label of success or failure on a newcomer. We all tend to do this at least within ourselves, until after a time we find we have been 99 9/10% wrong; and then we take the sensible attitude. *Anyone* may make it; and *anyone* may not make it. There is again only one prognostication we can with certitude give the new fellow: "If you follow the A.A. program sincerely, you *will* make it *no matter who you are, what your background is, what your problems are or whatever else may or may not be present in the circumstances of your living.* All that is needed is *willingness*—nothing else.

23) *Don't tell a new member whether he or she is alcoholic or not.* Much damage and many slips have resulted in some wiseacre's judging that so-and-so is *not* an alcoholic. When younger fellows and gals began coming to A.A. some years back, a lot of slips were caused because some old buck in his self-appropriated wisdom, told such a person: "You an alcoholic? Why you're too young to be an alcoholic." Of course in these days it is quite well known and understood by all that even in the teens one can already be an alcoholic. But still one hears very frequently, "Why, I don't think you're an alcoholic; you ain't drunk enough liquor to be one." So the poor guy or gal goes and finds out for sure—the hard way.

To quote from the A.A. Book, "If one says he is an alcoholic he is ready for A.A." The *only* one to make the judgment therefore *is the individual himself.*

24. *Don't OVER-TWELFTH-STEP.* Although we can fundamentally never give too much, still circumstances can make it so that our giving becomes excessive. So in twelfth-step activity, in making calls, in sponsoring new members, we can *overdo* it by taking ourselves away from our family too often or by over-tiring ourselves.

An axiom of Alcoholics Anonymous is: "A.A. comes first." But that does not mean A.A. *activities.* "A.A. comes first" means that the *principles we have learned in A.A.* come first. And one of the first principles we learn is *"First things first."* And the order of prudent charity tells us that *we come first.* For we are told to "love our neighbor *as ourselves*" which means we must love ourselves *first.* So if our twelfth-step activities of making calls, sponsoring, etc., are *injurious to us,* then it is time to eliminate some of those activities. And if it is over-tiring us, *we are definitely being hurt and badly.* Because many an otherwise good, sincere A.A. has learned the hard way—by a slip—that *as alcoholics we cannot tolerate becoming over-tired for a prolonged period. If we do we are in danger of setting off that craving for drink over which we will have no control.*

We also learn from true charity that *our families come next.* So if our twelfth-stepping is hurting our home relationship and causing us to neglect our family, *they come first* and we should eliminate some of the twelfth-step activities.

25) *Don't hesitate to use any reasonable adjunct to help you to help the new fellow stay sober.* In many groups there are traditions of procedure wherein varied psychological helps are employed in twelfth-step activity to give an added help in helping the other fellow. We shall only mention a few and pass them on for anyone who may wish to use them.

The use of "tokens" we feel is very effective and experience in many groups has borne this out. They work something like this:

The new fellow is given a white poker chip on the first contact. And his sponsor tells him that the chip is merely a *token* of his sobriety. And he also tells him that if he should ever be tempted to take that first drink he can do one of two things: 1) *Throw the token away before he takes the drink, or* 2) *Ask God for help before he takes the first drink.*

We have had some very dramatic happenings as the result of this token-therapy, and some are truly amazing. To mention but one:

John Doe was given a white poker chip by his sponsor when he made the call on John. He explained its purpose. Some weeks later, on a business trip, everything went wrong for John and in his resentment he decided to get a drink. He took his car keys from his pocket to start the car and lo, the token came with them. He looked at it, hesitated, then mused: "Well, I'll drive over to the next town before I get the drink." He came to the next town, drove up to the tavern and went in. He reached into his pocket for some change. Out came the token. His conflict heightened. He veritably crushed the chip in his clenched hand. Then he thought: "God—ask for help." That's what his sponsor had said. And as John so proudly relates his story, "And, gentlemen, for the first time in my life I said an humble sincere prayer. And I left the tavern relaxed and relieved and to this day I still haven't taken that first drink." This actually happened—nine years ago!

In groups using the poker-chip token, a white one is given for the first three months, then a blue one, then a red one (nine month danger?) and at the end of the first year a silver pocket-piece with A.A. on one side and the sponsor's and the sponsee's initals on the other side with the dry date. On receiving it he is told: "That is not a reward nor a gift, but only a *token of sobriety* given to one who has been sober for a year and is *beginning* to catch on."

The "nickel-therapy" is used effectively in very many groups as a psychological adjunct to the program. It is very simple. The new fellow or gal is given a nickel by the sponsor and is told: "Here, if you are ever tempted to take the first drink, use this to call me *before* you take the drink." And if he *does,* he *won't* take the drink! (Now almost everywhere we would have to substitute the "dime-therapy"—phone calls have gone up!)

Then there are numerous "physical adjuncts" such as vitamins, etc. But we'll leave them all to the medics. It is in their province to advise and to prescribe what may be helpful. Suffice it to say that there are today some very effective and some very recent discoveries in the fields of both glandular therapy and nutrition which are very helpful to most alcoholics in their body needs and which in turn prove at times dramatically helpful to sober the alcoholic in his problems of health and bodily welfare. We should never forget that the physical side of the alcoholic sickness is a very important one. And it is a tried and true axiom coming down to us for centuries: "Mens sana in corpore sano" which tells us the fact that there is usually a "healthy mind in a sound body." Modern experiments in psychosomatic medicine are more and more proving the validity of this axiom. Wherefore

26) *Don't neglect the alcoholic's PHYSICAL needs.* This fact in sponsorship is many times sadly neglected. For much can be done to smooth the rugged first weeks or months of the newcomer by pointing out to him and stressing the fact that the *body has a lot to do with the alcoholic sickness,* and that the average body *needs a lot of nutritive re-conditioning and re-adjustment before normalcy sets in.* And we should not fail to

point out also to the new member that proven fact *that most of his or her physical symptoms* (those "intangible symptoms and feelings and pains") *which many times are frightening to the alcoholic in the beginning of sobriety WILL EVENTUALLY LEVEL OFF and clear up.* These are usually simply some of the processes of the body's and the nerves' attempt to re-adjust to sobriety and life without alcohol. Particularly we should stress the danger of *too much analysis and thinking and worrying about these intangible inner reactions.* Convince the newcomer that neither the feeling nor the pain will be harmful, *but thinking and worrying about them too much might* prove harmful by leading to an acute neurosis or at least by accentuating the symptoms already present. *Tolerance, acceptance and ignoring them is* the solution on the alcoholic's part. And a *competent* physician, i.e., one who is thoroughly acquainted with alcoholism and its particular needs, can then immensely help the body to "level off" and re-adjust. Such a doctor can and will also point out body needs that will prove very helpful to the alcoholic *for the rest of his or her sober life.* For such medical men tell us that the average alcoholic's physical processes will have specific and added needs for all of the years of sobriety.

So even though your prospect does not need hospitalization, *practically every alcoholic can with great profit consult a competent physician after he quits drinking,* and it is the course of wise sponsorship to *guide your new fellow or gal to a doctor* —but to a *doctor familiar with alcoholics and alcoholism.*

We stress the necessity of contacting a "doctor familiar with alcoholics and alcoholism." We do this for two very definite and solid reasons:

1) Such a doctor will be familiar with the latest therapies in physical and psychosomatic discoveries in the field of experimentation with alcoholism; and

2) Such a doctor *will not presume to prescribe sedatives, particularly barbitals, to the alcoholic.*

And at this juncture we feel that it is of paramount importance to say a word or two about the grave dangers inherent in the use of barbitals and sedatives by the alcoholic.

Previously we gave what in our opinion were the three principal causes of "slips" in A.A. At that time we listed in their order of importance and in frequency of cause as 1) Reservations in the first step; 2) Neglect of meetings; and 3) Neglect of prayer. But today a cause has ousted all of these three out of first place, and that cause is *sedatives and barbitals.* And we now are convinced that it not only is the primary cause of "slips," but more and more proving to be a *most serious menace;* a contention which is borne out also by the excellent recent pamphlet published by the A.A. Publishing Co. and titled: *"Sedatives and The Alcoholic."* And it is our conviction that *every member of A.A. should familiarize themselves with this pamphlet.* And we feel, too, that so widespread is the barbital-sedation danger becoming, that such a brochure should by all means be incorporated in any future reprint of the big A.A. Book. For today it is becoming as much a part of the alcoholic problem as alcohol. And what is still more distressing is the fact that *many either unscrupulous or unknowing physicians still will prescribe barbitals and other sedatives to the alcoholics* as a "specific for what ails you." And some even go so far as to advise their use freely and add: "and they won't hurt you in the least." Fortunately fewer and fewer doctors fall into this class, but the writer has knowledge of many, too many, who still prescribe sedation freely to alcoholics. One widely read syndicated medical adviser wrote recently in his column: "The ideal medication of the alcoholic is *Dexedrine in the morning and a barbital at night!"* Shades of the merry-go-round! We also know another alcoholic who went through one of the outstanding clinics and at the end of his examinations was given *two boxes with a hundred barbituric acid derivative pills in each and was told to take "one every three hours!" We* certainly do not profess to know much about medicine, *but we do know beyond any shadow of a doubt and after contact with thousands of such cases that an alcoholic cannot without grave danger to his sobriety and sanity take any sedation except under strict institutional supervision.* And, Doctor, if you still say "He can," we still must emphatically and categorically reply, "Maybe, just *maybe he CAN but we are darn sure he WON'T.*"

So, the wise sponsor will see to it that his or her new prospect is warned in advanced of these dangers. And we even feel it might not be a bad idea to advise him: "If there ever comes a time when you must have sedation *take a stiff drink, chum, it will be a thousand times easier to come off of it!*"

And as the twelfth step says, in all of our calls and our sponsoring and in "all of our affairs, we *practice* these principles." And practice means REPEAT day in and day out, hour in and hour out and if necessary, minute in and minute out. "Practice makes perfect" is an old axiom. And in A.A. it is the secret of success and of serenity. A great artist in the musical world sometimes reverts to mediocrity, even to oblivion. Why? He stopped *practicing.* He kept on *playing,* i.e., *applying* his musical knowledge and skills, *but without practice he soon lost both knowledge and skills.*

So too with many A.A.'s—they learned "these principles," but they sooner or later *ceased practicing them.* And then—they *lost* both principles and sobriety. Ask any "long-time slippee."

"Practice these principles in *all* of our affairs" means that we must *continue to GIVE* in *all* of our living. And *giving* all of these principles may be summed up in one final sentence, one final *give,* one final *"should"*—we should

Give an EXAMPLE of TOTAL SOBRIETY in all that we do!

a) In business
b) In social life
c) In our home life
d) In our spiritual life
e) In our A.A. group life

TOTAL sobriety—that means happy sobriety; calm sobriety; virtuous sobriety; honest sobriety; loving sobriety; willing sobriety; open-minded sobriety; ever using *all* of the principles we have learned in A.A. in *all* of our affairs and *ever ready and willing to share and to give all that we have to whomsoever asks when they ask.*

Take a quick look around A.A. We see thousands who are not only sober, but who are happy; they are *totally* sober. Would you like to join their ranks? Then GIVE—GIVE—GIVE, again we say GIVE. Else you will remain with "the other nine"—possibly sober, but not happy; possibly still an A.A., but missing many meetings; possibly still "dry," but gradually, oh so gradually "slipping"; yes, possibly *drunk,* . . . for this is above all else a GIVE program.

And need we remind you that *you are sober today only so that* "you being sobered, you may in turn sober your fellowman"? And need we stress again the paradox which is the essence of A.A. and which should motivate every member in his "giving," namely *that in the process of sobering your fellowman, you in turn will be strengthened in your own sobriety? SELFISH-GRATITUDE!*

For, "what we give away—we keep; for it is in the giving that we receive . . . and *when we die, we take with us only that which we have given away.*"

There ain't no choice!

PRACTICE

"... and PRACTICE these PRINCIPLES in all our affairs"

In our college days, we attended a school which was surrounded by people of German descent. The townsfolk mostly all spoke German, our professors all knew German, and all of the workers at the college spoke German. And so in such an atmosphere, one could hardly help picking up at least a few choice German expressions. Some we made our own: "ya," "nein," "was ist das" and other similar, but simple phrases. However, there was one axiom that always fascinated us. Why, we do not know, but its phraseology, its sequence, and its almost resonant quality seemed always to cause it to stand out above all of the rest. It has an English counterpart and translation, but such never seemed to carry the depth of meaning as did the precise phrasing of the German which even in its absolute literal translation is far more meaningful in our language that the English axiom.

In German this phrase is: "Die übung macht den meister." The English axiom is: "Practice makes perfect." The English literal translation would be: "Continuing repetition makes the master." We feel "practice" denotes experiment, whereas "Übung" means as little bit more and means to "repeat" and to "repeat" and to "repeat" the SAME identical action, word, phrase or what have you, not necessarily until it is "perfect"—for "perfect" is too idealistic—but a "continuing repetition" until one has the ability to automatically repeat it at will or until one is "master" of said action, word, phrase, etc., under any circumstance and in any situation. So to become the master of anything it is necessary to repeat, and repeat and repeat—day in and day out—hour in and hour out—and, if necessary, minute in and minute out. All else can but beget mediocrity.

All of us have known at times famous people either personally or through reading about them. Always there have been the very few of every field of endeavor who have "mastered" their work or art or sport. And it is precisely this "mastery" that makes them stand out above all others in their chosen field.

All of us, too, have had the experience of realizing that some such artist, or musician, or sport figure has suddenly faded from the spotlight and has been relegated back again to the ranks of the mediocre or even into oblivion. It is then that we ask ourselves, why? What happened to cause them to fall from fame?

It was one such great violinist who gave the insight into what was behind these "failures" when he made the following statement: "If I fail to PRACTICE one day, I shall notice the difference in my playing; if I fail to practice two days, my family will notice the difference in my playing; if I fail to practice three days, my public will notice the difference in my playing."

Why such failures? What happened? They quit PRACTICING. They either gradually or suddenly discontinued that constant repetition that made them masters, and which was necessary to maintain the mastery once acquired. "Repeat and repeat and repeat, day in and day out, hour in and hour out and, if necessary, minute in and minute out."

The above fact was behind the seemingly endless and, to us, foolish repetitions of our school lessons. It is the reason behind the success of the few who achieve the "top" in any profession. It is behind those very, very few who STAY at the "top"—who remain "masters" in their field of endeavor.

And do you know something? It is that same almost startling truth that is behind those who achieve and maintain *mastery* in A.A.—not masters of drinking, but masters of sobriety—which means maintaining complete, total sobriety under every circumstance and in any and every situation. It is the truth behind those few in A.A. who achieve and maintain serenity and happiness and peace of mind in spite of the changing vicissitudes of life and in the face of any and all obstacles. It is the truth behind those many who have now gone from A.A. through the portal of death—sober and happy, and courageously meeting their final curtain call. Not necessarily perfection; but mastery.

And do you know something else? It is also the above truth that is the missing factor in all of those A.A.'s who were sober or at least "dry" for awhile, or for a few years, or even for many years and who then suddenly "slipped" into the oblivion of drinking again. What happened? Why do A.A.'s slip? Why does the old-timer in A.A. often disappear from our ranks? All of these questions can be answered by the same answer—the same identical truth: THEY QUIT PRACTICING. They "learned" A.A.; they "learned" the twelve steps; they "learned" all about alcoholism and the alcoholic. But they QUIT PRACTICING ALL OF THOSE THINGS THEY LEARNED. They seemed to have forgotten that all the twelve steps are necessary for obtaining sobriety and happiness; and that *all* of the TWELFTH STEP is necessary for MAINTAINING SOBRIETY AND HAPPINESS—for RETAINING the MASTERY IN SOBRIETY. They never learned, or they forgot, or they never accepted the truth that to "PRACTICE THESE PRINCIPLES IN ALL OF OUR AFFAIRS" means to REPEAT AND REPEAT AND REPEAT—DAY IN AND DAY OUT, HOUR IN AND HOUR OUT, and, if necessary, MINUTE IN AND MINUTE OUT those PRINCIPLES we learned in A.A. in ALL OF OUR AFFAIRS, i.e., in EVERY area of living:

In our home life.
In our social life.
In our business life.
In our financial status.
In our spiritual life.
In our emotional life.
In our physical life.
In our thought life.
In our A.A. life.

All slippees, all unhappy people in A.A., all unhappy people—period, have never begun to, or have not continued to apply, the most important part of the whole program for continued sobriety and happiness:

"TO PRACTICE THESE PRINCIPLES IN ALL OF OUR AFFAIRS"

THE PRINCIPLES OF A.A.

"... *and practice these PRINCIPLES*"

What principles have we learned in A.A.?

We do not here refer to those underlying truths and principles with which most of us have been familiar prior to joining A.A.—the principles of justice, the ten commandments, etc. We refer to the APPLICATION OF THESE SAME AGE-OLD TRUTHS TO THE ALCOHOLICS PROBLEM and to the alcoholic. The principles that "worked" for the alcoholic; all the "how" of using the truths many of which we already knew, but which we seldom used or used wrongly or badly; the principles we, as alcoholics, NEED to use in our living, if we ever hope to achieve—not perfection—but MASTERY of living AS ALCOHOLICS, MASTERS OF SOBRIETY. And SOBRIETY, total sobriety, means not only freedom from alcoholic indulgence, but also peace of mind, contentment, happiness, peace of soul, ADJUSTMENT TO LIFE, to REALITY, to GOD'S WILL AND MAN'S PRESENCE.

Again, what principles? Here they are. And most of these, dear reader, every member of A.A. has heard or will hear discussed, or at least mentioned, somewhere along the path of A.A.

1. *I AM AN ALCOHOLIC.*

This is the primary principle, the basic beginning of sobriety. In the past we never knew what an alcoholic really comprised; or we never accepted the fact that we were alcoholics; or we never PRACTICED AND APPLIED this truth to our living. This is the principle brought home to us in the first step in A.A. And the refusal to accept and/or practice this principle we found was the CHIEF obstacle to sobriety, to happiness, to adjustment to life. We shall thoroughly analyze and apply and learn how to *practice* this principle in a subsequent chapter of this present volume.[1]

---

[1] In subsequent chapters of this volume we have tried to give a thorough analysis of the first two principles enumerated here. God willing, it is our intention and hope that we may be able to do the same with the remaining principles through the coming years.—The author.

2. *FIRST THINGS FIRST.*

The second principle is like unto the first and tells us to put the first one first. It brings out the startling, yet amazingly simple truth that *if we always put first things first we shall always have all of our actions, thoughts, living, wishes, etc., etc., orderly and without conflicts.* It is only when we ATTEMPT to put *second* things *first,* and first things second, or third, or fourth, or last, that disorder and conflict, and unhappiness, and friction, and frustration, and all those things that made the life of the drinking alcoholic and the life of the non-drinking neurotic so burdensome and so unhappy and so hopeless, come into existence.

Alcoholics cannot for long tolerate conflict and stay sober. It is only by putting first things first that conflict disappears. Remember that only when every particle of paint, even the most minute, is in its exact juxtaposition to the whole that we have the MASTERPIECE!

3. *EASY DOES IT.*

When an alcoholic drank, his day was usually one round of pressure, speed, stubborn determination, unbending aim, and blind rushing through life irrespective of the outcome. A writer once wrote of such: "When one begins to flee the realities of living, each step is with increasing speed and with each step vision narrows." In A.A. we learn that neither speed nor pressure, nor stubborn determination, nor unbending aim, nor blind rushing EVER ACHIEVED MASTERY. Mastery comes in EASY stages, for mastery of the whole is only the result of MASTERY OF ALL OF ITS PARTS. Even in taking the twelve steps, we learned: ONE STEP AT A TIME IS ENOUGH FOR ME—EASY DOES IT. We learned that when we could not go *through,* we could most of the time GO AROUND—EASY DOES IT. We learned that if we *couldn't* do it today, there would always be a tomorrow, IF WE WERE MEANT TO DO IT—EASY DOES IT.

Life is to be "sipped"—not "swallowed," if we wish happiness and sobriety. Our primary job in life is US, but we have a lifetime to do it. *Mastery* is not achieved in a day, nor a month, nor a year, but only through long, patient and repeated practice—day in and day out, hour in and hour out, minute in and minute out—concerted practice without concern—EASY DOES IT .

4. *THERE BUT FOR THE GRACE OF GOD GO I.*

The almost pathological egotism of the drinking alcoholic placed him high upon a pedestal of his own making. Everybody else's pedestal was lower. Everybody else was beneath.

No other humans were equal to him. Some were the lowest of the low in his estimation. His tolerance as a result was "nil." And so was his happiness and sobriety.

In A.A. we learn that we can never look "down" upon "the lowliest of God's creatures, nor the worst of man's mistakes." We learned that THERE BUT FOR THE GRACE OF GOD GO I. And so necessary is tolerance to the sobriety and happiness of the alcoholic, and so imporatnt is this principle in attaining and maintaining it, that we placed this truth on most of our meeting room and club room walls: THERE BUT FOR THE GRACE OF GOD GO I. And there but for the grace of God I DO go, no matter WHOM I MAY BE CONSIDERING! "He GIVES the grace BOTH to will and to accomplish."

5. *TWENTY-FOUR HOURS AT A TIME.*

In our early drinking days we escape reality constantly either by dreaming of past pleasures, or accomplishments, or victories, or by a like dreamful anticipation of future pleasures, or accomplishments, or conquests. Thus we became perfectionists, dreamers, procrastinators. Then as we approached the chronic stage of drinking we progressively drank more and, instead of pleasureful anticipation and rememberings, we either indulged in repeated sieges of remorse in respect to the past or in soul-shaking fear in respect to the future. We were constantly split between those two awful eternities—yesterday and tomorrow.

When we came to A.A. we learned that the alcoholic temperament above all, and even more than so-called normal people, must practice TWENTY-FOUR HOURS AT A TIME. We learned that we MUST, if we wanted peace of mind, serenity and sobriety, leave the past, and ALL of the past to God's mercy; and that we must leave the future, ALL of the future in the hands of God's Providence; that actually we never had nor ever will have aught but TODAY to live. We found that thus we bring life down to a size we can handle. And we learn the principle that the burdens of TODAY no matter how great never drive men mad; but that the persistent and constant thoughts of WHAT MIGHT HAVE BEEN, or WHAT MIGHT BE often crush even the strongest man, whereas ANYONE can bear the HEAVIEST burden—JUST FOR TODAY. And so we learn to live twenty-fours hours at a time—day in and day out, hour in and hour out, minute in and minute out, BUT taking EACH day, and EACH hour, and EACH minute IN ITS OWN TIME.

"Lord, for tomorrow and its needs,
I do not pray;
Keep me, my God, from any sin,
JUST FOR TODAY.

"Let me both diligently work,
And duly pray;
Let me be kind in word and deed,
JUST FOR TODAY.

"Let me be slow to do my will,
Prompt to obey;
Help me to discipline myself,
JUST FOR TODAY.

"Let me no wrong or idle word,
Unthinking say;
Set Thou a seal upon my lips,
JUST FOR TODAY.

"Let me in season, Lord, be grave,
In season gay;
Let me be faithful to Thy Grace
JUST FOR TODAY.

"And if today, my tide of life
Should ebb away;
Give me then Thy Grace divine
O LORD, TODAY.

"So, for tomorrow and its needs
I no longer pray;
But guide me, Lord, and keep me
JUST FOR TODAY.

6. *THE DANGER OF RESENTMENT—SELF-PITY.*

In the alcoholic, frustration begot resentment, resentment begot self-pity, self-pity begot drinking, and drinking begot grandiosity and grandiosity begot frustration, and frustration begot resentment and resentment begot self-pity and on and on and on . . . in an unending cycle, until faced with the three-pronged choice: sobriety or insanity or death. "You take your choice and. . . ." And we chose sobriety in A.A. But you know something? Along with A.A. came the truth, the principle that IF THE ALCOHOLIC REPEATED ANY *PART* OF THAT CYCLE, THE *CYCLE* WOULD REPEAT *ITSELF*—"IN TOTO."

We learned the principle therefore that to the alcoholic—no matter how longer sober—RESENTMENT AND SELF-PITY would ever remain his number one twin-enemy, and that IF HE PERMITTED HIMSELF TO INDULGE IN SUCH FREQUENTLY OR FOR PROLONGED PERIODS OF TIME he would again set off that compulsion to drink—automatically.

Resentment and self-pity bring untold unhappiness to all people; to the alcoholic they bring *drinking*. The true alcoholic simply CANNOT tolerate resentment or self-pity.

7. *THE VALUE OF APOLOGY.*

APOLOGY is for weaklings and cowards. Such was the motto in the drinking days of the alcoholic, or even before his drinking days. In fact there was never anything to apologize for. Wasn't everybody else wrong; and were not we always right?

In A.A. we learn that it is necessary to be diligent in our mental hygiene; that apology, when apology is in order, is a necessary part of mental keeping house; that to omit such MIGHT, just MIGHT cause serious drink cravings even on the level of the subconscious. It has happened!

John Doe hadn't had a drink for six years in A.A. He suddenly one day got a terrific craving for one. And in spite of all he could do and no matter how much or how often he "talked it out" with other members, it still remained—day in and day out, hour in and hour out, minute in and minute out. Frantically and frightened he kept seeking advice. Then one day an A.A. came up with the question:

"Was there by chance anything or anyone that you deliberately LEFT OUT OF YOUR MAKING AMENDS? Was there anyone to whom you WILLFULLY REFUSED TO APOLOGIZE?"

John thought hard. Suddenly he stammered, "Yes, it was my brother-in-law, the so-and-so, BUT *HE* WAS TO BLAME! And even as late as two weeks ago he wrote me a snotty letter! Why, that . . . hey . . . two weeks ago, why that was the day this thing began!"

His friend looked straight at him, grinned, and said, "Well, what are we waiting for? Where does this brother-in-law live?"

It was a long trip. John took a plane. He went to his brother-in-law's office. He apologized asking no corners. And to this day he has had no further craving for a drink. This is a true story! "When wrong, *promptly* admitted it. . . ."

"Made DIRECT amends. . . ."

8. *THE VALUE OF A FULL DECISION.*

Life is always a terrific burden to the alcoholic. It is likewise to all neurotics. And it is the same to many people WHO GO THROUGH LIFE NEVER MAKING FULL DECISIONS; who always tack on to every decision some reservation: some "if," some "but," some "maybe." In all of life's decisions they "keep a door open." And at other times, in fact MOST of the time, they tried to avoid a decision altogether, and were, as a result, victims of that terribly de-enervating force—PROCRASTINATION, the end product of indecision.

In A.A. we learned in the very first step that a DECISION, a FULL DECISION was the only real difficult part of the whole program. Given that, the rest would be follow-up. And then we learned as we went along that MOST failures came from INDECISION; that MOST nervous, emotional, and physical tension inside comes from INDECISION.

On the other hand we learned that MOST JOBS AND OBLIGATIONS IN LIFE WERE NOT AT ALL DIFFICULT; that a FULL DECISION with no "if's," "and's" or "but's," would make the most difficult job a thousand times easier to accomplish. It is not the obligations of life that tear one down, but THE INDECISIONS. So it was suggested that we PRACTICE, day in and day out, hour in and hour out, minute in and minute out, DECISION, a FULL decision, and that in doing it, HALF the weight of living would be lifted. Want to prove it? Try it!

9. *A.A. COMES FIRST.*

Which means that these PRINCIPLES we learn in A.A. MUST BE PARAMOUNT IN OUR THINKING AND LIVING. If not, we might lose our sobriety, and being alcoholic, sobriety IS THE MOST IMPORTANT THING IN OUR LIFE BECAUSE, IF WE LOSE THAT THEN WE CAN NEVER BE ANY GOOD TO ANYTHING OR ANYBODY, NEITHER TO GOD, NOR TO OUR NEIGHBOR NOR TO OURSELVES.

We might remind our readers that this principle does NOT mean A.A. *ACTIVITY* COMES FIRST. Such activity must often be relegated to the background if it interferes with higher obligations. But it means: ALL THOSE THINGS *NECESSARY* FOR SOBRIETY MUST COME FIRST—INSIDE US.

10. *"MENS SANA IN CORPORE SANO."*

Pardon the language, but it is an age-old principle, the truth and value of which is becoming more and more recognized today. In simple language it means: "A healthy mind in a healthy body," or: THE PHYSICAL CONDITION OF OUR BODIES *CAN* HAVE A VERY SERIOUS BEARING UPON OUR THINKING, OUR EMOTIONS, OUR LIVING. And in every particular this means to the alcoholic that there is a very close tie-up between OVER-TIREDNESS, OVER-HUNGER, and OVER-THIRST and the DRINK COMPULSION AND CRAVING.

From *wide* and in some cases very sad *experience* we have learned the principle that *an alcoholic will inevitably tend to crave a drink again if he permits himself to become too frequently or for too prolonged periods of time OVER-TIRED, OVER-HUNGRY, or OVER-THIRSTY.* We do not know exactly *why* this is so. But we are positive—from the experience of thousands—that it IS SO. Many an otherwise sincere A.A. has learned this principle the "hard" way—after a slip.

11. *HONESTY IS THE BEST POLICY.*

Many learned this phrase in school days. But MOST people didn't and don't believe it, or at best don't PRACTICE IT. The alcoholic during his drinking days, and perhaps even before, did everything possible to DISPROVE this principle. He thus became a pathological liar. At first he "whitened" his lies; then he "blackened" them. He lied and he lied, both to himself and to others. And then he had to manufacture a few more lies to get out of the difficulties and tight spots brought about by his lying and dishonesties. Through this mode of operating he became a past expert at "excuse-making."

Then came the day. Either . . . or. Sobriety, insanity or death. "We admitted. . . ." AN *HONEST* ADMISSION. But that was only the beginning. From then on it MUST BE HONESTY—day in and day out, hour in and hour out, minute in and minute out. Or else . . . "for these there is less chance for recovery. They are not to blame. They seem not to be able to adapt their living to a way of life that demands RIGOROUS HONESTY." (The A.A. Book) And "WILLINGNESS, HONESTY AND OPENMINDEDNESS ARE ESSENTIALS for recovery, but they are INDISPENSABLE." (Id.)

In the early days of A.A., before the Book or the Twelve Steps came into existence, we had only three suggestions: Get HONEST with yourself, clean house, and help others. And that, in the writer's opinion, is still the *core* of the A.A. program of sobriety. HONESTY *IS* THE BEST POLICY.

12. *WE KEEP WHAT WE HAVE BY GIVING IT AWAY.*

The alcoholic, drinking, tried his best to GRAB everything he could get his hands on—"free-for-nothing"! And he always ended up with NOTHING but empty purse, empty stomach, and empty head. And that made room for the "Brooklyn-boys"!

In A.A. we are first GIVEN sobriety. And then we are advised that WE WILL KEEP AND ENLARGE UPON IT IN DIRECT RATIO AS WE GIVE IT AWAY. So, "having had a spiritual awakening as the result of these steps, we tried to carry this message to alcoholics. . . ."

And so in all of our living, the MORE WE GIVE, the MORE WE'LL GET—for ALL gifts are given to us so that we may in turn give and share them with our fellow man. A.A., we learned, is a GIVE program; and life too, we learned, to be happy MUST also be a "GIVE" program.

13. *ACTION IS THE MAGIC WORD.*

To listen to most alcoholics who are still drinking, and to some who are no longer drinking, one would get the idea that they had ALL of their problems solved—in fact, all of the world's problems solved. However, on closer analysis of ourselves and others we find that all of these problems had only been solved

MENTALLY. Again, the dreamer, the perfectionist, the procrastinator!

The alcoholic learns in A.A. that "wishful thinking" and "analysis" never *solved* ANY problem. So, to the alcoholic, A.A. gives the principle of ACTION—ACTION IS THE MAGIC WORD. And in applying and practicing this principle—day in and day out, hour in and hour out, minute in and minute out —we find that MOST problems of life will be solved or removed IF WE *DO* SOMETHING ABOUT THEM—*NOW!* ACTION IS THE MAGIC WORD! Let us remember the twelve steps are written in the PAST tense—they presume ACTION!

14. *THE EFFICACY OF ACCEPTANCE.*

Most alcoholics had been alcoholics and had lost control YEARS before they approached A.A., but they had never ACCEPTED THAT FACT. They, by every possible ruse and rationalization, had constantly endeavored to PROVE to themselves and others that they were NOT alcoholics, that they DID have control, or that eventually they WOULD have control.

The KEY TO SOBRIETY was then given to us in the first step. "We ADMITTED we were powerless over alcohol. . . ." —i.e., we ACCEPTED the fact, we ACCEPTED a so-called UNSOLVABLE PROBLEM, and lo and behold, we found that IN THE ACCEPTANCE LIES THE SOLUTION.

So in living, the easiest, the quickest, and the surest way to peace of mind is *acceptance,* ACCEPTANCE, *ACCEPTANCE!* Most things we cannot change, but ALL things we CAN, if we WANT to, ACCEPT. It truly is the MOST *EFFICACIOUS ROAD TO HAPPINESS AND SOBRIETY*—THE SOLUTION IS IN ACCEPTANCE!

15. *THE NECESSITY OF TOLERANCE.*

The alcoholic either by his nature or through his drinking had become the most intolerant of people. He basically didn't want anything or anyone to exist without his almighty will willing it. He came to dislike everything and everybody. And so people and circumstances, instead of being "props" to living happily, became burdens to his living and only goaded him forward in his progressive drinking.

In A.A. we had to learn or re-learn the law of love. We learned the necessity of loving God and our fellowman. But, above all, we learned that we simply MUST, if we could not LOVE certain of our fellowmen or certain of the circumstances in our lives, *TOLERATE* THEM, THEIR OPINIONS, AND ALL THE CIRCUMSTANCES. In this we learned the hard way what "RIGHTS OF OTHERS" meant. It was a MUST for us, because INTOLERANCE whether it be of race, creed, or circumstance, WOULD INEVITABLY, WHETHER WE WILLED IT OR NOT, LEAD TO "STINKING" THINKING, AND THEN DRINKING THINKING, AND THEN TO DRINKING.

16. *WEAKNESS IS STRENGTH.*

Without much faith in God, or without knowledge of God, or without practice of that faith in God, the alcoholic was frantic to always build up and assure himself of HIS OWN STRENGTH IN HIMSELF. To him that was the only security—physically, mentally, spiritually, materially. Self-sufficiency was our goal—especially in drinking. "Just to be able some day to retire and to drink gracefully!" Then the explosion!

A.A. suggested that "self-sufficiency" was fine as far as it went. But it never went far enough. True strength comes by admitting our own weakness (which is truth) and then by substituting for our own selves "a Power greater than ourselves" —i.e., God. "We admitted we were POWERLESS . . . came to believe a Power greater than ourselves could restore. . . ."

Enigmatic in terms, but truth in reality: WEAKNESS IS STRENGTH. Of ourselves we are nothing, but we can DO ALL THINGS IN HIM WHO STRENGTHENS US. "My grace is sufficient for you, for POWER IS MADE *PERFECT* IN *INFIRMITY.*" (II Cor. xii, 9.) It really IS—IN ALL OF OUR AFFAIRS.

17. *THE MYTH OF PERFECTION.*

Less there be misconceptions and misunderstandings of the foregoing which might lead the perfectionist alcoholic to the extreme and to false expectancy of accomplishments, particularly PERFECT accomplishments, we learned that IN REALITY THERE WERE VERY FEW PERFECT PEOPLE IN THIS WORLD, IF ANY. We learned that ALL are, and would remain, burdened with weak human nature ever pock-marked with flaws, and faults, and failings. Accepting this principle, we arc not so apt to suffer constant disillusionment both with ourselves and with others. We found we COULD become saints, but not QUICK! We are advised in A.A., "We are not saints. We only try to GROW along spiritual lines." So, we honestly keep TRYING—not EXPECTING perfection in ourselves, but always AIMING at it.

For the same reason, we no longer EXPECT PERFECTION in others. We used to do so. Remember? Your parents? Your sweetheart? (And then you were married!) Your profession? Your family? Your children? We EXPECTED PERFECTION, but when we found instead imperfection, faults, failings, even serious ones, we became so disillusioned—which was only a vicarious self-pity. So, we retreated from the reality, and kept looking for the non-existent PERFECTION IN OURSELVES AND IN OTHERS. What was our motive although often subconscious? That pathological pride which demanded the "TOP" for us and all of "ours." How often does this same egotistical pride not keep one from admitting and doing something about alcoholism in OUR folks, in OUR children, in OUR profession, in OURselves! MY dad an alcoholic? Why it's impossible! An alcoholic in OUR family? Why, impossible! I, an alcoholic? A Jones an alcoholic? Preposterous! Or as one matronly proud soul once exclaimed to the writer when approached about the alcoholism of one of her children: "An alcoholic in OUR family? Why, there has NEVER been weakness in OUR family!" Or another proud, sad, but stubborn mother: "MY Charley has NEVER done a wrong thing in his life!" Or in short: "It CAN'T happen to US" and which translated means "WE are PERFECT!" Funny thing though, it DID and we AIN'T!

So, now we no longer EXPECT PERFECTION; with the conviction that even those nearest and dearest to us, INCLUDING OURSELVES, ARE and probably will ALWAYS BE just POOR, WEAK, IMPERFECT HUMAN BEINGS. We look for perfection ONLY in GOD. HE alone has it in Himself and gives to each the degree HE WILLS, WHEN He wills it. But you know something? He usually gives perfection in direct ratio to one's *humility*—and the FIRST step in humility is HONEST ACCEPTANCE OF THE FACT THAT IN OURSELVES WE ARE ONLY THOSE POOR, WEAK, HUMAN CREATURES EXPECTING *EVERYTHING FROM HIM* and looking for nothing from either ourselves or others, with the conviction that ANYBODY is liable to do ANYTHING, and ANYTHING, ANY FAULT OR ANY WEAKNESS, CAN "pop up" in ANYBODY, even in OURSELVES AND IN OUR OWN—and many such PROBABLY WILL!

So we *practice*: by asking ourselves in all of our affairs NOT "How am I doing?"; but "How am I TRYING!" For GOD and GOD alone will *give* the SUCCESS—the perfecting; or *permit* the failure. And we? Just ACCEPT, and DO WHAT WE CAN with every failure—day in and day out, hour in and hour out, minute in and minute out. Just HONEST TRYING, to help ourselves and to help others to help themselves, not expecting PERFECTION, but constantly amazed that we or they are not worse. And IF we have TRIED to ACCEPT and DO something about EVERY FAILURE, in the end we can TRULY say WE HAVE NEVER REALLY FAILED.

18. *THE NECESSITY OF MEDITATION.*

An alcoholic is a sad "critter." Confused, fearful, mistrusting, arrogant, proud, vain, empty, he frantically avoids ever looking within himself. He doesn't dare! For, "with desolation is the land made desolate because there are none who thinketh in their hearts."

Then comes A.A. We clean house. And "in prayer and *meditation . . .*" we find clarity, and faith, and trust, and humility, and modesty, and a full heart and a full life giving, day in and day out, hour in and hour out, minute in and minute out, RELAXATION, AND PEACE, AND COURAGE, AND SERENITY, AND HAPPINESS.

Many of us used this before in our lives at sometime or other. BUT WE LOST THE SENSE OF NEED OF IT. And, finally, the only time we meditated was when we had to—at the end of a binge. Remember? What a meditation! "Nightmare" would be a better term.

But now we learn, and learn to keep, the CONVICTION OF THE TRUTH: THE ONE WHO MEDITATES EVERY DAY WILL NEVER HAVE THE DAY COME WHEN HE HAS TO MEDITATE. Repeat and repeat and repeat—PRACTICE meditation, day in and day out, hour in and hour out, minute in and minute out.

19. *THE PRINCIPLE OF THE "SERENITY PRAYER."*

> *God Grant us the serenity to accept the things*
> *we cannot change;*
> *The courage to change the things we can;*
> *And THE WISDOM TO KNOW THE DIFFERENCE.*

Through the years we had always attempted to change NOT those things we *could,* but EVERYTHING THAT DID NOT SUIT US, OR WHICH DID NOT GO ACCORDING AS WE WILLED. The result: frustration, unhappiness, drinking excessively, alcoholism.

Then in A.A. came the "serenity prayer." Again, not a new prayer, and not a new principle (there can be no such thing as a NEW truth. Truth is always truth—it is eternal and unchanging, BUT IT CONSTANTLY FINDS NEW EXPRESSIONS OF ITSELF) but ideally fitted to the alcoholic who realized that for continued and contented sobriety he HAD TO HAVE SERENITY—EVEN IF THE FRANTIC VARIETY!

So, we learn the many things we CAN change—those we do change; the many things we CANNOT change, those we accept. We go to GOD for the WISDOM to know what to change and what not to change—day in and day out, hour in and hour out, and, if necessary, minute in and minute out. Already He has given us quite a "lead": MOST OF THE THINGS WE CANNOT CHANGE ARE ON THE OUTSIDE OF OURSELVES, IN OTHERS AND IN THE CIRCUMSTANCES OF OUR LIVING, MOST THINGS WE CAN CHANGE ARE ON THE INSIDE, IN OURSELVES. And therein is a whole lot of WISDOM!

20. *THE NECESSITY OF A CONTINUED INVENTORY.*

What a "forgetery" the average alcoholic developed in his drinking days! The drinking, the binge, the trouble, the pain —and then FORGET IT—*QUICK!* Just to close our eyes to all the mess INSIDE AND OUTSIDE. And then—a container can only hold so much—even garbage. So we finally reached the explosion stage—"sobriety, insanity or death." "You takes your choice. . . ."

A.A. helped us get the first of these. Then it was suggested that we THOROUGHLY clean house; that we take an HONEST inventory; and that we EMPTY ourselves, NOT AVOIDING ANYTHING INSIDE OR OUTSIDE OF OURSELVES.

And then it was suggested that "we *continue* to take personal inventory"—lest almost imperceptibly we fill up again with "stinking thinking, drinking thinking, drinking." Either . . . or! Inventory—regularly; with its concomitant peace, and happiness, and serenity and all that goes into adjusted living. OR no inventory; BANKRUPTCY. Again, "you takes your choice. . . ."

21. *WE ARE NOT DIFFERENT.*

Many, many alcoholics put off doing anything about their drinking because (or they thought) they were DIFFERENT from others, and because NO ONE (so they thought) had quite the problem that they had. THEY were DIFFERENT. So being different, the ordinary course of solution and cure was not for them. What an excuse, even though at times sincerely believed!

There are millions of people today other than alcoholics who do not attempt the solution of their problems, because they *THINK* THEY ARE *DIFFERENT*.

The principle? The truth? NONE OF US ARE BASICALLY DIFFERENT FROM OUR FELLOWMAN. That guy or that gal to whom you talked or whom you met or whom you saw today—in fact ALL of the ones with whom you came in contact today HAVE THE *SAME* BASIC PROBLEMS, THOUGHTS, TEMPTATIONS, AND DIFFICULTIES *THAT YOU HAVE*. You say, "They do!?" Surprised? But they do—really they do. Remember the impact of that, the first time when another alcoholic told us, "Yea, I KNOW, I went through the SAME things; I have the same difficulties that you tell me of." It was then, maybe for the first time, we BECAME CONVINCED of the fact that WE ARE NOT DIFFERENT—no matter whether we be rich or poor, ignorant or educated, Catholic, Protestant, or Jew, black or white, clergyman, lawyer, doctor, beggar or thief. Take a good look at the next guy you meet. Then with a relaxing smile muse to yourself: "Hmmmm . . . you too!" Really, chum, "there ain't no difference"—only on the outside. You know something, this writer has a theory, that on judgment day the commonest exclamation of all will be: "Hmmmm . . . you too!"

22. *THE PRINCIPLES OF THE LORD'S PRAYER.*

We will venture to guess that most alcoholics in their drinking years knew and/or used the *Lord's Prayer*. But to most it was only a pattern of words—lip-expressed.

In A.A. we heard all of the rest repeating this same Lord's Prayer at the close of every meeting. And, we learned the PRINCIPLES it taught and contained. And we found that these principles—again, not new—would give anyone the strongest of foundations for living happily and spiritually IF PRACTICED. Let's quickly enumerate these principles:

a. *"OUR FATHER, who art in heaven . . ."*

Here we found the basis for the "Fatherhood of God, and the brotherhood of men": that we are ALL, without exception, BROTHERS under one common FATHER Who is God. Now, take a good look—that guy sitting next to you, or living next to you IS YOUR BROTHER having the *SAME* FATHER, the *SAME* RIGHTS, the *SAME* PRIVILEGES, the *SAME* OBLIGATIONS, and the *SAME* DESTINY that you have! That's right! IF one PRACTICES this first principle of the Lord's Prayer, it will be truly "OUR Father . . . NOT *MY* Father." What a landscape of reality and happiness and tolerance and peace and contentment and security stretches out before the one with an OPEN MIND. An *open* mind! The *willingness to learn!* ". . .Openmindedness . . . are ESSENTIALS for recovery, but they are INDISPENSABLE!" (From the Big A.A. Book.)

b. *"HALLOWED be Thy NAME . . ."*

Blessing, success, happiness, peace and contentment follow all who "HALLOW" God's Name. But these things are, or will eventually be, far from the one who uses it in vain or in cursing or irreligiously.

c. *"THY will be done . . . on earth as it is in Heaven . . ."*

There is one startling truth brought home by this simple prayer: IN PLAIN ENGLISH, *DISCONTENTMENT* IN LIFE IS NOTHING MORE NOR LESS THAN *KICKING AGAINST THE WILL OF GOD.* If we always really WANT God's Will, then we will always HAVE OUR OWN, because GOD'S Will is ALWAYS done. "Oh, what a beautiful morning, everything's going HIS way" . . . it always will.

d. *"Give us this day, our daily BREAD . . ."*

Another soul searching truth. GOD WILL ALWAYS GIVE US WHAT WE *NEED,* NOT NECESSARILY WHAT WE ASK. *BREAD*—the necessities of life!

e. *"Forgive us our debts, AS WE FORGIVE our debtors . . ."*

We suddenly realize that all the problems which we had, have been of our OWN ASKING. "Forgive... AS WE FORGIVE." What if God ALWAYS took us at our word!? Whom *can't* you forgive? You CAN (and WILL) if you *want to*... BE FORGIVEN!

f. *"Lead us not into TEMPTATION..."*

Here we found that HE WHO TOYS WITH TEMPTATION *WILL* FALL. God will give us the strength to overcome ALL temptations PROVIDED we, on our own, DO THE FOOTWORK IN AVOIDING TEMPTATION THE BEST WE CAN. Then no matter how severe the unforeseen temptation, GOD WILL PROVIDE. "In ourselves we are NOTHING...." Remember?

g. *"But deliver us from EVIL."*

All evil will be eventually eliminated but ONLY BY GOD. "Evil has its day." And for its solution or elimination, we must GO TO *GOD*, and not become self-appointed REFORMERS. Yes, PRAY that *GOD* will "DELIVER US FROM EVIL."... Another very potent truth becomes evident in this principle: NO *HUMAN* CAN LEGISLATE *MORALITY*. So why try? We can ONLY *LEAD*—GOD alone can, in HIS time and in HIS way take care of evil and evildoers if such they be. Here is THE principle which, if practiced, will keep one from ever becoming so-called "guardians of the morals."

h. *"For thine is the kingdom, and the power, and the glory forever."*

A doxology—used by some, omitted by others. In A.A. we all, without exception, approach God "AS WE UNDERSTAND HIM."

i. *"Amen."*

A very small word, but a very BIG principle. It is from the Hebrew and means: "SO BE IT.:" It brings home to us the basic truth of all spirituality and relationship with God: THAT AS WE PRAY SO WILL IT BE DONE TO US! IF therefore our prayer—*all of it*—is HONEST, then EVERY part will be answered, BUT IF our prayer in part or in whole is DISHONEST; IF WE are not willing to or do not do THE FOOT-WORK, then we are ON OUR OWN. "Willingness HONESTY, and open-mindedness are ESSENTIALS for recovery . . . they are INDISPENSABLE." Once more: "You takes your choice and. . . ."

23. *NO ONE STARTS AT THE TOP.*

Scene: An alcoholic pre-A.A. is reading the paper. He is a singer of sorts. He reads aloud:

"John Doe, internationally known singer, was given another increase of salary by the XYZ Company who sponsors all of his programs. John Doe now has an income of $10,000 a week, which is top salary for his profession."

The alcoholic takes another drink. He beams. "Ahhh . . . one of these days *I*, too, will be top—JUST LIKE THAT, when my ship comes in! Come on, fellows, let's all drink to the world's greatest tenor—ME!"

Final Scene: Flop house on the Bowery. Pre-A.A. alcoholic is lying on a mess of messy rags on a messy floor in a mess. He mumbles: "Thash me—the world's greatest shinger, hic, JUST LIKE THAT!" Pre-A.A. alcoholic passes out JUST LIKE THAT. Curtain!

It is a funny thing about life, NO ONE EVER STARTED AT THE TOP! There is only one place to *begin* and that is at the *beginning,* which therefore when we want to "ascend" is AT THE BOTTOM. (Our friend above has finally reached the starting line!)

But it is also a queer twist of many people's thinking and living, and of ALL alcoholics' thinking and living: THEY ARE DETERMINED TO BE A GREAT PERSON WHEN SOMEONE MOVES OVER AND SAYS, "HERE IS THE TOP ALL READY FOR YOU."

Also spiritually, many alcoholics at one time or other, in a fit of remorse or otherwise motivated, decided to be a saint

JUST LIKE THAT! But evening came, and a month passed, and six months passed, and our alcoholic, still far from sanctity and still very much a sinner, attempted to speed up the process with the help of a "little drink"!! We GROW along spiritual lines from the bottom!

And also in the material world, like our friend described in the little skit above, most alcoholics set out to be the world's *top* musician, doctor, clergyman, dentist, lawyer, actor, technician or just plain bum (but the BEST bum!) JUST LIKE THAT! Some few reached success, the TOP (*in their own estimation*)—all you had to do was ask them! We ascend any ladder—regardless of the goal ONE STEP AT A TIME—yes, even the twelve steps! And there are A.A.'s here and there who became the TOP A.A., JUST LIKE THAT—sober a month and they know all the answers! Just ask *them!*

There is in the world only one creature who reaches the top JUST LIKE THAT, and that is the *"gad-fly."* You know what a "gad-fly" is? A "gad-fly" is a little moth-like creature hatched on the lakes and streams mostly in the north. And having hatched they immediately ZOOM to a great height over the water JUST LIKE THAT, but almost as quickly they fall down on the water, DEAD, JUST LIKE THAT—fish food!

24. *A.A. IS A SELFISH PROGRAM.*

Many a time in his drinking "career," the alcoholic attempted sobriety to "please" his wife, or friend, or boss, or superior. But such sobriety was rather short-lived. For, as soon as they were "pleased," there was no longer any reason why we couldn't have "just a little drink."

Also, many come to A.A. just to "please" someone else or because someone else pressured them to come. Such also seldom retain their sobriety very long UNLESS THEY COME TO THE POINT WHERE *THEY WANT SOBRIETY FOR THEMSELVES.*

"A.A. IS A SELFISH PROGRAM" means that we are sober because WE WANT SOBRIETY *FOR OURSELVES.*

It is the only motive that works for the pathologically proud alcoholic. He isn't "BIG" enough to STAY sober permanently for the sake of someone else; he IS *"SMALL"* ENOUGH, HOWEVER, TO STAY SOBER FOR *HIMSELF*. This is a "selfish" program.

And so *all* of the areas of living of the alcoholic are best approached FROM A SELFISH viewpoint, i.e., WE ARE DOING WHAT WE ARE DOING, WHATEVER THAT MAY BE, FOR *US*. It is dangerous to the sobriety of the alcoholic to become "apostolic" in his motive.

We stay sober FOR *US;* we practice virtue FOR *US;* we keep our health FOR *US;* we practice mental hygiene FOR *US;* we are good to others FOR *US;* we control our emotions FOR *US;* we take part in twelfth step activity FOR *US;* we *DO ALL THINGS* in order that WE may keep the sobriety we have and that WE may in turn get more sobriety FOR US.

Is this a NEW approach? Well, hardly. Centuries ago a certain saintly king remarked: "I have kept Thy commandments, O Lord, BECAUSE OF THE REWARD!" His name was David, and he too had a proud messy past!

A.A. *IS* A "SELFISH" PROGRAM!

25. *THE PRIMACY OF THE SPIRITUAL.*

Most alcoholics either did not judge spiritual values or they judged by very confused spiritual values. Most of the time it was the *material* values that came first and which motivated their decisions. But material values relate to "things" and "ALL things are passing." So nothing was ever laid up; nothing of *lasting* value was ever acquired.

Then came A.A.; and meditation; and realization THAT before all else THE *SPIRITUAL* VALUE IS PARAMOUNT. And just what is this PRIMACY OF THE SPIRITUAL? It is a truth which tells us that *nothing in this old world really matters except God and His Will; that a penitent returning to God is far more important than the return of a lost fortune to its rightful owner; that a group of men united in humble sincere prayer is far more effective and necessary for the preservation of peace than all the machinations of the world's most astute diplomats; that dependence on God—day in and day out, hour in and hour out, minute and minute out—will keep the worst alcoholic sober and happy; that it makes little difference whether men confuse Aristotle with Aristides, but it makes a lot of difference whether men confuse gold with God; that a short fifteen minutes of meditation each day will more surely give peace of mind, and a thousand times sooner, than endless days and nights spent amidst the world's finest amusements; that there is in reality only one supremacy, and that is God; that there is only one rue primacy of value, and that is the primacy of the spiritual.*

And so, just once again, "YOU TAKES YOUR CHOICE . . ." EITHER—

The *principles and practice*—with *mastery* of *sobriety* and *happiness;*

OR: NO principles, NO practice, then no mastery, not much, if any, happiness, no contented sobriety—and inevitably, sooner or later, and soon at the latest: NO MORE SOBRIETY!

"YOU *HAS* YOUR CHOICE. . . ."

THE TWELVE STEPS

1. We admitted we were powerless over alcohol—that our lives had become unmanageable.
2. Came to believe that a Power greater than ourselves could restore us to sanity.
3. Made a decision to turn our will and our lives over to the care of God *as we understood Him.*
4. Made a searching and fearless moral inventory of ourselves.
5. Admitted to God, to ourselves, and to another human being the exact nature of our wrongs.
6. Were entirely ready to have God remove all these defects of character.
7. Humbly asked Him to remove our shortcomings.
8. Made a list of all persons we had harmed, and became willing to make amends to them all.
9. Made direct amends to such people wherever possible, except when to do so would injure them or others.
10. Continued to take personal inventory and when we were wrong promptly admitted it.
11. Sought through prayer and meditation to improve our conscious contact with God *as we understood Him* praying only for knowledge of His Will for us and the power to carry that out.
12. Having had a spiritual awakening as a result of these steps, we tried to carry this message to alcoholics, and to practice these principles in all our affairs.

Imprimatur:

✠ Paul C. Schulte, D.D.
Archbishop of Indianapolis

March, 1955